A COLOUR FILM FOR TELEVISION

with

GEORGE CLAYDON
as Little George The Photographer

IVOR CUTLER
as Mr. Buster Bloodvessel

SHIRLEY EVANS
as The Accordionist

NAT JACKLEY
as Happy Nat The Rubber Man

NICOLA
as The Little Girl

JESSIE ROBINS
as Ringo's Auntie

DEREK ROYLE
as Jolly Jimmy Johnson The Courier

VICTOR SPINETTI
as The Recruiting Sergeant

MANDY WEET
as Miss Wendy Winters The Hostess

MAGGIE WRIGHT
as The Lovely Starlet

MADE IN ENGLAND BY THE BEATLES

"Magical Mystery Tour" Book Edited by Tony Barrow
Editorial Consultants (for Apple): Neil Aspinall & Mal Evans
Photographs: John Kelly   Drawings: Bob Gibson
(c) 1967, NEMS ENTERPRISES LTD.

The BEATLES
Magical Mystery Tour
and Yellow Submarine

Compiled by Bruce Spizer

With additional contributions by

Bill King,
Al Sussman,
Frank Daniels,
Piers Hemmingsen
and other Beatles fans

The Billboard, Cash Box and Record World chart data used in this book was taken from books published by Record Research, including Billboard Pop Album Charts 1965-1969,Billboard Pop Album Charts 1970 and The Comparison Book 1954-1982. Images provided by: Beatles Book Photo Library (109, 166 and 192); Eric Cash (page 183 drawing); Rex Features/Shutterstock (page 103); Garry Marsh (page 130); Stephen M.H. Braitman (page 138); Simon Mitchell (page 139); Leslie Samuels (page 143); Wayne Olsen (page 144); Robert Koenig (page 147); and Koh Hasebe/Shinko Music (page 169). The Canadian images (pages 93 and 95) were provided by Piers Hemmingsen. Most of the other collectibles shown in the book are from the collections of Bruce Spizer, Jeff Augsburger, Frank Daniels, Gary Hein and Perry Cox.

Print edition ISBN 9780983295785

Printed in U.S.A.
1 2 3 4 5 6 7 8 9 0

Nothing's Gonna Change My World

In the 1960s, the Christmas season officially began with Santa Claus' appearance at the end of the Macy's Thanksgiving Day parade. But for me and most Beatles fans in 1967, the festivities started a few days earlier when Top 40 radio stations began playing an incredibly catchy new Beatles song, "Hello Goodbye." The song was placed in heavy rotation, meaning it was played about every 90 minutes or so. I first heard the single at the start of Thanksgiving week on WTIX in my hometown of New Orleans. That Sunday night I saw the Beatles, on film from London, perform the song on The Ed Sullivan Show.

My family always celebrated both Chanukah and Christmas. We faithfully lit the Chanukah lights for each of the eight nights and we had a Christmas tree. Chanukah usually preceded Christmas, so I would often get a few Chanukah presents prior to Christmas. But in 1967, the first night of Chanukah was not until the evening of December 26. There would be no pre-Christmas presents for me. That made Christmas presents all the more special as they would be the first of the season.

I am sure that my parents got me something nice for Christmas that year, but I have no memory of what it was. The only present I remember was the one from my sister Dale. It was a little bigger than 12" by 12" and was relatively flat. I eagerly ripped off the paper and saw the cover to the new Monkees album, *Pisces, Aquarius, Capricorn & Jones Ltd*. That was quite a treat for me as I was a huge Monkees fan. But under that record was an even greater treasure, the Beatles *Magical Mystery Tour*. It was the perfect present in every sense of the word. And while both albums spent a ton of time on either the portable record player that I "borrowed" from my older sisters or the family stereo in the living room, *Magical Mystery Tour* clearly got the most spins.

During the holiday break, I was invited to a neighborhood party. In those days, kids frequently brought some of their records to parties to ensure that there would enough good music. Normally one would bring singles. We would print our names on the labels to make sure we got our records back when we left. That's why you see names on so many of the records from the sixties. Although we collected as many records as we could afford, we were not "Record Collectors." And while I do not remember who gave the party, I do know that I brought the most prized new disc that I owned, the *Magical Mystery Tour* LP. In fact, there is photographic proof. The picture below shows me ready to depart my house, album in hand.

One afternoon in early March 1968 I heard a new Beatles song on WTIX on the Newman school bus. It was quite different from the psychedelic songs the group had released the previous year. The dominant instrument was the piano, which was played in a style similar to all those great Fats Domino singles I grew up with. And hearing it through the tinny radio speaker of the bus, I first thought it was Ringo trying to sound like Elvis. It wasn't till I played the 45 at home that I became certain the vocalist on "Lady Madonna" was Paul. I also enjoyed the single's lovely B-side, "The Inner Light."

As 1968 came to a close, I finally got to see the *Yellow Submarine* cartoon in the theater. In addition to being blown away by the bright colors, cool-looking villains and new Beatles songs, the thing I remember most about the film was its incredible number of puns. My mom was always quick with a pun and by that time I had become a wicked punster. And yes, by George, I did see the film on a "Sitarday" afternoon.

I bought the *Yellow Submarine* album at Studio A the weekend it came out. After being spoiled with 30 new Beatles songs on *The White Album*, the LP was a bit of a let down, having only four new tracks by the group. And while I knew the songs were not among the best the Beatles had released, I still enjoyed them all. I also found myself playing the George Martin side more than I thought I would.

A few years later my familiarity with his orchestral score became an asset. In my senior year in high school, I took a film course that required the production of a short film. I teamed up with my friend David Newhouse, who was also a big Beatles fan and played drums in my rock band. David was a wonderful person: talented, creative and very smart. He was clearly the driving force behind the film, writing the script, lining up the actors and working the camera.

The plot involved a well-dressed black business-man being followed and hunted down by a group of young white thugs for the crime of being in their neighborhood. My main contributions were making sure there was film in the camera, lining up locations, which included a chase over railroad tracks and through a lumber yard, and selecting the film's music. I chose bits and pieces from George Martin's *Yellow Submarine* score, with "March Of The Meanies" adding drama and intensity to the thugs' pursuit of the innocent man and his murder. The film tied for first place in the Louisiana High School Film Festival. Sadly, David died this year.

"Across The Universe" has always been one of my favorite Beatles songs. By my senior year in high school I had learned of the Wildlife version, which I preferred over the Spector-enhanced track on *Let It Be*. My senior year book quote and picture are below.

"Sounds of laughter, shades of life are ringing through my open ears inciting and inviting me. Limitless, undying love which shines around me like a million suns and calls me on and on across the universe. Jai guru deva om, nothing's gonna change my world."

John Lennon

Roll Up for the Magical Mystery Tour

In the introductory pages of my last published book, *The Beatles Finally Let It Be*, I paraphrased the ending of the James Bond films from the sixties by stating that "The Beatles Album Series Shall Return..." When I wrote those words, I thought I knew what book would be next, but when travel restrictions were imposed due to Covid 19, I needed to work on a book that I could research from home. I quickly determined that there was a lot of information on the Beatles activities during 1967 and 1968 that was available online. That led me to switch plans and produce a book covering *Magical Mystery Tour* and *Yellow Submarine*. As the songs for both projects were recorded after *Sgt. Pepper* and before *The White Album*, the pairing seemed quite natural, particularly since the four new Beatles songs appearing on the *Yellow Submarine* album would have made for a very small book!

You will notice that, unlike the first four books published in the Beatles Album Series, the British section precedes the American section. The previous books covered albums that were essentially the same in both countries, so I started with the American records because they were the ones I grew up with and because the United States was the Beatles biggest market. For this book, I started with England because the Capitol *Magical Mystery Tour* LP was an expansion of the British EP. When I get around to the remaining books in the series, which will cover the Beatles albums released before 1967, they will also start with the British perspective followed by what went on in America.

In researching this book, I went through tons of magazines primarily from 1967 and 1968, with a heavy focus on the British music weeklies. I also returned to Mark Lewisohn's *The Beatles Recordings Sessions* and *The Complete Beatles Chronicle*. For those interested in learning more about *Yellow Submarine*, I highly recommend Dr. Robert R. Hieronimus' books *Inside The Yellow Submarine* and his latest, *It's All In The Mind (Inside The Yellow Submarine, Vol. 2)*. And the full story of The Beatles Saturday morning cartoon series can be found in Mitch Axelrod's excellent book *Beatletoons*.

I assembled the same team utilized in the previous volumes in this series. Piers Hemmingsen provided the Canadian perspective. Beatlefan editor Al Sussman wrote about the Beatles being a part of Our World. Frank Daniels contributed a chapter on the friendly rivalry between the Beatles and the Stones. Beatlefan publisher Bill King returned with more fan notes. Jeff Augsburger, Perry Cox and Gary Hein provided images of memorabilia from their collections and inventory.

The Fan Recollections chapter has always been an important part of my album series books. Once again I was able to compile a wonderful collection of memories from Beatles fans of all ages, including two people who appeared in the *Magical Mystery Tour* TV film.

On the technical side, Diana Thornton worked her magic to make the book look terrific as always and Kaye Alexander coordinated the interactions with our new printer in Clarksville, Tennessee. Proofreaders included Diana, Frank, Al, Anthony Robustelli, Beatle Tom Frangione and Warren Huberman. In the tradition, my thanks to my family, Sarah, Eloise, Barbara, Trish, Big Puppy and others too numerous and crazy to name.

And yes, The Beatles Album Series Shall Return...

words About Author

Bruce Spizer is a lifelong native of New Orleans, Louisiana, who was eight years old when the Beatles invaded America. He began listening to the radio at age two and was a die-hard fan of WTIX, a top forty AM station that played a blend of New Orleans R&B music and top pop and rock hits. His first two albums were *The Coasters' Greatest Hits*, which he permanently "borrowed" from his older sisters, and *Meet The Beatles!*, which he still occasionally plays on his vintage 1964 Beatles record player.

During his high school and college days, Bruce played guitar in various bands that primarily covered hits of the sixties, including several Beatles songs. He wrote numerous album and concert reviews for his high school and college newspapers, including a review of *Abbey Road* that didn't claim Paul was dead. He received his B.A., M.B.A. and law degrees from Tulane University. His legal and accounting background have proved valuable in researching and writing his books.

Bruce is considered one of the world's leading experts on the Beatles. A "taxman" by day, Bruce is a Board Certified Tax Attorney with his own practice. A "paperback writer" by night, Bruce is the author of 13 critically acclaimed books on the Beatles, including *The Beatles Are Coming! The Birth of Beatlemania in America*, a series of six books on the group's American record releases, *Beatles For Sale on Parlophone Records*, which covers all of the Beatles records issued in the U.K. from 1962-1970, and his new series of books on the Beatles albums. His articles have appeared in Beatlefan, Goldmine and American History magazines.

Bruce Spizer at the controls of St. Charles Avenue street car No. 910 in New Orleans, Louisiana.

He was selected to write the questions for the special Beatles edition of Trivial Pursuit. He maintains the popular website www.beatle.net.

Bruce has been a speaker at numerous Beatles conventions and at the Grammy Museum, the Rock 'N' Roll Hall of Fame & Museum and the American Film Institute. He has been on ABC's Good Morning America and Nightline, CBS's The Early Show, CNN, Fox and morning shows in New York, Chicago, Los Angeles, New Orleans and other cities, and is a frequent guest on radio shows, including NPR, BBC and the Beatles Channel.

Bruce serves as a consultant to Universal Music Group, Capitol Records and Apple Corps Ltd. on Beatles projects. He has an extensive Beatles collection, concentrating on American, Canadian and British first issue records, promotional items and concert posters.

contents

DISC

and MUSIC ECHO 9d

JULY 15, 1967   USA 20c

BEATLES:
'Love' leaps
in at six!

HOW IT ALL BEGAN: SEE PAGE 2

The Beatles Magical Mystery Tour Through the U.K.

The cover to the July 15, 1967 issue of Disc and Music Echo ("Disc") featured a color picture of the Beatles and the bold headline "BEATLES: 'Love' leaps in at six! How it all began." Love, of course, was a reference to the Beatles new single, "All You Need Is Love," which would jump from six to number one in the Disc chart the following week. The picture was taken at EMI's Abbey Road studios prior to the Beatles rehearsal of the song they had written for the June 25 worldwide broadcast of the television show Our World. How it all began was part of the fascinating story of the various projects the Beatles were considering to follow-up *Sgt. Pepper's Lonely Hearts Club Band*.

News of the Beatles post-*Pepper* plans began circulating even before the album's release on June 1. The May 27 New Musical Express ("NME") reported that the Beatles would provide one of Britain's two contributions to the first-ever worldwide TV hook-up which would utilize five satellites to reach an audience of over 500 million people. The program, titled Our World, would be broadcast on BBC-1 on Sunday, June 25, from 8-10 pm, and simultaneously to 30 other countries. The Beatles five-minute segment would show the group live from EMI studios recording a brand new song written specially for the show. Before recording the song, the group would be seen discussing the song with their producer, George Martin. The recording might also feature an orchestra. John and Paul were keeping the lyrics simple for the benefit of the foreign viewers.

That same week Disc also ran an article about the program, informing readers that the Beatles would make history when they starred in a two-hour BBC special beamed by five satellites to 500 million viewers. The story contained much of the same information that appeared in NME, but added a few more details. The Beatles segment would be covered by a four-camera BBC crew and was scheduled for 8:45 pm, about halfway through the show. Disc noted that the song written for the program "has been kept 'simple' with basic English words so that it will be more easily understood by the vast foreign audience." The article also mentioned that the Beatles were planning an all-color spectacular based on *Sgt. Pepper*. No further details were available.

Prior to the Our World broadcast, fans learned of additional Beatles projects. The June 10 NME reported that the Beatles would begin filming their next movie, *Shades Of A Personality*, in September. The group hoped that they would be able to complete their planned TV spectacular based on their *Sgt. Pepper* LP prior to starting the film. NME also announced that the Beatles would be the subject of a full-length color cartoon, tentatively titled *Yellow Submarine*, that would be made in America by King Productions who had made a series of TV cartoons of the group for the American market. *Yellow Submarine* was intended for theatrical release and was expected to eventually be screened in the U.K. The film would feature three new Beatles songs as well as prior hits.

The following week NME provided additional information on the cartoon film, correcting some of the errors in its previous story and adding some new errors. Executive producer Al Brodax described the project as a "Beatles musical Fantasia" and went on to say: "The songs they have been recording for us this week are brilliant...incredible. They are using sounds I have never heard nor could have imagined." This misled NME to report that the Beatles were currently recording three new Lennon-McCartney songs for the film. [The group had already recorded the film songs the previous month, with two of the compositions being written by George Harrison.] Brodax claimed that the Beatles were very enthusiastic about the film: "They have been calling us at all times with ideas – we have even had discussions at two o'clock in the morning – and their suggestions are very good. So far all the Beatles ideas are being incorporated into the movie." The article indicated that the 90-minute color cartoon had started production in London and would be released the following spring through United Artists.

That same week the June 17 Disc ran its first article on the project, telling readers that the Beatles had written three new songs for a full-length animated feature film based on the lyrics of their hit song, "Yellow Submarine." The group would appear in caricature form, similar to Walt Disney's *Fantasia*. Disc correctly identified the name of the production company as King Features. Once again, Brodax made exaggerated claims about the Beatles involvement, telling Disc that "a good majority of the ideas for it are theirs." The film would also feature "Lucy In The Sky With Diamonds," "She's Leaving Home" and "Eleanor Rigby." Brodax added: "It will be very like 'Fantasia' – except that the score will be Beatles music. George Martin will probably do the incidental music."

Britain's music industry trade magazine, Record Retailer, reported on the Beatles participation in the Our World TV show in its June 22 issue, noting that the song recorded for the show would "almost certainly be their next single." This was confirmed the following week, with the magazine disclosing the song titles and noting that "All You Need Is Love" had received massive promotion on the Sunday broadcast. EMI announced an official release date of July 7 (a Friday, in keeping with industry practice), but hoped to get the disc in shops by Wednesday, July 5, for immediate sale.

All four of the weekly music magazines reported on the Beatles segment from the June 25 Our World TV broadcast in their July 1 issues. The similarity of content among the articles suggests that much of the information came from a press release. Disc, under the headline "Beatles TV Track Will Be New Single," informed readers that "All You Need Is Love," the Lennon-McCartney song written specially for the Our World TV broadcast, would be one side of a world-wide rush-release Beatles single. Tapes were sent to New York and other overseas centers within 48 hours of the Sunday recording session. Copies of the record were to be in U.K. shops within a week. The B-side was another Lennon-McCartney tune, "Baby, You're A Rich Man," originally written as one of three songs for the Beatles cartoon film, *Yellow Submarine*. John sang lead on both sides, joined by Paul and George. During the TV show, viewed by over 400,000,000 people in 24 countries, John was shown adding the final vocal track to "All You Need Is Love." This was the first time the group had written a song for a specific occasion. They were accompanied by 13 session musicians. It was noted that the Beatles will have released two singles and an album within 18 weeks, making this their most prolific output of songs since the early days of 1963. Record Mirror ran the same basic content under the headline "Surprise Beatle disc – details...," while Melody Maker's front-page article led with "A SURPRISE new single from the Beatles!" NME's rewrite of the press release ran under the headline "Beatles World TV Single."

That week, NME's Andy Gray penned a separate piece on the Our World broadcast, noting that the group made pop history by plugging their new record "to the whole world at the same time!" He described "All You Need Is Love" as an "up-beat, joyous-sounding, simple-lyriced song." He detailed the proceedings and how the sound and pictures went out from EMI studios via BBC TV and across the world on three satellites. Gray observed that the new number had a chorus reminiscent of four years ago and should be a big hit as it was simple and easy to sing.

The July 1 Disc also featured Penny Valentine's initial thoughts on the song. "'All You Need Is Love' sing the Beatles... proving that their minds are well in the flower areas and this is their way of taking good feeling and gentleness round the world." The song was a "fascinating exercise on how the Beatles take an exceptionally simple idea...and turn it into something grand." John sang lead, "coming along in a rush just a few notes later than you expect...knocking you out completely." The song opens with the triumphant brass of "The Marseillaise" followed by "warm backing voices which continue all the way through." The track "weaves splendidly with brass and violins and goes wild at the end." Valentine concluded: "It is every bit what we expect from the grand lads. And the world will sing along!"

All the weeklies ran reviews the following week. In the July 8 Disc, Valentine agreed with her prior comments, but thought the "end freak-out goes on too long and makes the record sound as though it wasn't recorded seriously." She described the B-side, "Baby, You're A Rich Man," as "An enthralling controlled lurching that sounds tremendously influenced by classical Indian dance rhythms," noting that "you can almost see brown arms swaying and bare feet tapping." Valentine called the single the "best actual 'sound' on both sides that the Beatles have had to date." In Melody Maker, Nick Jones touted the song as "another milestone in their very phenomenal careers." It was a "cool, calculated contagious Beatles' singsong" with a "beautiful sound [that] is easier to absorb than the more complex 'Strawberry Fields.'" The B-side was pleasing and would score lots of plays. Record Mirror's Peter Jones called the disc an "obvious number one...which is likely to go on for ever." It had a choral sound, a violent guitar solo and a finale which goes on a bit but is good-humored. The song was very catchy and involved a world message. As for the B-side, Jones thought: "Some will prefer this, oddly enough—and it is odd enough. Interesting sounds all the way." In NME, Derek Johnson noted that the song harks "back to the early Beatles—with added cellos and brass as the only concession to their present progressive style." It was a "very pretty sing-along tune, soloed by John, with Paul and George chanting 'Love' over and over behind him." He thought the track went about a minute too long, with the orchestra going "berserk while the boys chant the title phrase 42 times" and the strings play "Greensleeves." Johnson believed that "Only the Beatles could make such a classic out of such uncomplicated material...even though one can almost hear the group's tongues firmly planted in their cheeks!" The B-side had an "Oriental instrumentation and an unusual shuffle beat." Johnson's verdict: "The whole effect is startling and packed with interest from the word 'go.'"

Beatles manager Brian Epstein was extremely pleased with the new single, calling it "the best they've done" and further telling Melody Maker: "This is an inspired song because they wrote it for a worldwide programme and they really wanted to give the world a message. It could hardly have been a better message. It is a wonderful, beautiful, spine-chilling record. When you say 'All You Need Is Love' you are saying everything."

Music Publisher Dick James told the story behind his rapid printing of the sheet music and EMI's rush pressing of the "All You Need Is Love" single in the July 15 Disc in an article titled "Launching a new Beatles hit: all you need is speed." James called the endeavor his biggest challenge yet: to have the new Beatles song rolling off the presses and in shops in the fastest time possible after the show. He did not want fans to feel frustrated if the song was not in stores after they already heard it performed by the Beatles on TV. He was also concerned that unscrupulous people would take the transmission and rebroadcast it, adding that this happened in France and in the United States. James indicated that the surest safeguard was to get copies of the record out as soon as possible. EMI sent out promotional demonstration records to radio stations four days after the show, with shops stocking the disc within eight days.

James told of his first hearing the song during a visit to EMI Studios, when George Martin told him that the boys were going to be featured on Our World recording a special song for the show. Knowing that there would be immediate demand, everyone agreed that the song should be the A-side of the next Beatles single and that it should be rush-released within days of the program. After hearing John sing the melody line over the backing track, James "could see right away it would be another massive hit." Disc reported that the single had advance orders in excess of 300,000 copies and was expected to sell between 500,000 to 600,000 in the U.K., which was good for summer when sales were normally slow. The Beatles Our World segment was re-broadcast on Top of the Pops on July 6.

"All You Need Is Love" entered the Record Retailer chart at number two on July 12, while "A Whiter Shade Of Pale" by Procol Harum was at the top. The following week it moved up to number one, holding off the new Monkees U.K. single. The song was "Randy Scouse Git," but was re-named "Alternate Title" for the British market. It referred to the Beatles as "the four kings of EMI." "All You Need Is Love" topped the charts for three weeks before giving way to another Summer of Love anthem, Scott McKenzie's "San Francisco (Be Sure To Wear Flowers In Your Hair)." The Beatles single charted for 13 weeks, including seven in the top five. Melody Maker debuted the disc at number three on July 15 before moving it to the top for three weeks. During its 11-week run, the song was in the top five for seven weeks. "All You Need Is Love" debuted at number one on the July 12 NME chart and remained at the top for a total of four weeks. The single entered the Disc chart at number six before moving to number one for two weeks. The song also topped the BBC chart. After the disappointing failure of the group's previous single to top all but one of the U.K. charts, the song's overwhelming success was a welcome relief. The single was awarded a silver disc from Disc on July 22, 1967, indicating sales of 250,000. By year's end, it had sold over 500,000 copies.

Andy Gray reported in the July 22 NME that some fans were furious with "All You Need Is Love," calling it "trash and rubbish." However, Gray pointed out that unlike "Strawberry Fields Forever" and "Penny Lane," the song topped the charts. He observed that the "simpler tune has caught the imagination of the public." Paul said the group was "taking a look back with a new feeling." After being told that the Beatles would be seen recording the song by the whole world, Paul said "we had one message for the world – 'LOVE.' We need more love in the world."

The BEATLES

QMSP 16408

MONDOVISIONE

EMI's Italian branch, Dischi Parlophon, issued the single in a thick paper stock picture sleeve.

Readers of the monthly publication The Beatles Book learned of the group's participation in the June 25 worldwide TV hook-up in the magazine's June 1967 issue (No. 47, *Sgt. Pepper* Special). The Beatles would be shown live from EMI Studios playing a new song which they planned to write specially for the show.

The August 1967 issue (No. 49) had extensive coverage about the recording of the song performed during the group's Our World segment. Editor Johnny Dean, who was one-in-the-same as Publisher Sean O'Mahony, told readers that he was in the studio with the boys a few weeks before the broadcast when John first played the song to the others. "He sat down behind the piano and banged out the basic chords over and over again while George, Paul and Ringo experimented with different ideas. A couple of hours later they taped the basic backing, but at this stage it was about ten minutes long." When Dean later heard them rehearse "All You Need Is Love" the day before the TV show, he realized it was the same tune, but "with the most incredible number of extra ideas added." He observed that no record could have previewed to a larger audience, joking that it "beat Juke Box Jury by a big margin!" Prior to the Saturday rehearsal, the boys held a photo session, facing over 100 flashing cameras for over 30 minutes. It had been a while since their last general photo call, causing Paul to comment that if felt as if they were back in 1963.

Road managers Mal Evans and Neil Aspinall told of how "All You Need Is Love" was recorded. The initial session was held at Olympic Studios on June 14. The backing track consisted of John on harpsichord, Paul on Arco string bass, which he played with a bow, Ringo on drums and George on the violin for the first time in his life. The group then moved to EMI, where Paul added bass guitar, Ringo played drums, George recorded his guitar solo and John just sang. The song's orchestral accompaniment consisted of two trumpets, two trombones, two saxophones, an accordion, four violins and two cellos. George Martin played piano at the very beginning. The Beatle News section talked of a special June 25 session that took place in the huge Studio No. 1, which is used for orchestral and operatic sessions. Although the Beatles sometimes had friends in the studio when they were recording, this time there was a big crowd for the show. The session musicians wore dinner jackets. The backing track had been previously recorded. The live performance broadcast on the TV show was not the same as the single. The song's ending included "In The Mood," the traditional old English tune "Greensleeves" and a little bit of "She Loves You" thrown in for fun.

Previous issues of The Beatles Book provided information and clues about another Beatles project. The May 1967 issue (No. 46) contained an interview of Paul by Johnny Dean. When asked about the next Beatles film, Paul responded: "Before we start the film anyway, we want to do this television show. There's so much rubbish on television that it shouldn't be difficult to produce a good show. But, here again, we want to do it our way, to put our ideas into the show. We're tired of using other people's ideas and so often they're all wrong, so the only answer is to do it ourselves."

In his Editorial in the July 1967 issue (No. 48), Dean told of his conversation with Paul about the new television show, which, according to Paul, was coming along nicely. The boys had come up with a theme, so the show would not be a series of unconnected songs and guest artists like so many other shows. Dean noted: "The great thing about the Beatles is that they are always completely unruffled when faced with creative problems....Original thought just seems to flow from the Beatle brains in a continuous stream, John and Paul of course, bearing the main brunt. And whatever they do certainly makes everyone think." That same issue contained a day-by-day report by Mal of his time in the States with Paul, who was visiting his girlfriend Jane Asher on her 21st birthday, including the following entries. April 6 (Denver): "Took charge of Hertz rented car. Drove Paul and Jane into the Rockies for what I can only describe as a real Magical Mystery Trip." April 7: "Paul filmed Jane....Paul getting quite excited about ideas for The Beatles' TV Special. Idea going at the moment is for some sort of mystery tour. 'Roll up for the grand mystery trip!'" April 11: "Once we were on the plane Paul started working out ideas for the song he thinks might be the next single."

In their report on "All You Need Is Love" in the August 1967 issue, Mal and Neil indicated that the Beatles had already written and recorded the backing track to another song which was in line for the A-side of the Beatles second single of 1967 and would be the theme song for the 60-minute color TV special they've been waiting to do. Mal and Neil said it was too early to let readers in on the secret and tell them the title of the song, which might be the Beatles next single in a month or two, or might be a track on their next LP. The TV special was intended for showing all over the world. John and Paul decided not to finalize the lyrics until they finished filming the TV show. They might want to make last-minute changes in the words of their theme song to fit in with changes regarding the program's content.

The Beatles BOOK

No. 46
MAY
1967

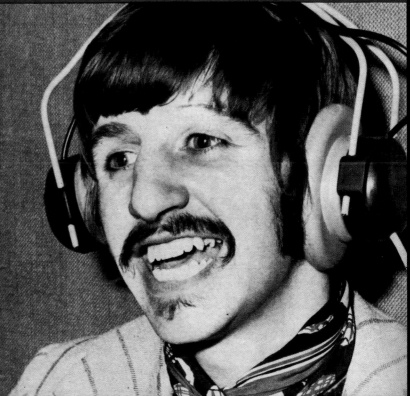

The Beatles MONTHLY BOOK

No. 48
JULY
1967
4th
YEAR

EVERY MONTH   Price TWO SHILLINGS

The music weeklies first reported on the Beatles planned TV special in their July 1 issues, most likely sourced from the same press release on "All You Need Is Love." Disc indicated that the group had modified its plans for the hour-long color TV spectacular based on material from *Sgt. Pepper*. Instead they were writing new songs and would shoot a new spectacular between now and the end of August. The program would be produced and devised by the Beatles. John and Paul had written a new song which would serve as the theme for the entire program. The group had recorded the backing track, with vocals to be added later. The song was originally intended as the band's new single, but now might be a later release or appear as a track on their next album, set for fall release. Special guest stars would be invited to participate in the spectacular. Melody Maker ran a similar report, informing readers that the Beatles would concentrate on writing new compositions for a television special. NME said that the Beatles would devote most of July and August to the preparation and filming of their hour-long TV spectacular. John and Paul had already written the theme song, which might be released as a single to coincide with the screening of the show. The group would write several more new numbers for the spectacular, which would also include existing songs. Guest artists might be invited to participate in the show. The July 22 NME reported that Paul and John were composing new numbers for the TV spectacular and that these numbers might make up a new album or some singles. Paul said the TV show was in the "thinking about" stage: "We like to take our time and make certain what we write is good."

On Thursday, August 24, the Beatles attended a lecture at the London Hilton on transcendental mediation by the Indian philosopher/teacher Maharishi Mahesh Yogi. The next day, with massive press coverage, they traveled by train to Bangor, North Wales, to spend five days studying meditation with the Maharishi. The press was skeptical of the group's newfound interest, calling the train the "Mystical Special." While in Bangor, they learned of the death of their manager, Brian Epstein, on August 27, causing an early return to London. The newspapers, tabloids and music weeklies speculated on the Beatles future, including who would manage the group. The September 2 Melody Maker raised the possibility of the group managing themselves for a while. In Disc that week John said: "We're all going to India soon for a couple of months to study transcendental mediation properly. The only plans we had, before Brian died, were to make a record, do a TV show and make a film. But meeting the Maharishi has changed our thoughts a bit, and Brian's death changed it a lot. It makes it more worthwhile now, somehow, going over to India."

Tributes to the man who revolutionised British pop by giving the world the Beatles . . .
BRIAN EPSTEIN

HE was 26 when he was asked for a record called "My Bonnie" by the Beatles by a Liverpool teen-ager. He was running the record department of his father's store. He hadn't the record, but he thought he'd have a look at the group. He saw a future in their happy, energetic sound—AND HE DID SOMETHING ABOUT IT. He gave it to the world and became world famous himself as the man who managed the Beatles—Brian Epstein.

Right up until his untimely, sad death at the age of 32, he was planning new enterprises for his Beatles and other artists, like Cilla Black. His great strength was his faith in their entertaining ability and the way he guarded this by never selling it cheaply.

In the beginning he spent money promoting the Beatles when they were almost unknown. He toured London with their tapes. Record companies turned them down. EMI put George Martin on to the Beatles. George was with Parlophone, till then a label concerned with comedy records. But the Beatles changed all that.

Brian Epstein had several tempting offers to sell his contract with the Beatles. But the Beatles didn't want him to, so he

ANDY GRAY

didn't want to either. As one of the Beatles said on hearing of his death: "He was one of us."

The fifth Beatle did more for British show business than any manager, agent or impresario has ever done—he tore down "closed shop" signs in America and allowed many, many recording stars to win fame there and, in consequence, all over the world. Show business owes a great deal to Brian Epstein.

Cilla:
The news is so awful I scarcely know what to say. He was so much more than a manager to me. He was a close friend and adviser.

Gerry:
There will never be another manager like Brian. When I heard the news I was completely shattered. I knew Brian about ten years and he was my manager for five.

Elvis:
Deepest condolences on loss of a good friend to you and all of us.

John:
I can't find words to pay tribute to him. It is just that he was lovable and it is those lovable things we think about now.

Paul:
This is a great shock. I am terribly upset.

George:
He dedicated so much of his life to the Beatles. We liked and loved him. He was one of us. There is no such thing as death. It is a comfort to us all to know that he is okay.

Ringo:
We loved Brian. He was a generous man. We owe so much to him. We have come a long way with Brian along the same road.

The personality I knew

Norrie Drummond

THE last time I met Brian Epstein was just over a week ago. We had dinner together in a small Italian restaurant in Soho. He was in excellent spirits and, as always, was planning great things for the future.

He talked enthusiastically about the Beatles' big television show, and of the plans he had for Cilla Black.

He was much happier than he had been for some time. "I'm delighted with the way things are going now," he told me. "In fact, everything's grooving along so nicely."

He talked about his visit to America which he was to have made next weekend. In the past year he had turned down many offers to appear on TV, but had accepted this one invitation to host his own spectacular in the States "because I have a lot of say in the show."

Brian Epstein knew hundreds of people, but had very few close friends. Those he trusted and confided in amounted to no more than about half a dozen — the Beatles, Peter Brown, his right-hand man, Robert Stigwood, joint managing-director of NEMS, his younger brother Clive.

He was one of the most complex men I have ever met, a man of extremes—with him there were never half measures. He was either deliriously happy or miserably depressed; he either liked or disliked a person.

He was also one of the most honest men I've ever met. He always kept his word and was tremendously loyal to the people whom he admired or respected.

Naturally he made enemies with other agents and promoters, largely because he always wanted the best for his artists. But he never held grudges against any of those he had quarrelled with in the past.

When I first met Brian Epstein during the Beatles' first major concert tour of Britain he dressed rather like a young advertising executive, giving the impression of being slightly above the pop business. He appeared aloof and silent. But this I later discovered was only a shield for the shyness

Continued on page 9

The BEATLES were in Bangor, Wales, on a meditation course conducted by their new hero, Indian mystic MAHARISHI MAHESH YOGI (right), who told them to have happy thoughts of Brian and they would reach him.

The following week the September 9 music magazines ran stories on the television film. In an interview by Norrie Drummond in NME, Paul said that the group was still trying to work out the format and had been recording songs the past few nights. He indicated that the band enjoyed recording, but wanted to go even further. "I would like to come up with a completely new form of music, invent new sounds."

A separate NME article told of the upcoming start to the filming of the color spectacular. On Monday (September 11) the Beatles and a film crew would depart London for Devon and Cornwall in a 60-seat yellow and blue coach with "Magical Mystery Tour" emblazoned on its sides. The group would make unscheduled stops along the way to scout locations for the TV special and planned to work on the project spontaneously without a script or director. The hour-long film was to be completed in November and might be shown during the Christmas season on BBC-2, which had recently added color programming. The previously planned *Sgt. Pepper* TV spectacular was canceled when the group agreed to do a song for Our World. *Magical Mystery Tour* was its replacement, but some *Sgt. Pepper* songs might be used in the film. A new single was expected in November while the group was in India. It might be the title song for the show, "Magical Mystery Tour," which had been recorded in April and recently revised. It was unlikely that the group would issue an album featuring the film songs, which might appear on one or two singles and an extended play (EP) disc. NME reported that the show would feature a song by George Harrison, but inaccurately stated it was written during his recent visit to India to see Ravi Shankar. [George actually wrote the song in Los Angeles during a visit there where he met with Shankar and saw him perform at the Hollywood Bowl.] There would be a "major guest attraction" in the TV spectacular, as well as non-musical guests, possibly Shankar and/or the Maharishi. After the group completed its location work, there would be two weeks of studio filming. Press officer Tony Barrow said that the group wanted the film to be screened at Christmas. The show would be offered to TV stations around the world.

The September 9 Disc ran a similar story teasingly titled "Beatles Plan Mini-Tour!" But this would be a four-day tour by coach, location-hunting to film scenes for their TV spectacular, *Magical Mystery Tour*. Melody Maker ran a brief cover story on the Beatles Mystery Tour, informing readers that the group was setting off on a four-day coach tour of the south of England, picking random locations and filming their hour-long TV show.

In their September 16 issues, NME and Disc covered the Beatles first week of filming. NME's article was headlined: "Beatles Take a Bus to Magic Land! West Country Will Never be the Same." It focused on the group's retro clothing. Paul wore a Fair Isle pullover jumper and striped Al Capone-type trousers. John had a striped tie and trousers. Ringo was set for a city desk of 20 years ago. George looked like he stepped out of a Hollywood gangster film. The group had no idea what the story would be when they began filming other than it being built around four new songs written by John and Paul and be connected to their motor coach outing with their fellow travelers. Disc also emphasized the clothing in its story, "Beatles in Squareville for Mystery Tour," observing that the Beatles had "cast aside their now-familiar beads and bells in favour of...old-fashioned outfits." The film was a "coach journey through the West Country" full of "typical holiday atmosphere complete with beer and sandwiches and pub stopping places." Most of the first day was spent filming inside the coach filled with 43 people including comedians Ivor Cutler and Nat Jackley, actress Maggie Wright, Jessie Robbins as the Fat Lady and George Claydon as the Small Man. Mal said: "People were lining both sides of the road in Teignmouth. Police were called....It was back to the days of Beatlemania."

The September 23 music magazines ran articles on the first two weeks of filming. Melody Maker reported that *Magical Mystery Tour* would feature a striptease sequence. The Beatles had been filming at secret locations in and around London. The Monday (September 18) filming of the Bonzo Dog Doo Dah Band [performing "Death Cab For Cutie"] was delayed because their instruments had been stolen the night before. The magazine also ran a story on how some of its staff, including Chris Welch, went looking for the Beatles on their mystery tour filming that threw Cornwall into chaos. The group decided to stay at the Atlantic Hotel in Newquay because they liked the area. During this time they "made lightning forays into the countryside for spontaneous filming of improvised antics." John and George directed a comedy bit at the hotel's swimming pool involving a lady accordionist, a comedian and a bevy of girls in swimming suits who jumped into the freezing pool water.

NME placed three pictures of the proceedings on its cover with the caption: "The Beatles 'Magical Mystery Tour' is in the can and the West Country has returned to normal." The text said there were "surprises all the way," including Spencer Davis being roped into doing scene with Paul. Record Mirror ran a shot of the Beatles at Plymouth Hoe.

Disc ran two articles on the project. The first was of a general nature. The next Beatles single would probably be the theme song from *Magical Mystery Tour* or there could be a four-song EP. The previous week the Beatles were in Devon and Cornwall, while this week they would be primarily in film studios. On Monday, the Bonzo Dog Doo Dah Band was filmed performing at Raymond's Revuebar in Soho. After shooting ended on Friday, the group would work on the musical soundtrack for two weeks. Upon completion of the film, the Beatles would leave for India and return for Christmas. The second piece was an inside story on the first week of filming by Beatles Fan Club Secretary Freda Kelly. She and three other lucky girls were asked to join the Beatles on the "slow coach to Cornwall!" Paul and Ringo directed the coach scenes, while John and George handled beach scenes and those around the swimming pool with girls in bikinis. According to Freda, "There was no prepared script as such. They just put their heads together the night before and prepared some ideas." Spontaneous filming included lunch and the coach failing to get over a bridge. When Spencer Davis and his family happened along, they were put in a scene. Freda and the other girls got to chat with the Beatles on the bus. Her experience: "I loved every minute of it. A nice all-expenses-paid holiday!"

The November 1967 edition of The Beatles Book (No. 52) contained separate reports from Freda and the three Fan Club Area Secretaries who traveled with the Beatles along with several pictures. The previous issue (October, No. 51) had multiple reports on the film. Editor Johnny Dean told readers that all the boys had been "busy thinking up ideas for the special," with John, Paul and George "doubly occupied writing new songs." Dean assured readers that many of the new numbers were "absolutely fascinating," causing him to believe that their next LP would be better than *Sgt. Pepper.* The Beatle News page told of Paul signing autographs while waiting for the Mystery Tour coach to pick him up. The Beatles were joined on the 43-seat bus by seven technicians, Mal, Neil, Tony Barrow, an elderly couple and friends. The Beatles had planned the Mystery Tour themselves and were directing it. On September 13, John directed a scene with Scotch comedian Nat Jackley chasing girls around a swimming pool. When the Beatles learned that all film studios around London were booked, they located an empty hanger in West Malling, Kent to shoot the interior scenes for the show. Neil's report on George's trip to California included the story of how George was inspired to write the song "Blue Jay Way" on mini-organ while waiting for Derek Taylor to join them at the house they were staying at in the hills of Hollywood on Blue Jay Way. The song would be included in *Magical Mystery Tour.*

The music weeklies continued their updates on *Magical Mystery Tour* in their September 30 issues. Melody Maker reported that the Beatles had finished filming and would spend the next three weeks editing and writing and recording the incidental music. This would delay the Beatles trip to India until late October. Record Mirror and Disc indicated that Paul had asked Traffic to appear in the TV spectacular. Traffic would make their own insert film, most likely for their new single, "Around The Mulberry Bush." Disc also reported that the Beatles had completed filming. One of the final scenes, featuring Ringo buying his tour ticket from a shopkeeper played by John, was shot in a village shop in West Malling, Kent. The Beatles spent most of the past week filming at the former United States Air Force base in West Malling. Barrow indicated that the base's large hangers were excellent substitutes for sound stages and indoor sets. The group would spend the next three to four weeks editing the film and completing and recording songs. NME ran a photo of the Beatles and stripper Jan Carson from the film's striptease scene along with the caption: "Studies in expressions from the Beatles....Would Maharishi approve? That bears meditating over!"

The October 7 music magazines ran similar stories on the project. The group had spent the entire week in the studio recording songs for the film, which would feature up to seven new compositions by the Beatles, including an instrumental and one by George Harrison, "Blue Jay Way." Tony Barrow indicated that no decision had been reached on when or how the songs would be released, but a single and an EP might come out while the Beatles were in India. The group had begun editing the film. They would also write and record the incidental music, but could not start on this until the editing was completed and the group determined what was required. As this could take a few weeks, the Beatles trip to India might be delayed until November.

The October 21 NME reported that the Beatles had received over 40 offers for screening rights to *Magical Mystery Tour*, including 11 from Europe and others from Japan, Australia, South Africa and Mexico. All three major U.S. networks were competing for the show, with the winning bid expected to exceed one million dollars. Although the British broadcast rights had not been finalized, the Beatles were still hoping for a Christmas date in the U.K. With the completion of the project taking longer than anticipated, the group might need to postpone their trip to India until next year. The following week Disc confirmed that the Beatles were delaying their India trip until the following year.

DISC
and MUSIC ECHO 9d
NOVEMBER 11, 1967   USA 20c

Beatles: new single!

See Page 4

See Page 4

DAVE DEE TV SERIES ★ TOM on a HIT TOUR

Beatles during shooting of their TV "Magical Mystery Tour" which goes on world TV at Christmas.   Picture: John Kelly

Russia celebrates the 50th year since the Revolution
. . . and Britain today celebrates 5 years of the BEATLES!
The pop Revolution began 5 years ago this week with
'Love Me Do.'   A 4-page Beatles special starts on page 10

Fans learned of the new Beatles single, "Hello, Goodbye" c/w "I Am The Walrus," from the November 11 music weeklies. The record was set for release on November 24. Disc reported that "Hello, Goodbye" was specifically written to be a single and was completed the previous week. Paul was the lead singer, backed by himself, John and George. Tony Barrow indicated that "the boys wanted to write a completely new song to be the topside of the new single release so they come up with 'Hello, Goodbye.'" The flip side, "I Am The Walrus," was recorded a few weeks before and was one of the big production numbers from *Magical Mystery Tour*. John sang lead, with the voices of John, Paul and George heard in the backing. The Beatles were filming a promo clip of "Hello, Goodbye" for television broadcast. The final sequences needed to complete *Magical Mystery Tour* were shot at Ringo's Weybridge, Surrey home on Friday (November 3). The other film songs would be released in December. Next year's plans called for a new LP and a new film to follow up *A Hard Day's Night* and *Help!* Barrow added: "Though 'Magical Mystery Tour' is a TV film, this is the first time they have produced, scripted, cast and starred in a film. This may well prove to be a prototype of their next film assignment." In other news, the *Yellow Submarine* cartoon, with 12 Beatles songs including four new ones, was set for release in March or April.

NME's article on the new single contained additional information. In discussing the upcoming release of the six film songs, a Beatles spokesman said: "There is too much for an EP, and not enough for an LP. This means the material will probably be put out as a special presentation package." The promo clip for "Hello, Goodbye" would most likely be screened first on BBC-1's Top Of The Pops. It would also be available throughout the world. The clip was being made by Subafilms, a company formed by Brian Epstein. George Martin was named as musical director for *Yellow Submarine*. The film, produced by King Features and Subafilms, utilizes the most advanced animation techniques ever. "The drawings, influenced by pop and psychedelic art, are styled to set off the 'Mod world of the Beatles.'" The cartoon, written by Al Brodax, Jack Meldonsohn and Erich Segal, was a musical comedy with a chase and rescue.

Melody Maker ran a cover story on the new single, providing much of the same details on the record as Disc and NME. The magazine added that the Beatles were still finalizing the editing and recording for *Magical Mystery Tour*, which was expected to be seen on British TV this Christmas. Record Mirror provided the titles to the single.

Three of the music magazines reviewed the single in their November 18 issues. In Disc, Penny Valentine called the record "great, shattering and marvelous." "Hello, Goodbye" was simple and direct, but showed "how the Beatles can make even the most ordinary lyrics sound something special." The song had lines like "You say high, I say low," "but massed and compressed with a mammoth cathedral backing, a hold-back ending, and then everyone coming crashing back sounding like panting West African tribesmen." It was "immediately attractive and immediately catchy." "I Am The Walrus," with John's "grating, sad voice," was more difficult to grasp. "It has shades of 'Alice In Wonderland' and extraordinary things going on in the backing that nobody will understand." The song contained a "few jolly dodgy Lennon lines and...[was] crazy and weird and somehow desperate." In a separate article, Disc reported on a controversy over "I Am The Walrus" for the line "Crabalocker fishwife pornographic priestess boy you been a naughty girl you let your knickers down." John said, "The words just appeared that way." Paul added, "this is quite a commonplace saying—to be caught with your knickers down is to be taken by surprise....It's quite harmless."

In NME, Derek Johnson marveled "how the Beatles always succeed in creating a minor sensation out of something incredibly simple!" "Hello, Goodbye" had "a repetitive lyric repeated over and over by Paul, while John and George chip in with vivid tonal harmonies...set to an urgent strumming beat, accentuated by maracas, clanking piano, occasional twangs and some solid Ringo drumming." The track's false ending was followed by a Polynesian-flavored fade-out. His conclusion: "Supremely commercial, and the complete answer to those feel the Beatles are going too way out." "I Am The Walrus" featured John growling out nonsense lyrics, backed by a complex score with violins and cellos. Johnson observed: "You need to hear it a few times before you can absorb it." In Melody Maker, Nick Jones noted that "Hello, Goodbye" seemed "ordinary" and lacking the "weaving hallucinogenic sounds that we've grown to love." But its "soul and feeling" shown through "with the strong repetitive lyric punctuated occasionally by a searing guitar note or a chugging piano riff." It was a nice sing-along that "fades and ska-beats back into a stronger, louder, and generally more positive ending." "I Am A Walrus" had "whining, sad blue strings behind John." Although not as complex as some of the Beatles previous efforts, "it builds nicely to a chattering, spinning cacophony of electricity and hissing gongs behind a barely audible conversation." Jones predicted the single would be a "Christmas number one, keeping the realms of pop within the boundaries of insanity, being as witty and as subtle as ever."

HELLO GOODBYE

I AM THE WALRUS   PARLOPHONE R 5655

Peter Jones reviewed the single in the November 25 Record Mirror. "Hello, Goodbye" was a "deliberately repetitive medium pace item" with typical McCartney vocals. It sounded like a send up. Although the lyrics mean nothing, the track's "insidious compelling brain-storming" would take it to number one. Jones preferred John's "I Am A Walrus" with its "fantastic wailing production" complete with "interesting acidy sounds throughout and catchy strange lyrics." It was a "very long side with the usual Beatles psychological tricks being played throughout."

The music industry guide, Record Retailer, called the single "tremendous" in its November 22 issue. The magazine went on to say: "Again the impact comes from the great progression of ideas, though the top deck is basically a very simple tune, with even simpler lyrics. But the Beatles delve deep, break all sorts of pop rules and come up with another sure number one. Flip is an amazing potpourri of sounds, words (controversial in one part) and electronic control. Brilliant popular music."

"Hello, Goodbye" debuted in Record Retailer at number nine on November 29 while "Let The Heartaches Begin" by Long John Baldry was topping the charts. The following week it moved to number one where it remained for seven straight weeks. The disc charted for 12 weeks, including nine weeks in the top ten. The single entered the Melody Maker chart at number 3 on December 2. The next week it moved up to number one where it remained for four weeks. "Hello, Goodbye" spent ten weeks on the charts, eight of which were in the top ten. The single also debuted in NME at number 3 on December 2. The next week it spent its first of six straight weeks at the top. The disc charted for 10 weeks, including nine in the top ten. The BBC also reported the single at number one. The December 2 Disc reported that "Hello, Goodbye" had sold over 300,000 copies, earning the Beatles another silver disc award. By the middle of the month, over a half-million copies had been shipped. The record reportedly sold over 700,000 copies.

The December 2 Disc reported that the BBC had refused to show the "Hello, Goodbye" promotional clip prepared by the Beatles because it violated the Musicians Union ban on miming. Instead, viewers of the November 23 Top Of The Pops heard the new single but saw extracts from the Beatles film *A Hard Day's Night*. The clip was also pulled from the BBC-2 color program Late Night Line-Up and replaced with the Condon Jazz Four playing Beatles songs.

DISC
and MUSIC ECHO 9d

DECEMBER 2, 1967   USA 20c

LONG JOHN: film star?

TOM JONES on Elvis

SCAFFOLD get a hit

A STONE goes solo

CENSORED! THE NEW BEATLES PICTURE MISSED BY 15 MILLION TV VIEWERS!

CHRISTMAS LP SPOTLIGHT

4-PAGE SPECIAL STARTS ON PAGE 12

'HELLO, GOODBYE' HITS THE CHART AT 3

HERE IT IS! Exclusive to Disc. The picture they wouldn't let you see — banned from TV last week. John, Paul, George and Ringo onstage at London's Saville Theatre, where they made three promotion films for their new single, "Hello, Goodbye," which enters the chart at number three this week.

The Beatles singing and playing — and a troupe of pretty girls in Hawaiian costume dancing — would have been seen on "Top Of The Pops" last Thursday, BUT for a ban by show producer, Johnnie Stewart. He turned down the film clip because of the Musicians Union ruling on miming.

Being asked to dance for the Beatles was an envied experience for the girls. And Disc spoke to the three in our picture — Jenny Rufus (seen with Paul), Christine Schiefinger (near Ringo) and Karen Collett (with John)—for their impressions.

It all happened about three weeks ago when the group were shooting movie inserts to promote their latest single. Half-a-dozen dancing dollies were swiftly recruited, draped in grass skirts and adorned with flowers.

And as John, Paul, George and Ringo sang their way to another hit in front of the cameras the girls ran through a specially-prepared routine to suit the song.

"It was an exciting experience for us," explained 23-year-old Karen Collett. "We were thrilled at the opportunity to meet the boys.

It's a nice thing to look back on—after hearing so much about them."

Said Brighton belle Christine Schiefinger, also 23: "It was a lovely day. There was a lot of hanging around and the Beatles were very sweet. They bought us coffees and Cokes and handed out cigarettes. We all chatted freely. There was nothing high - and - mighty about them."

Full story: page 4

By mid-November 1967, Beatles fans had been wondering for over two months how the group was going to release the songs from their *Magical Mystery Tour* film. Some articles speculated that the tracks might be issued on one or two singles and an EP. The problem was that were not enough songs for an album but too many for an EP. The answer finally came in the November 18 music magazines. The six songs would be released in a special book containing two 45-rpm discs and 32 pages of color and B&W illustrations priced under a pound at 19s 6d on December 1.

NME praised the product as a "spectacular package presentation." Disc described it as a "Beatles' Christmas bonus." Record Mirror observed that the Beatles had "again created their own rules." Melody Maker provided the most detailed description of the package, informing readers that the special book would have one disc in a sleeve inside the front cover and the other disc inside a sleeve in the back cover. The six songs were spread across the records as follows. Disc 1, Side 1: "Magical Mystery Tour" and "Your Mother Should Know." Disc 1, Side 2: "I Am The Walrus." Disc 2, Side 1: "The Fool On The Hill" and "Flying." Disc 2, Side 2: "Blue Jay Way." The records would be issued in mono and in stereo. In addition to photographs from the film, the book had six pages of a color cartoon depicting the *Magical Mystery Tour* story drawn by Beatles Book artist Bob Gibson and written and edited by Tony Barrow. The center of the book contained a pull-out supplement with the lyrics to the songs. According to Barrow, "The Beatles were anxious to keep the cost of the whole production under one pound and EMI cooperated in this." In America, the *Magical Mystery Tour* songs would be placed on one side of an LP, with five Beatles singles on the other.

The November 25 NME contained an article by Norrie Drummond on his visit to a Beatles editing session for *Magical Mystery Tour* held in a small Soho studio. Upon arriving, he heard a barrel-organ arrangement of "She Loves You." John indicated that they had a few more weeks to go, but were happy with what they'd done. Paul said: "Film-making isn't as difficult as many people imagine...'Magical Mystery Tour' was an experiment and so far it's been successful...We learned so much from working on our own." That same week Melody Maker also reported that the Beatles were editing the film at a Soho studio. The magazine added that the segment prepared by Traffic would not be in the film due to difficulty fitting it in. Fans learned that the songs from *Magical Mystery Tour* would be played on Saturday (November 25) on BBC Radio One's program Where It's At. John would be interviewed by Kenny Everett.

★ Direct . . . from the Beatles TV film track . . . half a dozen hits on a pair of 45 r.p.m. discs!

★ Buy the Magical Mystery Tour book, and records, complete for only 19 6d . . .

★ A 32-page full colour book packed with exclusive pictures— a strip cartoon of the Magical Mystery Tour story — plus the words to the songs in the show!

EMI

THE GREATEST RECORDING ORGANISATION IN THE WORLD

Record One : "Magical Mystery Tour"   Record Two : "The Fool On the Hill"
"Your Mother Should Know"   "Flying"
"I am The Walrus"   "Blue Jay Way"

AVAILABLE EVERYWHERE

NME, Disc and Melody Maker reviewed the *Magical Mystery Tour* EP in their November 25 issues. In NME, Nick Logan opens his review quoting from the left inside cover flap of the package: "Away in the sky, beyond the clouds, live four or five magicians. By casting Wonderful Spells they turn the Most Ordinary Coach Trip into a Magical Mystery Tour." He then heaps praise on the set: "The Beatles are at it again, stretching pop music to its limits on beautiful sound canvasses, casting wonderful spells beyond the clouds to turn the dullest plastic disc into a magical mystery tour of sounds fantastic, sounds unbelievable!" In keeping with the spirit of the package, Logan's piece reads like its own magical mystery tour. "The four musician-magicians take us by the hand and lead us happily tripping through the clouds...past the fool on the hill...into the world of Alice in Wonderland....This is the Beatles out there in front and the rest of us, a cast of millions, in their wake. This is *Sgt. Pepper* and beyond, heading for marvelous places."

The title track has "a lot of rollicking *Sgt. Pepper* type roll and swing...with an almost Herb Alpert trumpet going away in the background, a piano break in the middle and [a] fade out to tinkling bells and what sounds like the clatter of milk bottles." "Your Mother Should Know" is a "nice easy to sing along track," with "sadness and immediate appeal." "I Am The Walrus" takes the listener into "the world of Alice in Wonderland," a fantastic track with a "whole bagful of weird and eerie Beatle sounds like a ringing doorbell and somebody sawing a plank of wood." "The Fool On The Hill" has a strong McCartney vocal "with an off-key penny whistle piping out behind him." "Flying" is a "very odd instrumental" containing "Some tricky guitar work with chanting vocals in the background" which "soars away into the skies in a crescendo of tinkling piano and very weird sound effects." "Blue Jay Way" opens with a church organ and initially sounds like Procol Harum's "A Whiter Shade Of Pale." Although the disc identifies George Harrison as the composer, Logan erroneously attributes the vocal to John. The song is a "whirlwind of sound." When over, "We are back from beyond the clouds and down on mother earth to reality." Logan ends his magical listening tour with a sales pitch: "It will cost you 19s 6d and you can buy it on December 18. Happy Traveling!"

With stereo records finally beginning to make inroads into the British market in late 1967, Melody Maker devoted several pages to "The Swing to Stereo" in its November 25 issue. Bob Dawbarn seized on the opportunity to review the stereo EP package in an article titled "Magical Beatles—in stereo."

Dawbarn praised the set: "They've done it again—six tracks which no other pop group in the world could begin to approach for originality combined with the popular touch." "Magical Mystery Tour" was described as a "massive, storming piece with Paul singing lead over a ten-ton beat." The track featured guitars and brass with piano taking over at the end. "Your Mother Should Know" was propelled by "prominent piano and steady four-to-the-bar rhythm" and had "a tune that sticks in the memory first time around." For "I Am The Walrus," Dawbarn commented that "bits like the cello figures sound great in stereo," no doubt favorably comparing the stereo version of the song to the mono B-side of the new Beatles single. "The Fool On The Hill" had "immediate impact" and was a "typical Beatle lyrical ballad." He noted the gimmicky and "highly effective use of penny whistles instead of flutes" and thought the song would make an excellent A-side. [The song actually used a recorder played by Paul and three flutes by outside musicians.] "Flying" was a "weird piece, full of organ sounds" that ended "with a touch of the Dr. Who." George Harrison's "Blue Jay Way" had the "requisite Eastern overtones." It was a "sinister little tune" and the most difficult of the recordings "to assimilate at one hearing." In keeping with the swing to stereo theme, Dawbarn concluded that: "The stereo recording increases the effect of the Beatles harmonies and the action-packed arrangements."

In Disc, Penny Valentine gave a track-by-track account. She singled out "The Fool On The Hill," predicting it would be another Lennon-McCartney classic that would "be sung all over the world." It featured Paul "singing wistfully about a man everyone else considers a fool but who actually is the only one who SEES what's going on." The track was a "beautiful fly-away number" with gentle flute and penny whistles and piano and was "the Beatles offering of a new 'Yesterday.'" The title song was a "super send-up rock-'n'-roll thing" sung by John with the others "chanting like girls in the background." Valentine thought "Your Mother Should Know" was the least effective song in the set, but noted it was a "jolly little number ideal for coach singing, which is presumably what was in mind when it was written." The instrumental "Flying" featured "dark organ, gritty guitars and woodwind" and "Far away monk-like voices" chanting. The track "disintegrates like blancmange [a sweet gelatinous dessert made with cornstarch and milk] at the end." George Harrison's "Blue Jay Way" was a "strange, almost one-note number that needs a lot of listening" to appreciate. "I Am The Walrus" was the B-side to the group's new single. Valentine quipped that the song explained "why John is splendidly dressed in animal fur with two long white teeth on the cover."

Norman Jopling reviewed *Magical Mystery Tour* in the December 1 Record Mirror, describing the project as one in which the Beatles were able to "exercise their vivid imaginations." Unlike *Sgt. Pepper*, where "the effects were chiefly sound and only the album cover was visual," the latest project had a "visual side...in the shape of a TV film" that "dominated the music." Jopling noted: "Everything from fantasy, children's comics, acid (psychedelic) humour is included on the record and in the booklet." The title track was a "shouting, loud effective item with a hollow overall sound and an unusually different piano ending." "Your Mother Should Know" was a medium tempo ballad with a "corny sort of tune." However, the song's atmosphere was fantastic—"a hazy, stoned kind of sensation which reminds you of hearing old tunes, in smoky rooms." The single "I Am The Walrus" sounded even better in stereo. "The Fool On The Hill" was a "thoughtful reflective...ballad dealing with a perceptive person and the attitudes of those around him." Jopling described the track as "Deliberately disjointed." The instrumental "Flying" was a "ponderous medium pace effort which becomes strangely exhilarating" and ends with a "disturbing tuning-note." "Blue Jay Way" featured George's dry vocals up against a swooping church organ and an overall "seashell sound."

The unique 2-EP book package sold for 19 shillings, 6 pence (at a time when there were 20 shillings to one pound sterling and 12 pence to a shilling). While the price was about 61% the cost of an album (32 shillings or one pound, 12 shillings), it was nearly double the cost of a standard EP (10 shillings, 9 pence) and over three times the cost of a single (6 shillings, 8 pence). The price and unique format did not adversely affect sales as evidenced by advance orders in excess of 400,000 units and sales of over 500,000 by Christmas 1967. The EP was awarded a silver disc on December 23, 1967. By mid-January 1968, sales exceeded 600,000. Dealers ordered over 50,000 copies of the imported U.S. album and sold enough copies at 47 shillings, six pence for the LP to reach number 31 in the Record Retailer LP chart. By the time *Magical Mystery Tour* was released on December 8, 1967, the EP format had diminished to the point where Record Retailer had discontinued publishing a separate EP chart the week before. The magazine charted the set for 12 weeks with a peak at number two, second to "Hello, Goodbye." *Magical Mystery Tour* entered the Melody Maker singles chart on December 16, 1967, at number 17. Three weeks later on January 13, 1968, the EP replaced "Hello, Goodbye" at the number one spot. It charted for ten weeks, including three in the top five and five in the top ten. NME charted the set for eight weeks, including two weeks at two behind "Hello, Goodbye."

RECORD MIRROR

Largest selling colour pop weekly newspaper. 6d. No. 351. Every Thursday. Week ending Dec. 1, 1967

"MAGICAL MYSTERY TOUR" is another example of a subject in which the Beatles have been able to exercise their vivid imaginations. With "Sgt. Pepper", the effects were chiefly sound and only the album cover was visual— but with the latest project the visual side—in the shape of a TV film—has dominated the music, which comes in the form of six tunes on two EP's in an adventurous booklet of EP size, for only 19/6. Everything from fantasy, children's comics, acid (psychedelic) humour is included on the record and in the booklet. Depending on your involvement, you can read whatever you like into the "kiddies'" plots, told in the booklet with cartoons by Bob Gibson and captions by Tony Barrow.

"Magical Mystery Tour" is a shouting, loud effective item with a hollow overall sound and an unusually different piano ending. "Your Mother Should Know" is medium tempo ballad with a corny sort of tune—but the atmosphere developed is fantastic. It's a hazy, stoned kind of sensation which reminds you of hearing old tunes, in smoky rooms . . . one line is 'Lift up your hearts and sing me a song, that was a hit before your mother was born". You've all heard "I Am The Walrus"—it sounds even better in stereo. "The Fool On The Hill" is a thoughtful reflective type of number—a ballad dealing with a perceptive person and the attitudes of those around him. Deliberately disjointed. "Flying", the only instrumental on the EP's is a ponderous medium pace effort which becomes strangely exhilarating and features wordless vocal backing some way through. A disturbing tuning-note closes things and the instrumentation tapers off. "Blue Jay Way", written by George, features his dry vocals up against a swooping church organ. The story line, dealing with a human situation is enhanced by, to paraphrase Nick Jones, a 'seashell sound".

NORMAN JOPLING

Safe as Mirrec

PARLOPHONE 45 R.P.M. MMT-A1

NORTHERN SONGS NCB
℗ 1967 (7XCE.18435)
1
SOLD IN U.K. SUBJECT TO RESALE PRICE CONDITIONS, SEE PRICE LISTS
1

THE BEATLES
In Songs and Music from the T.V. Film "Magical Mystery Tour"
1. MAGICAL MYSTERY TOUR
2. YOUR MOTHER SHOULD KNOW
(Lennon—McCartney)
Producer: George Martin
MADE IN GT. BRITAIN

PARLOPHONE 45 R.P.M. MMT-A1

NORTHERN SONGS NCB
℗ 1967 (7XCE.18434)
2
SOLD IN U.K. SUBJECT TO RESALE PRICE CONDITIONS, SEE PRICE LISTS
2

THE BEATLES
In Songs and Music from the T.V. Film "MAGICAL MYSTERY TOUR"
I AM THE WALRUS
(Lennon—McCartney)
Producer: George Martin
MADE IN GT. BRITAIN

PARLOPHONE 45 R.P.M. MMT-B1

NORTHERN SONGS NCB
℗ 1967 (7XCE.18436)
3
SOLD IN U.K. SUBJECT TO RESALE PRICE CONDITIONS, SEE PRICE LISTS
3

THE BEATLES
In Songs and Music from the T.V. Film "MAGICAL MYSTERY TOUR"
1. THE FOOL ON THE HILL (Lennon—McCartney)
2. FLYING (Instrumental) (Harrison—Lennon—McCartney—Starkey)
Producer: George Martin
MADE IN GT. BRITAIN

PARLOPHONE 45 R.P.M. MMT-B1

NORTHERN SONGS NCB
℗ 1967 (7XCE.18437)
4
SOLD IN U.K. SUBJECT TO RESALE PRICE CONDITIONS, SEE PRICE LISTS
4

THE BEATLES
In Songs and Music from the T.V. Film "MAGICAL MYSTERY TOUR"
BLUE JAY WAY
(Harrison)
Producer: George Martin
MADE IN GT. BRITAIN

Beatles fans were treated to extensive coverage of the *Magical Mystery Tour* project in the December 1967 and January 1968 issues of The Beatles Book (Nos. 53 and 54). The December issue, which came out prior to the film's screening on the BBC, featured color photos on its front and back covers and contained a color center spread and 19 black and white pictures, described by Editor Johnny Dean as "the most unusual collection of Beatle photos you've ever seen." Dean emphasized that the film had been "devised, written, produced and directed by the four great musicians who have given us so much musical magic in the past." Mal and Neil provided their personal insights into *Magical Mystery Tour*, from the Beatles decision to stop personal appearances to the project's inception during Paul's U.S. visit to the planning to the filming to the editing to the contents of the special packaging that included a color cartoon strip by Bob Gibson and Tony Barrow. This was followed by an article by Barrow (credited to his pen name Frederick James) titled "The Mystery Partly Explained" in which he told the *Magical Mystery Tour* story without giving away too many secrets.

In the January 1968 issue, Mal and Neil took fans into the recording studios for their report on "How The Magical E.P.s Were Made." The book also contains a half dozen or so pictures from the filming of *Magical Mystery Tour* and eight photos from the production of the "Hello, Goodbye" promo clip.

The introductions to the main articles in the December 1967 issue spoke of the Beatles planned new direction. Barrow opened with: "There's never been a Television Show quite like it! And I doubt if there will be again until The Beatles make another TV film next year!" Mal and Neil went even further: "'MAGICAL MYSTERY TOUR' marks the beginning of a very important new stage in the career of The Beatles. For the first time they have created their own show for television. They have worked out the scenes, hired the cast, written the basic script, composed the songs and incidental soundtrack music, directed the actual shooting and edited the finished film. And, of course, they have taken part in the show—playing the parts of four Magical Mystery Tour coach passengers PLUS a number of other roles." They went on to say that if all goes according to plan, the group would be looking after every aspect of the scripting, shooting, direction and editing of their upcoming third motion picture. But despite the praises of Mal, Neil, Johnny and Tony and the magic of four or five magicians above the clouds, things did not go as planned.

The Beatles
MONTHLY **BOOK**

No. **53**

DEC. 1967

5th YEAR

2/-

JANUARY No. **54**

The Beatles BOOK

Price TWO SHILLINGS

The initial reviews of the *Magical Mystery Tour* TV spectacular that ran in the December 23 music magazines prior to the show's black and white BBC broadcast on Boxing Day (December 26) gave the appearance that the Beatles had once again successfully pushed the creative boundaries. In NME, Norrie Drummond said that "the Beatles should start planning their next full-length film immediately" and was "convinced they are extremely capable of writing and directing a major movie for release." He acknowledged that the group broke many of rules followed by established directors, but this "seemed to add to the delightful, free and easy atmosphere throughout the film." While sometimes the results looked like amateur holiday snapshots, that may have been the effect the Beatles intended. Drummond wrote that the story line is simple—the exploits of the weird and amusing characters on a coach tour. The cast included Victor Spinetti, who appeared in the prior Beatles films, Paul's brother Mike McGear, Mal Evans and the Bonzo Dog Doo Dah Band. The Beatles played multiple parts, including a "hilariously funny team of camp wizards." He put in special words of praise for Ringo, who "comes over very, very funnily" and complimented the clever sequences for the musical numbers, finding "The Fool On The Hill" to be "particularly beautiful—especially in colour." He lamented that most TV viewers will only be able to see the film in black and white. His bottom line was that "although everything appears to be unrelated, the film as a whole is immensely entertaining and never dull."

Penny Valentine, writing in Disc, also praised Ringo, calling him the best thing about the film. Although she revelled in the glory of Paul singing "The Fool On The Hill," the "mysterious mistiness" of George in "Blue Jay Way" and John's funny scene with the little girl on the coach, it was Ringo who "emerges in this hour-long fairytale as a delightful comedian with a real touch of brilliance." She found the film more interesting because the Beatles were free to do what they wanted. While she initially thought "very nice, but nothing very new," upon reflection she wondered "if it is not all too easy to criticise a group from whom, after all this time, you have really come to expect not just perfection but constant surprise, constant genius." Valentine described the show as a "light tale of imagination" that entertains and amuses, though at times drags. She enjoyed the strip club scene with the Bonzo Dog Doo Dah Band and the interludes with the Beatles as wizards above the clouds baking cakes and preparing spells. Her favorite bit was the tender love scene between the elderly couple on the beach. Record Mirror's Derek Boltwood wrote that "there was comedy, pathos and some beautiful fantasy scenes—all held together by the multi-colored magical mystery bus."

Beatles must make another 'Mystery Tour'

Says **Norrie Drummond**

IF they aren't already doing so, the Beatles should start planning their next full-length film immediately. After watching a rough cut of their "Magical Mystery Tour," which BBC-TV viewers can see on Boxing Day, I am convinced they are extremely capable of writing and directing a major movie for release on one of the major cinema circuits.

Certainly they break many of the rules which established directors stick to but this only seemed to add to the delightful, free and easy atmosphere throughout the film. Occasionally though it didn't quite work and the result looked a bit like Auntie Maggie's holiday snapshots—but then with the Beatles this could easily have been the effect they intended.

The story line is simple. The film opens with Ringo taking his enormous Aunt Jessie—played by Jessie Robbins—on a coach tour. John, Paul and George are among the weird and amusing characters on the coach, and the story basically is simply of their exploits.

There's the over-exuberant courier; the midget photographer, the dour middle-aged bachelor Buster Bloodvessel—played by Ivor Cutler—and a host of other incongruous personalities.

Victor Spinetti, who played the harassed TV producer in "A Hard Day's Night," re-appears in "Mystery Tour" as an even more harassed army sergeant.

Other familiar faces which crop up throughout the film include Mike McGear, Beatles' road manager Mal Evans and the Bonzo Dog Doo Dah Band.

The Beatles themselves appear in a variety of parts. John first of all as the travel agent who sells Ringo his tickets; then with his hair slicked back he becomes a leering, cowering waiter. Paul pops up as a stiff upper-lipped Army Colonel, and all four made up a hilariously funny team of camp wizards.

If you happen to be wondering how they manage to become any of these characters when the story is about a coach tour don't ask me!

But somehow, although everything appears unrelated, the film as a whole is immensely entertaining and never dull.

Clever sequences

The film sequences for the musical numbers are extremely clever and the scene where Paul sings "Fool On The Hill" silhouetted against a setting sun is particularly beautiful—especially in colour.

For "Blue Jay Way," George is seen sitting cross-legged in a swirling mist which materialises into a variety of shapes and patterns. It's a pity that most TV viewers will be able to see it only in black-and-white.

"I Am The Walrus" has four of them togged up in animal costumes switching at times to them bobbing across the screen as egg-men.

In the final scene in the film for "Your Mother Should Know," all four are dressed in immaculate white trousers and tails as they do a soft shoe shuffle through a team of ballroom dancers.

A special word of praise for Ringo, who more than the others comes over very, very funnily. But praise to all of them for making a most entertaining film. I only wish they would now put out a sequel made up from the parts they left on the cutting-room floor.

GEORGE, JOHN, PAUL and RINGO in one of the scenes from their "Magical Mystery Tour" to be seen on BBC-TV on Boxing Day.

The December 1967 Beat Instrumental, published by Beatles Book publisher Sean O'Mahony, foresaw the likelihood that critics were looking forward to berating the Beatles for having the audacity to produce their own film: "The critics are waiting for the first showing with bated breath. If it's all wrong, they'll be very happy." Unfortunately for the Beatles, with few exceptions, the critics were quite happy to tear apart the group and their film.

The British press was brutal in its condemnation of *Magical Mystery Tour*. The Daily Mirror reported that thousands of baffled viewers protested to the BBC, with writer Mary Malone describing the film as "chaotic." Her verdict: "Too Toot Tootsie John, Paul, George and Ringo as film makers. It's hello–and goodbye." Robert Ottaway of the Daily Sketch wrote: "This witless home movie...scotched the myth of their genius." Writing in the Daily Express, James Thomas called the film "tasteless nonsense" and "blatant rubbish," adding: "The bigger they are, the harder they fall. And what a fall it was...The whole boring saga confirmed a long held suspicion of mine that The Beatles are four rather pleasant young men who have made so much money that they can apparently afford to be contemptuous of the public." Henry Raynor wrote in The Times: "This was a programme to experience rather than to understand; I was unfortunate–I lacked the necessary key." The Guardian called the film "an inspired freewheeling achievement," but then described it as a "kind of fantasy morality play about the grossness, warmth and stupidity of the audience."

The TV critic for The Evening News, James Green, had this to say: "It's a long day's night since any TV show took the hammering that this Beatles fantasy received by telephone and in print. Take your pick from the words, 'Rubbish, piffle, chaotic, flop, tasteless, non-sense, emptiness and appalling!' I watched it. There was precious little magic and the only mystery was how the BBC came to buy it." In The Daily Mail, Douglas Marlborough reported that not only was the BBC flooded with protests, but that "mystified viewers" also phoned the newspaper, with one caller saying: "It was terrible! It was worse than terrible. I watched it in a room together with twenty-five other people, and we were all stunned!" TV critic Peter Black, who opened with "It's colossal, the conceit of the Beatles," called the show "Appalling!" The Sun's Richard Last reported that the "BBC switchboard was overwhelmed" by complaints, with some protesting that the program was "incomprehensible." Perhaps wanting the last word, Last called the show "a bore based on the proposition that improvisation and random selection are a valid substitute for organized art."

It wasn't just the press that criticized the film. The BBC's reaction index, arrived at by quizzing viewers who saw the program, was a dismal, historically low 23 out of 100. The evening after the show's broadcast, Paul was given the opportunity to defend the film on The Frost Programme. Host David Frost set the stage: "The Beatles' music brings unanimous enthusiasm and approval pretty well. Last night their television show did not bring unanimous enthusiasm and approval, and everyone seems to be discussing it today. Here is the man most responsible, Mr. Paul McCartney." When asked why the critics didn't like the film, Paul said he didn't know, but added, "I quite liked it myself." As to why people were puzzled, he thought people were "looking for a plot, and there wasn't one."

As for how the project came about, he explained the group had been waiting for a couple of years to make another feature film and "had been asking people to write stories and write plots," but that nobody came up with one. "So we thought, 'We'll do something which...isn't like a real film in as much as it's got a story and a beginning, and we'll just do a selection....We'd put together a lot of things that we like the look of, and see what happens." He talked of the contrast between recording an album and making a film. For an LP, "all the songs don't necessarily have to fit in with each other," but with a film "you seem to have to have a thread to pull it all together." He thought a mystery tour with things happening to a group of people on a bus would be enough of a thread. By calling it a "magical mystery tour...then anything might happen, and it wouldn't have a thread if it was magic." Paul added, "if you watch it a second time it does grow on you." This was another difference between film and records in that Beatles records were played multiple times with the listener often gaining a greater appreciation with each listen. When asked if the film was a success or a failure, Paul thought it was both. He admitted that it couldn't be called a success because "the papers didn't like it." He thought the next one would be better and "have a fat plot, as opposed to a thin plot." He reminded Frost that many people first thought "Strawberry Fields Forever" and "I Am The Walrus" were terrible. He predicted that "in about a year or two these things that didn't look like successes will look a bit more like successes."

The January 6, 1968 NME quoted Paul as saying: "We could have easily assembled a team of experts and asked them to come up with a first class show for Christmas which would star the Beatles. But that would have been easy. We wanted to try and do it ourselves and we were expecting criticism but nothing quite as bad as we got."

The film received a friendly review in The Sunday Times from Hunter Davies, who was writing an authorized biography of the Beatles. Davies described the show as "excellent entertainment, funny, clever and very professional looking," adding "They went into it all with their eyes closed to all the traditions, ignorant of all the ridiculous conventions which have hamstrung almost every British film director who ever wanted to make a film exactly as he wanted."

The January 6, 1968 music magazines reacted to the avalanche of negative reviews heaped upon the *Magical Mystery Tour* film by the British national press. In NME, Norrie Drummond stood by his prior assessment that the film was entertaining. He wondered if the vitriolic attacks by these highly-respected journalists were prompted by a dislike of the film and their personal dislike of the Beatles. Drummond singled out and responded to James Thomas, who accused the Beatles of being contemptuous to the public. "How wrong you are Mr. Thomas. The Beatles set out to make a film which they hoped the public would like and which would give them some sense of satisfaction." After viewing it for the third time, Drummond was even more convinced that the film had "great merit."

In Disc, Penny Valentine called the film "good but it wasn't a masterpiece." With the Beatles showing they were mere mortals, the critics came down like a "pack of howling wolves." The Beatles, "far ahead of any of their pop predecessors, went out on a limb and faced the consequences." Wondering if the film fell short for the audience it aimed for, Valentine solicited the opinions of other musicians. Alan Price "liked it because it was fresh." For him, the Beatles could do no wrong. Pete Townshend thought it was a great film. The reason it was not understood by so many was because it "wasn't the usual jolly Boxing Day stuff they expected." Spencer Davis enjoyed it, noting: "People should think back on coach tours and they'd see how true this was. It was an experiment, and for me it came off." Record Mirror had a massive response from readers with about two-thirds coming out in favor of the film. Melody Maker presented opposing views. Bob Dawbarn noted if the show "achieved nothing else, it underlined the remarkable gap between the generations." Although "amateurish in parts, confused at times," it entertained him for the full 50 minutes. Alan Walsh wondered why the Beatles made a film that failed to communicate with its audience. "The Mystery Tour was not so much a flop as a mass audience flop, even though it might have been a Beatles triumph."

NME printed letters from its readers in its January 6 issue. D. Millar was disgusted by the reviews, finding it a "marvelous film." Phillippa Dean was appalled by the savagery of the attacks by the press. While not a great film, the song sequences were brilliant and "there were some memorable moments." The Beatles deserved credit for the "beautiful music and a brave and interesting experiment in film making." Andy Smart was the lone exception, finding the film, apart from the songs, dull. He doubted Brian Epstein would have let them "turn out such a load of rubbish."

The January 13 Disc gave its readers the last word: "Groovy or Grotty?" Miss B. Toole wondered if the film needed to make sense, asking, "why not just sit back and accept it as a beautiful, crazy and amusing dream?" J. Jobes described it as "the best television show ever" full of laughs and terrific songs. Joe Fox thought the papers were "cruelly unfair to the Beatles," failing to give them credit for trying something different and risky and for their hard work. David Palmer called the film "the most fantastic and original TV show ever, proving once again they are the world's greatest performers." Eileen Read thought it was "magical, mysterious, full of fantasy, and exciting from beginning to end." Mrs. H. Murray wrote, "It was too stupid for words." A. Markus thought it was "a load of rubbish, though not bad for the first attempt." Peter Naylor wondered, "Are people so stupid as to need the plot printed in block capitals to be satisfied with the programme?" A.R. Wooster observed that "It was hopeless to think families sitting around on Boxing Day full of Christmas cheer would understand the intricate thought and construction behind it."

The color broadcast on January 5 changed some minds. Under the headline "Colour vital to Beatles film," Norman Hare of the Daily Telegraph ran the following reassessment: "In black and white it looked appalling...I took a second trip with the Beatles on their 'Magical Mystery Tour' on BBC 2 last night. Colour produced the magic that sadly seemed missing on the first coach outing. If there was a mystery it was why the BBC ever thought the film was suitable for screening in monochrome. They might as well have tried to paint a picture of a sunset with a tar brush."

Paul plugged the next Beatles film project in the February 10, 1968 Disc, saying it was likely to be screened in May and providing the following description: "The 'Yellow Submarine' film is about the pepper people–who are really flower people–and their battle with the blue meanies, who are the philistines trying to put down culture etc."

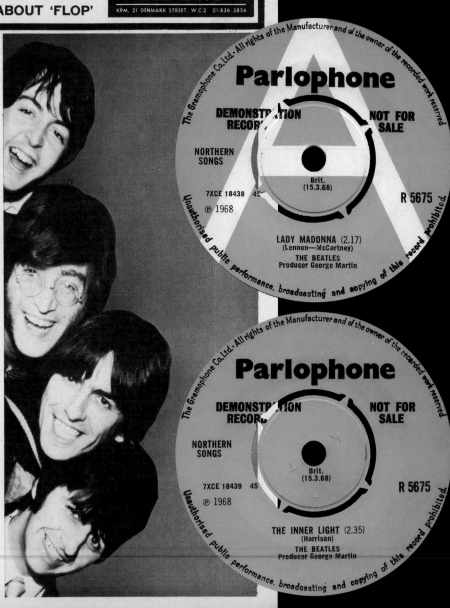

The February 17 NME reported that the Beatles next single would be issued on March 15. "Lady Madonna" was described as being "as close to rock 'n' roll as the Beatles could get in 1968." Paul, the lead singer, told NME: "It is not outright rock, but it's that kind of thing–we think the time is right." The B-side was "The Inner Light," a George Harrison composition, described by Paul as unusual and the most commercial song written by George. Its backing of Indian instruments was one of four tracks recently recorded in Bombay by George during a session for the *Wonderwall* film soundtrack. The vocals were added the previous week at EMI's London studios. The group also recorded a song specifically for the *Yellow Submarine* cartoon film, which fans would later learn was "Hey Bulldog."

That same week Disc reported on the upcoming "Lady Madonna" single, while Record Mirror mentioned that the Beatles were in the recording studio all of the previous week working on three new songs, including a George Harrison composition whose backing track was recorded in Bombay [now known as Mumbai]. Melody Maker ran a brief cover story on the "Lady Madonna" single, which was one of four songs recorded during a recent session. Sax players Ronnie Scott and Harry Klein were part of a four-piece sax section that played on the song. Scott said, "'Lady Madonna' is a rock 'n' roll thing on which I take a solo." The group was soon to fly to India to study with the Maharishi Mahesh Yogi. The following week Melody Maker provided information regarding the single's B-side, "The Inner Light." The March 2 Disc ran a story on Britain's recent Rock 'n' Roll Revival. The article noted that the Beatles had lent their name to the rock revival with "Lady Madonna," which had a blatant rock feel and marked a "swing away from Flowerpower and back to the big beat." The magazine added, "what the Beatles do, everybody does."

The first formal reviews of "Lady Madonna" began appearing in the March 9 music magazines. NME noted that the Beatles had turned full circle, "back to square one again with a rocker!" The track wasn't the "raw, blatant rock of the group's early days," but rather was "controlled, polished and impeccably produced...up-dated sophisticated rock!" The song opened with "clanking barrel house piano" and had guttural sax passages and a solid infectious beat. Paul sang lustily, backed by "'syncopated' harmonies–sometimes indulging in trumpet impressions reminiscent of the Mills Brothers." NME realized that the flip side, "The Inner Light," might not appeal to the masses due to its Indian instrumentation, but urged readers to keep listening as the song was really beautiful and tenderly sung by George.

Writing in the March 9 Melody Maker, Chris Welch thought that "Lady Madonna" wasn't so much a rock 'n' roll song, but "more an impressionist view of that riotous music of all our yesterdays." It had the same feeling as the group's last rocker, "Sgt. Pepper," with Paul clearing his throat "to jig up and down and shout the usual quaint Beatles words," this time about "some bird lying in bed and mending her stockings." His favorite part was the piano intro and he wondered why Paul sounded like Ringo. After advising readers to buy the record, he noted: "After all that progression, the best thing they could have done was to go backwards." Welch closed on a sarcastic note: "But I can't really see this being a hit, not when there's stacks of competition from Four Jacks And A Jill and Kay Starr."

Disc's Penny Valentine noted how easy it was to praise the Beatles, but "truth must out." While others listen to a "lot of re-hashed old Eddie Cochran numbers badly done, the Beatles turn up with 'Lady Madonna.'" In this rock-based effort, the Beatles use the "thumping, raving piano and drum combination" for its backing, but give the track "their very own special touch." The end result: "Instead of sounding like tired old baggy eyed rock given a new face lift, it sounds fresh and new without losing any of the brassy urgency we associate with Little Richard...Jerry Lee...Fats and Bill Haley." George's "The Inner Light" was a "weird, effective little Indian piece with nice vocals." Penny collected the thoughts of other musicians. Mick Jagger liked the words, but felt the track was "too relaxed with not enough raw excitement." Steve Winwood thought is was great, sounding like something Bob Dylan might do. It was different and couldn't be compared to anything else they've recorded. Winwood observed: "The Beatles have never been very far away from rock 'n' roll." Michael d'Abo of Manfred Mann described it as "nice, bright and happy," but he wasn't knocked out by the vocal. He noted a similarity in the rhythm with "Bad Penny Blues." Engelbert Humperdinck liked the recording, finding it unusual, adventurous and "very Presleyish on the intro voice." He admired the group's courage for doing something different every time. Cilla Black joked that it sounded like "Ringo singing in tune."

Record Retailer gave the disc a favorable review in its March 13 issue. After commenting on the record's place in the current rock 'n' roll revival, the magazine noted that the Beatles "switch styles from complex to simple with complete ease." The magazine described "Lady Madonna" as "instantly distinctive, almost frighteningly." Harrison's Eastern-influenced flip side was singled out as a "complete contrast on a tremendous double-sider."

Norman Jopling reviewed the disc in the March 16 Record Mirror. While he thought the song lacked the "sharp quality of genuine old rock records," it was "so beautifully performed and timed, with good lyrics" that it would be well received. Paul's vocal was backed by "repetitive exciting piano, virile percussion and six-five special sax." The flip side had an interesting background and a "bubbly oriental sound with plenty of potted pop philosophy."

In an interview in the March 16 Melody Maker, Ringo commented on the perception that "Lady Madonna" marked a return to rock and roll: "We've been trying to make a rock and roll record for five years. Because rock and roll has suddenly hit the headlines, the great revival, because this one is a rocker—a slight one anyway—people are saying it's a rock and roll record." When told that a lot of people thought he was the lead singer on the song, Ringo agreed some people did think that, but added, "It doesn't sound like me to me." When the interviewer commented that "Lady Madonna" was different from the songs found on the *Sgt. Pepper* album, he replied, "We're always trying to be different. If people hadn't been saying 'the great rock and roll revival' we most probably still would have done this record, and it still would have been just the new Beatles single. It would have been rock and roll Beatles." When asked if the record indicated a new direction for the Beatles, Ringo said, "It's not a backwards step, as some people have said. Because it doesn't freak out, people think you're going backwards. It's just another type of song from the Beatles." That same issue ran comments by British disc jockey Alan Freeman on the single: "After *Sgt. Pepper*, I don't feel they could have progressed any further and still made contact with their fans, and I do believe that, above all else, keeping contact with their fans is what they want to do. I don't hear this as rock and roll at all, just up-tempo Beatles, and anything of theirs is surrounded by an aura of magic."

"Lady Madonna" began its eight-week run in Record Retailer on March 20 at number 11 while the number one song was "Legend Of Xanadu" by Dave Dee, Dozy, Beaky, Mick and Tich. The next week it spent its first of two weeks at the top ahead of "Delilah" by Tom Jones. "Lady Madonna" entered the NME chart at six on March 23 and moved up to number one the next week where it remained an additional week before dropping to four behind "Congratulations" by Cliff Richard, "What A Wonderful World" by Louis Armstrong and "Delilah." The single topped the BBC chart, but stalled at number two in Melody Maker. Disc awarded "Lady Madonna" a silver disc on March 30, 1968.

Two of the music magazines informed readers in their March 9 issues of another recently recorded Beatles track, "Across The Universe." NME wrote that the group would likely contribute the John Lennon song to an all-star charity album. In Disc, Bob Farmer reported that "Across The Universe" would be released for charity. The song, written and sung by John, had the same "peace on earth" appeal as "All You Need Is Love," and started and ended with the sound of seagulls. Farmer incorrectly speculated that the charity benefiting from the song would be associated with the Maharishi. The March 23 Disc confirmed through Tony Barrow that the Beatles had been approached by comedian Spike Milligan to contribute a song for a charity album to aid the World Wildlife Fund. Barrow indicated that the song could well be "Across The Universe," but it was not definite.

Readers of The Beatles Book learned about "Across The Universe" in the March 1968 issue (No. 56). In a Beatle News bit on the new single, the magazine reported that the group had recorded three new titles for consideration in early February: "Lady Madonna," "Across The Universe" and "The Inner Light." Everyone who heard the songs thought that "Across The Universe" was "really fantastic and deserved to be the new single," but the group opted for "Lady Madonna." During the recording of John's "Across The Universe" on February 4, John and Paul decided that girls would be needed to sing a high falsetto vocal passage. Paul recruited two fans hanging out at the studio, Lizzie Bravo and Gayleen Pease. Lizzie said, "I still don't believe it happened!," while Gayleen added, "It was like a dream. The Beatles are so easy to get on with." Producer George Martin was satisfied with their performance: "Considering the girls had never done any recording before, I think they were really great." The magazine's next issue (April 1968, No. 57) ran a report by Mal and Neil on new single sessions. "Across The Universe" would appear on a special charity LP. The article told of the backing vocals by Lizzie and Gayleen, who sang "Nothing's gonna change my world" over and over again. George played sitar on the track. The following overdubs were added on February 8: organ by John and George Martin, maracas by George Harrison and piano at the end by Paul. The Beatles last session before leaving for India was on February 11. Cameramen filmed the group for a TV clip to promote the new single, "Lady Madonna." [The promo film premiered the night before the single's release on Top Of The Pops on Thursday, March 14, and was broadcast later that night on Late Night Line-up and on Friday on All Systems Freeman!] The group rehearsed and recorded a song for inclusion in the soundtrack of the *Yellow Submarine* cartoon, John's "Hey Bulldog."

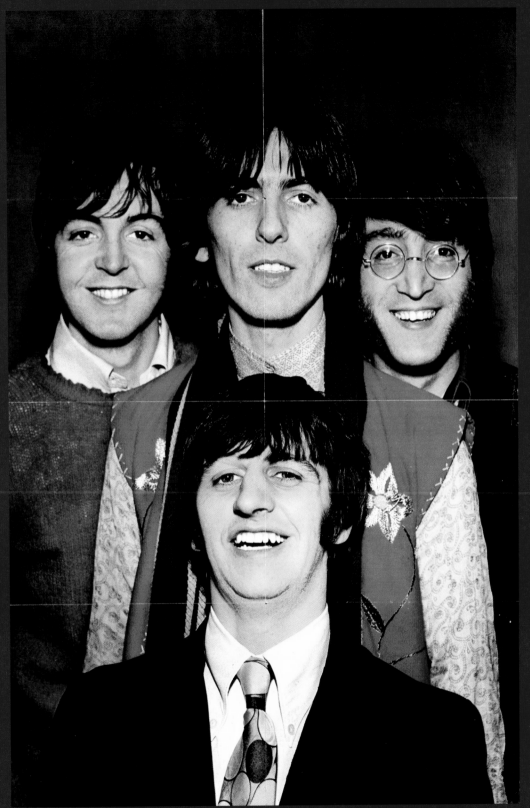

The Beatles 1968 Fan Club poster photo was taken at the February 1968 session.

The music magazines were also reporting on the *Yellow Submarine* cartoon. The March 23 Disc reported that the film songs would be issued around August, either on an EP or album. The May 18 Record Mirror revealed the titles of the four new Beatles songs written for the cartoon, but mistakenly attributed them all to Lennon and McCartney. The film told the story of the Beatles "traveling in a yellow submarine to defend 'Pepperland' against an attack of anti-music missiles and various other monsters." That week NME reported that the film's premiere was set for July 17. Disc and Melody Maker disclosed in their May 25 editions that the world premiere of *Yellow Submarine* would be held before an invited star-studded audience at the London Pavilion on July 17 with the Beatles in attendance. The June 1968 issue (No. 59) of The Beatles Book also reported on the July 17 premiere, claiming that the Beatles had taken a "close personal interest" in the making of the cartoon, "giving their enthusiastic approval to the drawings of themselves and expressing great delight at seeing all the curious characters...created for the story."

Yellow Submarine was shown to the press a week ahead of its release, enabling the July 13 music weeklies to provide reviews. Chris Welch raved about the film in Melody Maker, calling it "simply superb" and concluding that "Colour, humour and even an element of horror make it a far more impressive Beatle-tagged movie than their own 'Magical Mystery Tour.'" Welch described it as a "cartoon 'space odyssey' with the imagination and visual impact of Stanley Kubrick's '2001'" that captures the "essence of Beatles humour and humanity." He found the imagery to be "meaningful" and thought the music was great, singling out the jolly "All Together Now." The actors did a good job with the Beatles dialog and the "boys" make a "real" appearance at the end. Welch ended his review with: "Are the Beatles slipping?...Never!" NME's Andy Gray talked with Ringo, Paul and George at the press screening of the film, which he found "colourful, sometimes ingenious, but overall rather boring." Ringo said that *Yellow Submarine* was for the children, adding: "Kids are the most important people in the world today. They are the future." Paul wanted the Beatles next album to come out before the Christmas release of the *Yellow Submarine* LP with its four rather inconsequential songs written for the film. David Griffiths reviewed the film in the July 20 Record Mirror. He thought the film was "stunning" and visually overwhelming: "The dazzling colours and patterns and wild action sequences are so powerful that by the end of the picture I was over-stimulated and longing for a rest...It's an experience, a very artistic achievement, and not to be missed."

In Disc, Hugh Nolan proclaimed that the Beatles had revived psychedelia with the release of *Yellow Submarine*: "Britain is due for a mind-dazzling, super-coloured fantasy extravaganza...about ten times as psychedelic as anything which happened in last summer's flowerpower bloom." The Beatles had scooped a new and often ignored medium, cartoons, whose possibilities were limitless, even though nothing new had been tried with them since Walt Disney's masterpiece, *Fantasia*. Although the Beatles had inspired the film with "Yellow Submarine" and their *Sgt. Pepper* LP, they had little to do with it. After running through the plot of the film, Nolan turned to the music. Although none of the new songs were likely to become classics, the incredible cartoons accompanying "It's All Too Much" made it a "gas, gas, gas!" "Hey Bulldog" was "fairly freaky," "Only A Northern Song" was "pleasant" and "All Together Now" was "the one you'll be singing when you walk out of the cinema." As for the familiar classics featured in the film, the cartoons added "new meaning and a fresh approach to songs you've heard thousands of times." Nolan called the film a "trip through fantasy and imagination." It was technically brilliant with the "most astonishing colours ever seen in a cartoon." Beneath the surface, there were multiple symbols and allegories if you took care to look for them.

Although the British press was highly critical of *Magical Mystery Tour*, it raved about *Yellow Submarine*. The Sun described the film as a "kaleidoscopic psychedelic trip which is highly enjoyable." The Daily Express called the movie "a gem of a voyage," "an absolute joy" and "a sophisticated work of art for children and a comic-strip for adults, a constant delight to the eye." The Daily Mail described it as a "dazzled wild dream-like mosaic of mirth and melody" with "dazzling imagery...weird and witty fantasy" executed with "skill, charm and freshness." The Daily Mirror called it "lively, jazzy" and a "sure-fire hit," where the screen was "alive with movement and surprise." The Morning Star described *Yellow Submarine* as an "explosive new film dimension," "brilliant" and "a fantastic achievement," telling readers, "you've never seen anything like it before." The art critic for The London Observer described it as "an exhilarating crash course in today's visual tactics and equipment" that "packs more stimulation, sly art references and pure joy into 90 minutes than a mile of exhibits of op, pop and all the mod cons." Alexander Walker of the Evening Standard called it "the key film of the Beatles era...a trip through the contemporary mythology that the quartet from Mersey-side helped to create...a Mod-odyssey...that sails under the psychedelic colours of Carnaby Street to the turned-on music of *Sgt. Pepper*...that will appeal to teenage ravers and Tate Gallery-goers alike."

The October 12 NME reported that a "special Christmas 'bonus' Beatles LP" was scheduled for December. *Yellow Submarine* would be the same as the set issued in America—four new Beatles songs plus "Yellow Submarine" and "All You Need Is Love" on one side and the film's instrumental music by George Martin on the other. As per the Beatles wishes, the soundtrack LP would be released after the group's follow-up album to *Sgt. Pepper,* the two-disc LP *The Beatles*. When that album was delayed until November 22, *Yellow Submarine* was pushed back to January 17, 1969.

The January 15 Record Retailer praised the LP: "Six fun tracks from the Beatles plus six orchestrated George Martin compositions and his arrangement of 'Yellow Submarine' fit together to make what is probably the most entertaining Beatles album yet." Although the four new songs were "Not their best artistic venture," they gave the album great appeal. The January 18 Record Mirror said the LP was "Well worth any price." It described "Only A Northern Song" as a "technical experiment" that "comes off very well" and "All Together Now" as a "bouncy little jaunt sporting a jovial and interesting lyric." "Hey Bulldog" had a "gigantic beat" with heavy bass and pounding piano. "It's All Too Much" was the "best SOUND" on the disc. The pleasant George Martin tracks were a "tremendous achievement."

The January 18 Disc observed that the group charmed with everything it did and called the LP "Beatles entertainment at its best." It noted that George Harrison's songwriting skills were improving all the time, describing "It's All Too Much" as brilliant and "Only A Northern Song" as catchy. George Martin's orchestrations were clever, with an air of fantasy. In the January 18 NME, Allen Evans merely described the contents of the album, which included two former hit singles and "four so-so songs written for the film and sung by the Beatles" plus the flip side of six compositions by George Martin plus the orchestrated Lennon-McCartney tune "Yellow Submarine In Pepperland." Melody Maker waited until January 25 and also had little to say, listing the contents and concluding: "Great, but if you're short of readies [available money], better to get their new album."

The *Yellow Submarine* LP entered the Record Retailer chart at number 37 on January 29, 1969, while *The Beatles* (*The White Album*) was at number one. The following week it reached its peak position of three. The album charted for 11 weeks and was also listed as a "mover" for several additional weeks when the Record Retailer chart was restricted to numbering only 15 full-price albums. Melody Maker charted *Yellow Submarine* for nine weeks, including four weeks at its peak position of four, while NME charted the album for eights weeks with a peak of three.

"Across The Universe," finished with overdubs on February 11, 1968, was eventually issued on an all-star charity LP, *No One's Gonna Change Our World*, on EMI's budget Regal Starline label priced at just under a pound (19 shillings and 11 pence) on December 12, 1969. Royalties from sales of the album were donated to the World Wildlife Fund.

Rather than taking a well-deserved break after the final recording sessions for *Sgt. Pepper*, the Beatles soldiered on, entering a phenomenal post-*Pepper* phase from April 25, 1967, through February 11, 1968. In less than ten months, the Beatles recorded the songs for their self-produced *Magical Mystery Tour* TV show and the *Yellow Submarine* cartoon film, as well as three singles. The first track released from this fertile period was "All You Need Is Love," which was broadcast throughout the world via three satellites as part of the Our World TV show. The last completed recording released, "Across The Universe," appeared on the album *No One's Gonna Change Our World* and was later beamed across the universe into deep space by NASA on February 4, 2008, forty years after it was recorded.

NEW!
FOR CHRISTMAS

(S)MAL 2835

The Beatles Magical Mystery Tour In America

Although Beatles fans in the U.K. had four weekly music magazines to keep them informed of the Beatles activities and upcoming record releases, in 1967 most Americans still learned of new Beatles singles and albums by hearing the songs on the radio and seeing the new 45s and LPs in record stores and other retailers. By November 20, 1967, U.S. radio stations began playing a catchy new song by the Beatles titled "Hello Goodbye." Some stations even played its more adventurous flip side, "I Am The Walrus." A film of the group performing "Hello Goodbye" was shown on The Ed Sullivan Show on Sunday, November 26. While fans hoped this meant a new album was on the horizon, they could not be sure. After all, Capitol had failed to bring Christmas cheer in 1966.

Three years earlier, in 1964, Capitol had given fans a double disc documentary, *The Beatles' Story*, and the album *Beatles '65*, which contained the double-sided smash "I Feel Fine" b/w "She's A Woman." The 1965 holiday season brought even greater highs with a spectacular LP, *Rubber Soul*, and single containing two wonderful songs, "We Can Work It Out" and "Day Tripper," that were not on the album. However, in December 1966, the Beatles and Capitol failed to deliver. It was as if the Grinch had stolen Christmas.

But 1967 would be a return to form. Fans entering record stores in December were greeted with a bold red-background poster spreading holiday cheer. At the top, it proudly proclaimed: "NEW! FOR CHRISTMAS." Below was a colorful album cover with "BEATLES" spelled out in bright yellow stars. The lads, dressed in animal costumes, appeared above a rainbow-colored *Magical Mystery Tour* logo and a small white banner with "Includes 24-page full color picture book" in red. Above it all was a list of mostly unfamiliar song titles, the lone exception being "I Am The Walrus," the B-side to the group's latest disc. At the bottom was a list of recent Beatles singles. The packaging for the album was first class, with the gatefold cover containing a 24-page book full of pictures and a cartoon summary of the *Magical Mystery Tour* film. It also included the lyrics to the six songs appearing in the film. Once again the Beatles, with an assist from Capitol, had given fans good value for their money and a spectacular Christmas offering.

The Beatles followed up their landmark *Sgt. Pepper* LP with the single "All You Need Is Love," released by Capitol Records on July 17, 1967. Some lucky fans had already seen the group perform the song on the Our World TV show on June 25 or heard a tape of the song on radio stations such as New York's WOR-FM. Capitol quickly distributed promotional copies of the single to radio stations. Cash Box indicated that as of July 5, 37% of its reporting stations were playing the song. By July 12, 53% more stations added the song, bringing its total to 90%. "All You Need Is Love" entered the Billboard Hot 100 at number 71 on July 22. Four weeks later it reached the number one spot on August 19, displacing the Doors' "Light My Fire." The following week it slipped to the second spot, surrounded by the chart topping "Ode To Billie Joe" by Bobbie Gentry and the Monkees' "Pleasant Valley Sunday." During its 11-week chart run, "All You Need Is Love" spent five weeks in the top three. Cash Box charted the song for nine weeks, including six in the top five and two at the top. Record World reported the song at number one for two weeks during its ten weeks on the charts. The disc was certified gold for sales of one million units by the RIAA on September 11, 1967.

The single's B-side, "Baby You're A Rich Man," also received significant air play, with Cash Box indicating that 40% of its reporting stations had added the single by July 12. The following week this had doubled to 80%. Billboard charted the song for five weeks, with a peak of 34, although it was mistitled "Baby You're A Rich Man Now." The other trades charted the song at number 60, with Cash Box listing the song for four weeks, and Record World for five.

The trade magazines reviewed the single in their July 15 issues. Billboard described the top side as a "smooth rhythm offering that must be heard to the end for traces of 'In The Mood,' 'Greensleeves' and 'She Loves You,'" while the flip was called an "Eastern-flavored rocker with an infectious beat and intricate lyric." Cash Box raved about the disc: "Unbelievable is the genius behind the latest magic concoction of the Beatles. On their newest single, 'All You Need Is Love,' the foursome brews up a batch of disparate ingredients and blends them into an enchanting soft rock tune. Way-back sax rag, classical strains, snatches of old Beatles material and plenty of humor turn up between the 'Marseilles' opener and probably the longest fade in record history. Oriental psych finger-snapper on the flip." Record World kept it short and sweet: "The Beatles, riding the crest of their most publicized album to date, follow it up with a marvy love single, 'All You Need Is Love.'"

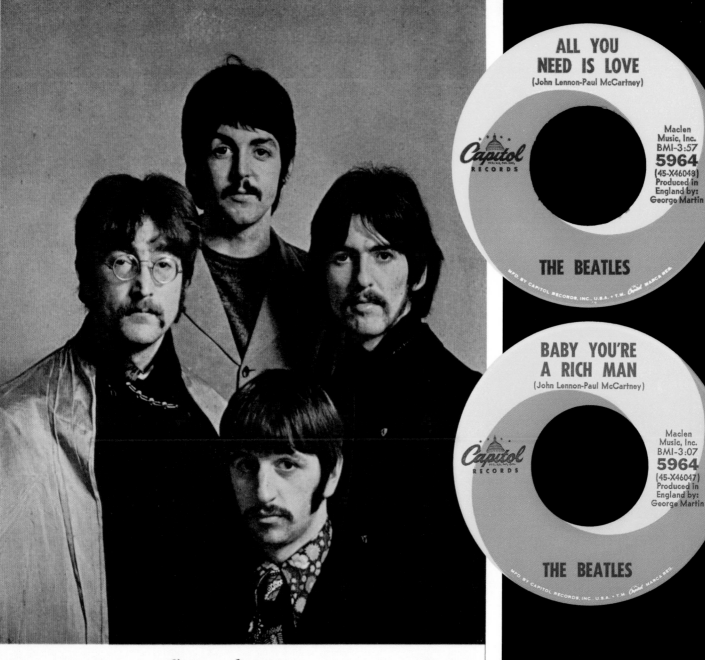

The Beatles ushered in the holiday season with the November 27 release of another marvy single. Paul's "Hello Goodbye" was an instant pop classic–a catchy, moderate-tempo rocker with beautifully textured instrumentation and vocals. The flip, "I Am The Walrus," was a masterful bit of organized chaos from John, assisted by George Martin.

"Hello Goodbye" entered the Billboard Hot 100 at number 45 on December 2. The following week it was at number eight, before climbing to three for two weeks. Finally, on December 30, "Hello Goodbye" took its rightful place at the top, knocking off the Monkees' "Daydream Believer." It remained number one for three weeks before dropping to three behind "Judy In Disguise (With Glasses)" by John Fred and His Playboy Band and Aretha Franklin's "Chain Of Fools." "Hello Goodbye" remained in the Hot 100 for 11 weeks before saying its goodbyes. Cash Box charted the song for 12 weeks, including two at number one. Record World charted the song for 11 weeks, with four at the top. The unconventional B-side also gained recognition, with Billboard charting the song for four weeks, with a peak of 56. Cash Box and Record World both reported the song at 46, with Cash Box charting the song for six weeks and Record World for five. Cash Box indicated that 50% of its reporting stations had added "Hello Goodbye" by November 22. A week later this had grown to 97%. "I Am The Walrus" also received air play, with 38% of the stations adding the song by November 22, growing to 66% by November 29. KJR in Seattle reported "Hello-Goodbye/Walrus" at number one in its December 15 and 22 surveys. The disc was certified gold by the RIAA on December 15, 1967.

The three music trades reviewed the single in their November 25 issues. Billboard noted: "With equal sales and programming potential for the top stop on the Hot 100, the Beatles have more exciting, creative material here." The A-side was described as a "strong, easy beat ballad," while "Walrus" was a "rocker with lyric content that takes some listening." Cash Box agreed. "Minimum of words, minimum of melody and practically no subject at all, yet the Beatles have a new side that packs a panchromatic rainbow of sound into the narrow limits that Lennon & McCartney have selected to work with on 'Hello Goodbye.'" The magazine praised the song's fade and predicted sales would match its brilliance. The flip side was called a "down and out session with a set of lyrics that will have many scratching their heads." Record World was more to the point. "New Beatles million-seller-to-be is the simplest of rock love songs about lack of communication." It made no mention of the not-so-simple B-side, "I Am The Walrus."

recorded by the BEATLES on CAPITOL records

HELLO, GOODBYE

words and music by JOHN LENNON & PAUL McCARTNEY

MACLEN MUSIC INC

75¢

SHEET
MUSIC
INSTITUTE
05201

While most Americans did not hear about *Magical Mystery Tour* until mid-December, some West Coast fans read a Tony Barrow report on the film in the October 7 KRLA Beat. Others learned about the project in November through a new publication, Rolling Stone. In its debut issue, cover dated November 9, 1967, Editor Jann Wenner indicated that they had "begun a new publication reflecting what we see are the changes in rock and roll and the changes related to rock and roll." Wenner further stated: "Because the trade papers have become so inaccurate and irrelevant, and because the fan magazines are an anachronism, fashioned in the mold of myth and nonsense, we hope we have something here for the artists and the industry, and every person who 'believes in the magic that can set you free.'"

It was only natural that the Beatles would be frequently featured in the magazine, starting with the first issue placing John as Private Gripweed from the film *How I Won The War* on its cover. The issue ran articles on the group's Apple boutique and their "Mystery Tour" project, reporting that the group had recently "finished filming their mysterious tour through Cornwall" and had spent the previous week at EMI's studios in St. John's Wood for the *Magical Mystery Tour* TV special, which would be shown worldwide at Christmas time. The show was to contain a George Harrison composition, "Blue Jay Way," inaccurately described as an instrumental written during Harrison's six-hour stay in San Francisco. The group planned to release a new single simultaneously in the U.S. and U.K. The remaining tracks would be released on an EP in England. The magazine doubted that Capitol would issue an EP in America.

The next issue, dated November 23, 1967, stated that three television networks, ABC, CBS and NBC, were bidding for the American broadcast rights of the film. Writer Nick Jones stated that "the show promises to be incredible." Most of the film had been shot in Southeast England around Cornwall and Devon, with the Beatles traveling "around the country in a brightly painted coach with actors and characters–loons all!" By early December, Rolling Stone's third issue, cover dated December 14, 1967, had been published. Its cover featured the Beatles and other cast members of *Magical Mystery Tour*, along with an article titled "New Thing for Beatles: Magical Mystery Tour." John Lennon explained, "Records can't be seen so it's good to have a film vehicle of some sort to go with the new music." The film would be shown in England at Christmas and in the States on NBC-TV in March 1968. Capitol would be releasing a "special Magical Mystery Tour LP shortly before Christmas."

ROLLING STONE

DECEMBER 14, 1967
VOL. 1, NO. 3

OUR PRICE:
TWENTY-FIVE CENTS

MFP

NEW THING FOR BEATLES: MAGICAL MYSTERY TOUR

"Records can't be seen so it's good to have a film vehicle of some sort to go with the new music," said John Lennon about the Beatle's television film, *Magical Mystery Tour*. As it is, we'll be seeing both. The film is complete and will be shown in England at Christmas, and in America on NBC-TV in March. In addition Capitol will release a special *Magical Mystery Tour* LP shortly before Christmas.

Magical Mystery Tour is full of visual and musical fantasy, dream sequences, and the Beatles. "A lot of laughs, some off-beat characters, a few very giant orous girls, a bit of dancing and quite a bit of magic," is how John describes it.

The plot involves the adventures of a bus-load of passengers on a Mystery Tour trip. It has a cast of hundreds, including teams of formation dancers who appear in a spectacular finale. Victor Spinetti, who has appeared in both Beatles films as well as 'How I Won the War,' makes a guest appearance as an Army recruiting sergeant. Some of the "off-beat characters and very glamorous girls," are Derek Royle as Tour Courier Jolly Jimmy Johnson, Mandy West as Tour Hostess Wendy Winters, midget actor George Claydon as Little George the Amateur Photographer, heavyweight actress Jessie Robins as Ringo's Auntie

Jessie, and Maggie Wright as Paul's girlfriend, Maggie the Lovely Starlet. Spencer Davis and The Traffic also appear.

The original idea to make a TV film about a bus tour was Paul's. He thought it up in April while on a week's vacation in America and started to work out the song *Magical Mystery Tour* on the plane back to London. It clicked with the rest of the group because, says John, "At the beginning of 1967 we realized that we wouldn't be doing any more concert tours because we couldn't reproduce on stage the type of music we'd started to record. So if stage shows were to be out we wanted something to replace them. Television was the obvious answer."

The Beatles also realized that if they were to have exactly what they wanted they would have to do the whole thing themselves: devise the format, write the script, cast, direct, and edit the film. (See Page 2. "What the Beatles should do is make this glorious, world's most expensive home movie. They should make it themselves." — Richard Lester.)

By September the world's Merriest Pranksters were bouncing around Devon and Cornwall, in southwest England, in a widly-decorated bus. They wore the oldest, straightest clothes they could find: Paul wore a hand-

knitted Fair Isle pullover and baggy pants in the manner of a typical English father, and the rest of the group wore Al Capone suits. Ringo looked very distinguished in his; George looked like an honest-to-God gangster in a bright-blue suit and 1940's hat; John wore a derby with a white feather and a white carnation in his buttonhole. All the paint and decorations washed off the bus in a heavy downpour.

The Beatle's approach to the filming was somewhat unconventional. They relied on improvisation rather than demanding that the cast stick to a written script. To make dialogue as natural as possible, the actors were given situations and reactions instead of lines.

"We knew most of the scenes we wanted to include," said John, "but we bent our ideas to fit the people concerned once we got to know our cast. If somebody just wanted to do something we hadn't planned they went ahead. If it worked we kept it in. There was a lovely little 5-year old girl, Nicola, on the bus. Because she was there and because we realized she was right for it, we put in a bit where I just chat to her and give her a balloon."

They only hired technicians who were absolutely necessary. Paul says there were no problems. "For the first couple of days when we set out with this big bus full of people we took things easy, let the ice break slowly, let everyone know what it was all about. Things just came together after that. Of course

we weren't using the right jargon when we talked to the sound men and the camera crew and they felt a bit strange to begin with. After a while they got to the stage where they were as enthusiastic as the rest of us. The main thing was to get rid of all the traditional tensions and hangups, cut through the red tape and get everybody interest-

—Continued on Page 4

BYRD FLIPPED; CLARK LEAVES

Les than a month after David Crosby was asked to leave the Byrds, leader Jim McGuinn has asked guitarist Gene Clark to leave as well. The friendly dismissal took place two weeks ago at the New York airport when Clark refused to board a plane for Chicago. Clark is afraid to fly and McGuinn insisted that, to be a Byrd, one had to fly.

The group intends to fill their 17 remaining engagements in 1967 as a trio, according to their manager, Larry Spector. Meantime a replacement is being sought.

Clark, who once before had left the group, plans to record another solo album, this one of country and western material. The forthcoming Byrds album, due around the first of next year, does feature material and work by David Crosby but the group does not know whether sessions with Clark will be included.

All three music trade magazines, apparently drawing from the same Capitol press release, reported in their November 25 issues that the Beatles 13th Capitol album, *Magical Mystery Tour*, was due in mid-December. Its title came from the forthcoming London-produced TV special featuring the group, which would broadcast in England during Christmas week and in America in early 1968 on NBC. The album would have 11 songs, including six from the television show. The remaining songs included the A-side of the group's new single, "Hello Goodbye," plus four songs previously unavailable on LP. The package came with a "full-color, 24-page book containing photographs and art work from the TV special." The album was the group's follow up to *Sgt. Pepper*. The magazines noted that the Beatles had earned 23 gold records (singles and albums), which was the most in the history of the RIAA.

Capitol's *Magical Mystery Tour* LP is a perfect example of Capitol understanding the American market. In England, the Beatles decided to release the six songs from their upcoming TV film, *Magical Mystery Tour*, on two 7" extended play (EP) discs packaged in a gatefold jacket with a 24-page booklet. When Capitol president Alan Livingston heard that the next Beatles release was to be a two-EP set, he wisely balked at the idea. Sales from the two Beatles EPs released by Capitol in 1964 and 1965 had been considerably less than sales of singles and albums. Even with the Beatles, the EP format was difficult to market in America. Livingston decided that the songs should be incorporated into an album for U.S. release. The proposed LP would contain the six songs from the film along with the A-side to the group's new single, "Hello Goodbye," plus the four songs from the band's previous two singles, "Penny Lane," "Strawberry Fields Forever," "All You Need Is Love" and "Baby You're A Rich Man," none of which had appeared on albums. There was just one hurdle that needed to be cleared. Under the group's new contract with Capitol, the Beatles and their management had final approval on the selection of the songs to appear on their albums.

Fortunately the Beatles and their advisors granted Capitol's request to convert the double-EP set into a gatefold LP packed with hit singles. The November 25 Billboard reported that talks between Capitol Records and the Beatles in London on November 10 resulted in a "decision to issue the six soundtrack recordings from the Beatles' forthcoming TV fantasy spectacular, 'Magical Mystery Tour,' on an album in the U.S." Most likely at the insistence of the Beatles, *Magical Mystery Tour* was a regularly-priced album despite the extra production costs due to the 24-page book.

Magical Mystery Tour
The Fool On The Hill Flying Blue Jay Way
Your Mother Should Know I Am The Walrus
All You Need Is Love
Penny Lane Baby You're A Rich Man
Hello Goodbye Strawberry Fields Forever

Includes 24-page full color picture book

In programming its album, Capitol placed all of the songs from the *Magical Mystery Tour* film on Side One. Because Capitol did not face concerns of how best to fit the six songs on four sides of two seven-inch discs, the company was free to program the tracks to maximize the listening experience. The side opens with the film's title track, a charming upbeat rocker, augmented with brass, that ends with a change-of-pace breakdown coda with lazy-sounding notes. This flows perfectly into Paul's dreamy piano ballad, "The Fool On The Hill," highlighted by his "round, round, round" vocals and the recorder and flute instrumental breaks. "Flying" is a mid-tempo instrumental track with "Tra La La La La" chanting vocals by all four Beatles, who are given co-writers credit on the label. This is followed by "Blue Jay Way," a psychedelic dirge, written and sung by George about friends who have lost their way in the thick Los Angeles fog ("There's a fog upon LA"). The song's textured sound, with its swirling vocals, organ and strings, conveys the feeling of fog rolling into the listener's room through the speakers. The mood then shifts to a music-hall, Hollywood send-up production number by Paul, "Your Mother Should Know." The song's "yeah-ah" ending leads into the side's final selection, John's "I Am The Walrus." The track's ominous opening, interesting lyrics, effective vocal shenanigans and intrusion of the King Lear death scene during the fade ending make the song an effective closer to the program.

The sequencing of the second side is equally effective. "Hello Goodbye" is the perfect opener, an infectious pop tune that grabs the listener's attention from the start. The recording's musical backing effectively reinforces the song's tale of mismatched lovers. As the track appears to come to an end, it continues with an equally catchy change-of-tempo end piece. This is followed by the Mellotron introduction of one of the Beatles greatest recordings, John's "Strawberry Fields Forever." The song's slow tempo and somewhat-psychedelic heavy instrumental backing provide a sharp contrast from the previous selection. Once again, the Beatles toss out a trick ending, with the recording fading out and then coming back until its final break down. The tempo picks up again with Paul's "Penny Lane," a wonderful piece of nostalgia inhabited by an interesting cast of characters and blue suburban skies. Highlights include Paul's walking bass part, multiple keyboards and an exciting piccolo trumpet solo. Although "Baby You're A Rich Man" is not in the same league with the hit singles that dominate the second side, it fits in nicely with the other songs, pulsating along with an interesting instrumental backing. The side ends with the perfect closing anthem, "All You Need Is Love."

The decision to package *Magical Mystery Tour* as an album proved to be a wise one. Officially released on November 27, 1967 (although it most likely did not appear in stores until a week or so later), the disc entered the Billboard Hot LP's chart at number 157 on December 23. The following week it moved up to number four, one notch behind the still popular *Sgt. Pepper's Lonely Hearts Club Band*. On January 6, 1968, the Beatles latest album replaced the Monkees' *Pisces, Aquarius, Capricorn & Jones Ltd.* at the top, holding off the Rolling Stones' *Their Satanic Majesties Request*. The Beatles LP spent eight weeks at number one before falling behind *Blooming Hits* by Paul Mauriat & His Orchestra and Bob Dylan's *John Wesley Harding*. Billboard (which in mid-1967 expanded its LP chart from 150 to 200 positions) charted the album for 91 weeks, including 14 in the top ten and 21 in the top twenty. Cash Box also charted the album at number one for eight weeks. It spent 34 weeks in the Top 100, including 13 in the top five, plus 17 weeks in the second tier chart listing numbers 101-140, for a total of 51 weeks. Record World charted the disc at number one for seven weeks during its 41 weeks on the 100 Top LP's chart, including 13 weeks in the top five. *Magical Mystery Tour* was certified gold on December 15. It sold over one and a half million copies before Christmas 1967 and nearly two million by year's end. As of July 25, 2000, the RIAA has certified sales of six million units.

The trade magazines reviewed *Magical Mystery Tour* in their December 16 issues, with two finding contrasts between the new release and the group's previous album, *Sgt. Pepper's Lonely Hearts Club Band*. Billboard indicated that the group's latest LP was in a "completely different style" from *Sgt. Pepper*, being a "non-psychedelic disc" whose "emphasis is away from musical and lyrical complexities." [Apparently the reviewer wasn't thinking about "Blue Jay Way" or "I Am The Walrus."] The magazine found the title track and "The Fool On The Hill" to be the most appealing of the film songs, which were on one side of the album paired with a side "comprised of their singles hits." Cash Box wrote that: "The Beatles have left the somewhat macabre and disturbing world of 'Sergeant Pepper's Lonely Hearts Club Band,' and they are now living, or perhaps just touring, a comparatively gentle land filled with 'magical mystery.' Colorful arrangement's haunting melodies, buoyant rock and fanciful lyrics are in evidence on Side 1, which contains five songs (and an instrumental) from the TV film." Cash Box noted that the double-fold package came with a 24-page color book and predicted that the LP would soon be number one. Record World made the disc its Album Pick of the Week, but rather than reviewing the LP, it merely provided a brief description: "The Beatles' new album, tagged after a new TV special they've concocted, is called 'Magical Mystery Tour' with new and old tunes."

From the very start, Rolling Stone magazine provided in-depth reviews of albums. But those expecting insightful renderings about the Beatles *Magical Mystery Tour* LP were truly let down. Although the magazine's January 20, 1968 issue showed black and white images of the album's cover and three pages from its booklet, the entire review consisted of: "'There are only about 100 people in the world who understand our music.'—John Lennon, 1967."

Mike Jahn took a much deeper approach in his review appearing in the December 30, 1967 Saturday Review. Jahn opened with a quote from the Bhagavad Gita, the Celestial Song of Hindu theology: "Who sees Me in all/and sees all in Me/For him I am not lost/and he is not lost for me." This was compared to the surprisingly similar "I am he/as you are he/as you are me/and we are all together." He credited the Beatles with introducing Yin and Yang, the doctrine of opposites found in Eastern religions, into Western rock through *Magical Mystery Tour*, which he rated as "easily their best album." He described the program as an "extravagant home movie" of the "adventures of travelers, on an imaginary tour bus, which is taken over and put through a weird series of events by the sorcery of five musicians—

the Beatles plus their talented producer, George Martin." He detailed the contents of the album and the packaging, including the comic strip rendition of the film "to pacify those teen-aged fans put off by the fact that the words 'love' and 'baby' do not appear once in the songs from the film."

For Jahn, the album's real innovation is the group's "personal involvement with Hinduism." While *Sgt. Pepper* was a great work of intricacy and beauty depicting everyday events, *Magical Mystery Tour* is "distinguished by its description of the Beatles acquired Hindu philosophy and its subsequent application to everyday life." "The Fool On The Hill" is about a "detached observer, a yogin, who meditates and watches the world spin," while in "I Am the Walrus," "the yogin tells what he sees." The latter song, possibly the most significant Beatle song yet, "mixes surrealistic imagery... with a line calling up the 'we are all together' thought." He adds that those having decent stereo equipment and a quick ear will notice that the track ends with a reading from King Lear. Jahn concludes that "*Magical Mystery Tour* may not be the best piece of musical composition to emerge in the twentieth century," but it is a "marvelous step in a very personal direction for the Beatles—one that they communicate well–and that is enough."

Richard Goldstein, who notoriously criticized *Sgt. Pepper* in The New York Times, reviewed *Magical Mystery Tour* in the December 31 edition of the prestigious newspaper. The title of his piece set the tone: "Are the Beatles Waning?" Goldstein calls the Beatles the "clown-gurus of the 60s," whose "jester's approach to 'serious' music and 'deep' thought clamors for interpretation" along with "their intentional embrace with ambiguity." Although he panned *Sgt. Pepper*, Goldstein acknowledges that the album had become "this year's most-analyzed piece of pop art," adding: "Never before has the critical establishment responded to a rock work with such vigorous acceptance." But Goldstein notes that the Beatles popularity is waning among the very young due to "the inevitable result of artistic complexity." If those under 20 were deserting the group, it was "because their former idols have departed from rock–its sound, its structure, and its specific brand of sensuality." For the Beatles, "The Beat is no longer implicit," having been replaced by a "collage of sound-images masquerading as Brechtian vaudeville." Sometimes "this free inquiry...stuns with resonant power," while "other times it seems capricious and gimmick-ridden." But for Goldstein, its most noticeable characteristic is that it rarely rocks.

The six new songs on the album represent "six distinct styles" in which the Beatles "vary tempo, orchestration, lyric structure and vocal color to achieve sounds which illustrate moods." When George sings "There's a fog upon L.A." in "Blue Jay Way," the listener is "engulfed with a waft of foggy music." When the protagonist in "The Fool On The Hill" sees the world spinning round, the music "whirl[s] gently amid dizzy rhythms." These touches take the group away from rock. The Beatles are now "so profoundly conscious of their own evolving style that they sometimes lose track of...melody and lyric in favor of ensemble effect." Goldstein's deepest cut: "Scratch the surface of 'Magical Mystery Tour' and it bleeds like show music."

Goldstein states that it was the group's "electronic posturing" that he "found fraudulent" in *Sgt. Pepper*, and that it is "even more apparent" in *Magical Mystery Tour*. Both the title track and "Your Mother Should Know" are "motifs disguised as songs" that are "as tedious and stuffy as an after-dinner speech." While Harrison's "Blue Jay Way" has "fascinating tones and textures," his writing is "obtuse and muddled." Goldstein likes "The Fool On The Hill," calling it a nice song that "says the right things about alienation." Paul's melody is "the most haunting thing on the album." "I Am The Walrus" is the group's most realized work since "A Day In The Life." It is "filled with eerie split-second glimpses of English life" that "struts, puns, and bristles in perfectly wicked Lennonese...a fierce collage."

As for the singles on Side Two of the album, he is fond of the "pomp" in "Penny Lane" and the "pageantry" in "Strawberry Fields Forever," but views "Hello Goodbye" and "Baby You're A Rich Man" as "interesting but subordinate." He is turned off by "All You Need Is Love," finding its sloppiness not only intentional, but fake. Goldstein does not think it is heresy to say that "the Beatles write material which is literate, courageous, genuine, but spotty." He concludes by saying: "They are inspired posers, but we must keep our heads on their music, not their incarnations. In that critical distance lies the deepest sort of respect."

In the January 1, 1968 Newsweek, Jack Kroll reviewed *Magical Mystery Tour* and the Rolling Stones' *Their Satanic Majesties Request* in an article titled "Beatles v. Stones." Kroll praised the Stones' new LP, but added that the Beatles had successfully challenged the Stones' challenge to *Sgt. Pepper* with yet another new album, *Magical Mystery Tour*.

Kroll concluded that "in scope and subtlety, the Beatles are still supreme." He lauded "All You Need Is Love" and "Hello Goodbye" for "their absolutely unique vein of deadpan but heartbreaking satire on the sentiments" and called "I Am The Walrus" a "brilliant piece of schizoid surrealism." As for "Strawberry Fields Forever," it was "surely one of the most beautiful musics of our time, a superb Beatleizing of hope and despair, in which the four minstrels regretfully recommend a Keatsian lotus land of withdrawal from the centrifugal stress of the age." Kroll noted that "two million buyers have taken home this message" in less than a month's time. He ended his article by praising the "revolutionary excellence of work" by both groups, which combined with their popularity, "has just about become the most amazing cultural fact of our time."

While Richard Goldstein claimed to have the "deepest sort of respect" for the Beatles when he criticized the group's music, the same cannot be said for Rex Reed. The most vicious piece on the *Magical Mystery Tour* album came courtesy of the famous New York movie critic in the March 1968 edition of HiFi/Stereo Review. Reed gave the following summary: "Performance: **Repulsive**; Recording: **Fair**; Stereo Quality: **Good**." From the outset, it is clear that Reed harbors resentment towards the Beatles, stating that their new album convinces him that "someone should do society a favor by locking them up." After noting that half of the album contains singles that most fans already own, he laments that Capitol is asking six bucks for the "salacious drivel on side one," adding: "Baby, you gotta be a rich man to shell out that much bread for something as revolting as this."

With the exception of the superb vocal treatment on the delightfully ingenious "All You Need Is Love" and the instrumental intonation on "Penny Lane," Reed believes that the Beatles do not perform their own songs well. While they write intelligently, "they are lousy entertainers and downright untalented, tone-death musicians." He claims that their "farcical, stagnant, helpless bellowing on the *Magical Mystery Tour* songs proves [his] point," but worse, the disc contains the first group of Beatles compositions that he "never ever want[s] to hear again performed by anybody!" He then examines "this creepy phenomenon," stating that: "Ever since the fellows gave up singing about narcotics in favor of meditation with the great Indian guru Maharishi, their music has become...totally divorced from reality." He complains that the group's musical gimmicks "don't compensate for confused musical ideas."

Reed dismisses the title track as a "Radio City Music Hall Parody" with nothing different or clever. He likes "The Fool On The Hill" for its "lovely flute work" and lack of distortion, but adds he will like it even more when it is recorded by "people who can sing." "Flying" reminds him of "the soundtrack of an old Maria Montez jungle movie...where she feeds the chanting populace to the cobras." "Blue Jay Way" is "boring as hell," with the Beatles "sounding as if they are singing under water or gargling with Listerine." "Your Mother Should Know" is "nothing more than a Gaslight Era cabaret tune full of da-das and yeah-yeahs." Finally, "I Am The Walrus," which "defies any kind of description known to civilized man," is "ugly to hear, lacking any cohesion of style or technique" and "utterly silly and pointless." He ends his attack by stating that "if you buy this platter of phony, pretentious, overcooked tripe, then you and the Beatles deserve each other."

The April 1968 Hit Parader raved about *Magical Mystery Tour*, proclaiming that "the beautiful Beatles do it again, widening the gap between them and 80 scillion other groups." After recognizing the group's team work with George Martin, the review states: "The master magicians practice their alchemy on Harrison's 'Blue Jay Way,' recorded perhaps in an Egyptian tomb and 'I Am The Walrus,' a piece of terror lurking in foggy midnight moors." The instrumental "Flying" has a gentle beat and ends with "soft, whipping outerspace sounds." As promised in the title track, the Beatles take us away on their Magical Mystery Tour. The review ends with: "You must listen in stereo."

Robert Christgau's review of the *Magical Mystery Tour* album in the May 1968 Esquire focused on the five "new" songs (meaning "I Am The Walrus" was not reviewed because it had been previously released as the B-side to "Hello Goodbye"). He described three of these songs as "disappointing." The title track was "perfunctory," while the instrumental "Flying" was "just a cut above Paul Mauriat, not bad but not Our Boys." He blasted "The Fool On The Hill" for being a "callow rendering of the outcast-visionary theme" and possibly "the worst song the Beatles have ever recorded." He joked that it would become a "favorite of the Simon & Garfunkel crowd and the transcendental meditators." Although he didn't like those songs, the album was worth buying for the singles and the tender camp of "Your Mother Should Know" and George's hypnotic "Blue Jay Way," which was an "adaptation of Oriental modes in which everything works, lyrics included."

Although NBC had planned to broadcast the *Magical Mystery Tour* TV special in March 1968, the network canceled its plans due to the film's poor reception in England. Writing in the January 27, 1968 KRLA Beat, Tony Barrow indicated that "A VIOLENT storm of controversy surrounded the London unveiling of *Magical Mystery Tour*," with the BBC "jammed with calls from baffled viewers." Barrow believed that "viewers were looking for too much reality in a film which relied upon the magic of fantasy, the mystery of unfamiliar happenings."

The first confirmed American theatrical screening of *Magical Mystery Tour* took place at midnight on Friday, May 10, 1968, at the Los Feliz Theater in Los Angeles, with a second midnight show the next night. According to Kevin Thomas of the LA Times, the screenings were held to benefit the striking KPPC-FM disc jockeys, who obtained the film from former Beatles press agent Derek Taylor with the proviso that it not be reviewed. Thomas honored this request, but indicated that the film was "not like any trip anybody ever took before." He added that the show richly deserved its enthusiastic reception from the 550 in attendance the first night and the sell out crowd of 770 the following evening. Attendees paid a $3 donation to benefit the Underground Radio Strike Fund. The film was also shown at Royce Hall on the UCLA campus on Thursday, May 16 for a $1.50 admission (see flier on page 138), and the following Friday through Sunday at the Esquire-Pasadena. *Magical Mystery Tour* had a few more limited showings in America during 1968 and 1969 before becoming the darling of college and midnight screenings a few years later.

Tom Nolan reviewed the film for the June 21, 1968 Los Angeles Free Press, an underground newspaper. Nolan wrote that the film was "superb, brilliant, great, heavy, boss, light entertainment, good clean fun, a Message Picture, an entertaining nightmare, and it has good rock and roll music," adding it was "by far the best of the Beatle films." He mocked the critics, implying that they wanted to see the Beatles fall flat on their faces. They thought the film was a "rambling...melange of disconnected dolly shots, spotty color, and general weirdness that fails miserably." Nolan disagreed. While it wasn't slick like *Help!*, it wasn't incomprehensible. He admitted that "in parts, it is very strange: surrealism more frightening–and at the same time grotesquely amusing–than anything Salvador Dali ever dreamt up for a Hitchcock flick." The film had: "Laughter, gaiety, songs, horror, wacky, zany, lyric, wistful, psychedelic color... something for everyone....It's a work of art. Well, you know, it's a magical mystery tour."

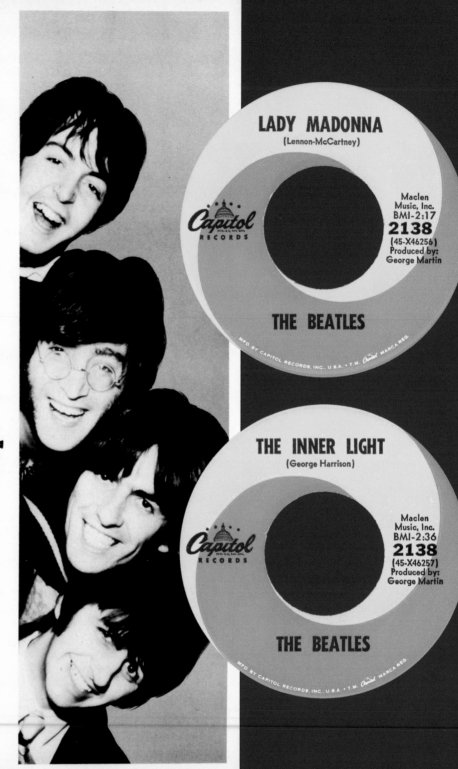

anewrockandrollcombo
directfromhamburgwith
themerseybeatnow
onemiladymadonna
childrenatyourfeet
wonderhowyou
managetomakeends
meetseehowtheyrun

THE BEATLES
LADY MADONNA
AND
THE INNER LIGHT

afabnewreleaseoutnowon

 2138

LADY MADONNA
(Lennon-McCartney)

Maclen
Music, Inc.
BMI-2:17
2138
(45-X46256)
Produced by:
George Martin

THE BEATLES

MFD. BY CAPITOL RECORDS, INC., U.S.A. • T.M. *Capitol* MARCA REG.

THE INNER LIGHT
(George Harrison)

Maclen
Music, Inc.
BMI-2:36
2138
(45-X46257)
Produced by:
George Martin

THE BEATLES

MFD. BY CAPITOL RECORDS, INC., U.S.A. • T.M. *Capitol* MARCA REG.

In early March 1968, Americans began hearing a new Beatles song, "Lady Madonna," on the radio. Cash Box announced that 25% of its reporting stations had added the song to their play lists by March 6, indicating that a relatively small number of stations had received the promo copy of the single from Capitol Records by that time. The following week the song was added by 67% of the stations, bringing its total to 92%. Capitol officially released the single on March 18. After making its Billboard debut at number 23 on March 23, the song entered the top ten at number nine the following week and worked its way up to number four on April 20. It remained there for three weeks, unable to move past Bobby Goldsboro's sentimental tear-jerker "Honey," "Young Girl" by the Union Gap featuring Gary Puckett and the Box Tops' "Cry Like A Baby." Billboard charted "Lady Madonna" for 11 weeks. The Beatles single fared better in the other trades, but failed to reach the top. Cash Box reported the disc at number two for three weeks during its 11-week run, while Record World showed a peak at two for one week during its 12 weeks on the charts. The single's remarkable Eastern-influenced B-side, "The Inner Light," received virtually no air play. Billboard listed the song for only one week at number 96 on March 30, while Record World reported the song for one week at 113 on April 6. Cash Box neither charted the song nor indicated it was being added to the play lists of its reporting stations. Although "Lady Madonna" failed to reach number one, Capitol claimed sales of over one million units within the disc's first week of release, giving the Beatles yet another gold record. The "Lady Madonna" promo clip was show on the March 30 Hollywood Palace. The RIAA awarded the disc platinum status on February 17, 1999.

The music trades reviewed the new Beatles single in their March 16 issues. Billboard described "Lady Madonna" as a "powerful blues rocker" and "The Inner Light" as "East-Indian oriented and timed right in with their meditation spell." After observing that "Every Beatles release is one of their best," Record World called the new single "terrific rock and roll and pungent social comment." Cash Box noted the single's change in direction for the group: "Taking one step back, the Beatles ease their progressive pace with this knocking rhythm side that features Ringo Starr in a rare vocal showing with hard-rock and kazoo orking and lyrics that view working class hardship with a pinch of salt." The magazine praised the flip side: "Lyrics from the transcendental meditation school and near-Eastern orchestrations on a very interesting coupler that could show sales as strong as the top-side." Cash Box was wrong on two counts. "Lady Madonna" was sung by Paul, not Ringo, and "The Inner Light" would sadly be neglected.

As "Lady Madonna" was heading up the charts, readers of Rolling Stone learned of a new Beatles project. The magazine's April 27, 1968 issue featured an article disclosing much of the plot of *The Yellow Submarine*, a full-length Beatles cartoon under the production of King Features Syndicate, the company that made the Beatles weekly cartoon show. The film, nearing completion, had a budget of a million dollars and was expected in theaters sometime after May. The article stated that "the film promises to be far superior and far more successful than *Magical Mystery Tour*." The Beatles were initially skeptical of the project based upon the "series of inane 'Beatletoons,'" but now viewed it as a "major artistic effort about them." The magazine incorrectly reported that the Beatles had "lent their own voices for the characters." It listed the following four songs as being written by the group for the film: "You Know the Name, Look Up the Number," "All Too Much," "Altogether Now" and "Northern Song." While the titles were slightly off, the last three did appear in the film. "You Know My Name (Look Up The Number)," while started around the same time as the others, would not be completed until a year later and was not suitable for the film.

Although *Yellow Submarine* was released in the U.K. on July 17, 1968, it would not be distributed in America until four months later. The film did, however, get favorable advance publicity in newspapers and a handful of magazines, including Seventeen, Look, McCall's, Eye and Newsweek. United Press International ran a story on the cartoon on June 21 that was picked up by several American newspapers. Producer Al Brodax touted the Beatles involvement, adding: "John called me once at 3 a.m. and said, 'wouldn't it be great if Ringo was followed down the street by a yellow submarine.'" The scene was included in the film. After seeing initial drawings, Ringo said, "My nose isn't long enough." The July 1968 Seventeen ran a column on *Yellow Submarine* in its Hollywood Scene section. The piece, written by Edwin Miller, was accompanied by seven frames from the film (shown on next page). The movie was described as a "witty and bizarre" feature-length cartoon in which the "ingeniously animated" Beatles journey by Yellow Submarine from Liverpool to Pepperland to save its citizens from the Blue Meanies. Because these grotesque creatures can't stand music, they drain all the color from Pepperland and lock up the instruments. The Beatles have "extraordinary adventures on their mad underwater odyssey" to Pepperland, where they eventually "do battle with various droll fiends." The film was made by the producers of the Beatles TV cartoons, but is "distinguished from anything that has gone before by the extraordinary flavor of its master designs" created by artist Heinz Edelmann.

Rolling Stone

ACME   APRIL 27, 1968   VOLUME I, No. 9, THIRTY-FIVE CENTS

CLAPTON BUSTED; KMPX STRIKE

Beatles' Battle The Blue Meanies

All photos © King Features–Subafilms, Ltd., 1968. A United Artists Release

THE HOLLYWOOD SCENE

Ingeniously animated Beatles fight the Blues in a fantastic fable

The trusty Yellow Submarine

John, Paul, Ringo and George

Max, the Chief Blue Meanie's aide

The Beatles and the Boob

The terrible Snapping Turtle Turk

John on the Tower of Love

John vs. the Dreadful Flying Glove

Witty and bizarre, "The Yellow Submarine" is a feature-length cartoon in which the Beatles are brought by submarine from Liverpool to Pepperland to save its citizens (descended from Sergeant Pepper of Lonely Hearts Club Band fame from the song of the same name), menaced by the Blue Meanies. Because these grotesque creatures can't bear music—it shrinks them—they attempt to drain all color from the Pepperland people (who while away their days and nights in song) and lock up their instruments. The Beatles have extraordinary adventures on their mad underwater odyssey. Voyaging through such areas as the Sea of Monsters, they meet the Vacuum Cleaner Monster (it swallows itself), all the while singing Beatle classics like "Eleanor Rigby" along with four new tunes. Eventually they do battle with various droll fiends.

Made by the producers of the Beatles TV cartoon series, "The Yellow Submarine" is distinguished from anything that has gone before by the extraordinary flavor of its master designs—imagine a psychedelic Hieronymus Bosch!—created by an artist named Heinz Edelmann. He designed the Beatles and everything else in the film, from the submarine's wallpaper to the mad monsters. Born in Czechoslovakia and trained in Germany, he sold his first canvas to one of his teachers in high school, went on to study etching, literature, psychology and philosophy before going to work as a commercial artist. A rabid science-fiction fan, he lists Francis Bacon, Arshile Gorky, Graham Sutherland and James Ensor among his favorite artists. Through special photographic processes and chemical techniques, Edelmann has blended live and animated action to create marvelous special effects. When he first arrived in London from Germany to work on the cartoon, he researched the super-mod Chelsea district because, he explained, "I had never seen a hippy or flower person before." They've never seen anything like Edelmann's whimsical beasties either.

More on page 40

THE YELLOW SUBMARINE

In which our British heroes (the Beatles) set out on a colorful fantasy adventure that outdoes the best of Disney

Presenting, in their first full-length cartoon film, all four of the super-incredible fantastic BEATLES— as you've never before seen them!

WORDS BY WILLIAM HEDGEPETH

© KING FEATURES—SUBAFILMS, LTD. 1968

...from a ...the ...'eanies' ...love.

All right, all whimsy, fun, folderol and psychedelic-drug stuff aside, lurking beneath the simple, childlike surface of *The Yellow Submarine* are deeper layers of just this same sort of innocent exuberance.

Pooh on those who try to conjure up allegories and symbols: the Beatles here are singing out a new hymn to plain enjoyable nonsense and self-parody. This deliberate naïveté of *The Yellow Submarine* may hail the beginning of a real renaissance of joyful absurdity in the best traditions of Lewis Carroll. Like *Alice*, *The YS* possesses all the impudent charm and pazzaz that appeal to the universal human thirst for simple lunacy.

The Yellow Submarine, inspired by the Lennon-McCartney fantasy-song, features four new Beatle tunes, plus eleven of their "classics." Visually, it is a dazzling, animated stream of leaping colors, exploding designs and zappy characters—all of which flowed from the head of German illustrator Heinz Edelmann. "Heinz," exults Paul McCartney, "is *ser* Dali." Edelmann was unimpressed with the movie's original outline, and put together an alternate involving hundreds of far-out villains: the Blue Meanies. After approval from a dozen script experts—including three Broadway authors, a Yale professor, American producer Al Brodax and director George Dunning—the Meanies joined the film, along with scores of other vivid creatures and stupefying creations that should make previous animated efforts seem antique. Beyond the drawings, tunefulness, Beatle wit and *Submarine's* totally preposterous freshness, there is the power of the Beatles themselves. With their infectious influence on public thought, this film may be the first burst in a whole new eruption of spontaneous glee.

"All you need is love": The Beatle bedazzles the Blue Glove by singing for himself a protective tower of babble.

The July 23 issue of Look ran a six-page spread on the Beatles and their new breakthrough movie with color images from the film and text by William Hedgepeth. The first page features an image of the Yellow Submarine and "all four of the super-incredible fantastic BEATLES—as you've never before seen them!" In the film, they "set out on a colorful fantasy adventure that outdoes the best of Disney." Hedgepeth writes that the Beatles, having done just about everything else, have "thrown themselves, in far-out cartoon form, into a beautifully fresh full-length fable." And just like other Beatles projects, the film "will be analyzed and scrutinized for its subtle social 'message' by critics, scholars and the Red Chinese." But over time, "what will remain is the sheer fun of an elegant fantasy romp that puts the quartet up against the most mind-blowing collection of creatures and circumstances since *Alice in Wonderland* or *Oz* or Tolkien's Middle-earth or that garish dream you had the night you raided the refrigerator."

Hedgepeth then runs through the plot of the mod-odyssey, which starts with "Old Fred fleeing occupied Pepperland in the Yellow Submarine and surfaces in Liverpool to ask the Beatles' help" in assisting the "flower-powered, tune-loving, love-loving people of Pepperland, who have been conquered by those anti-music happiness-haters, the Blue Meanies." The trip to Pepperland through the various seas becomes a "super pop-psychedelic panorama, complete with probably the most wildly original, kaleidoscopic bunch of beasts ever drawn—plus four Beatles so delightfully surreal as to relegate the originals into obsolescence." After they arrive in Pepperland, the Beatles engage in "a hard day's fight," clothe themselves in band uniforms and "sing color, joy and love back into faded Pepperland" until their music soothes the Meanies, "who become not only pop converts but hard-core Beatles addicts, like all the rest of us."

Hedgepeth puts down those who will "try to conjure up allegories and symbols." The Beatles are out for "enjoyable nonsense and self-parody," a naiveté that may start a "renaissance of joyful absurdity in the best tradition of Lewis Carrol." Visually, the film is a "dazzling, animated stream of leaping colors, exploding designs and zappy characters... from the head of German illustrator Heinz Edelmann," who McCartney refers to as "our Dali." The film's vivid creatures "make previous animated efforts seem antique." Hedgepeth reminds us that: "Beyond the drawings, tunefulness, Beatle wit and *Submarine*'s totally preposterous freshness, there is the power of the Beatles themselves." With their "infectious influence," *Yellow Submarine* may be the "first burst in a whole eruption of spontaneous glee."

The women's magazine McCall's, in its August 1968 edition, ran a feature titled "The Log of the Yellow Submarine," with the following credits: "Charted by Max Wilk, Designed by Heinz Edelmann." The introduction states that the "irrepressible Beatles" are on their way back "aboard 'The Yellow Submarine,' a full-length, animated fantasy film that may rival 'The Wizard of Oz,' Wonderland, and the adventures of Dr. Dolittle" during which the Beatles defy monsters and "sail to the rescue of Pepperland, a cartoon Camelot that lives on love and music." The magazine states that *Yellow Submarine* is now running in London and will reach New York in the fall. The film will be preceded by a "million-copy paperback-book version," which forms the basis of the McCall's feature. The preview is four pages long and contains text and color images from the book, telling the story in truncated form. Along the way we see illustrations of the mod-looking Beatles, Old Fred, the Boob, various villains and, at the end, a photograph of the Beatles warning us that "Newer and Bluer Meanies have been reported" and suggesting that we "start *singing*."

The *Yellow Submarine* book was published by the Signet Books imprint of The New American Library in both paperback (95¢) and hard cover ($1.95) editions on September 30, 1968, a month and a half ahead of the film's American debut. The full-color book is a novelization of the film and has 128 pages. As is often the case with book versions of films, there are some deviations from the film. Max Wilk is listed as the author.

The August 1968 issue of Eye has an article by Erich Segal, a young classics professor at Yale, who tells how he was recruited by *Yellow Submarine* producer Al Brodax to work on the film. The piece, written in the form of a movie script, starts with Segal receiving a phone call from Brodax in August 1967 asking if he can "write a complete film script in a month." After Segal explains his teaching obligations, Big Al starts dropping the names: "For the Beatles?;" "For John?;" "For Paul?;" "For George?;" "For Ringo!" When Brodax adds, "For money?," Segal agrees. The script then cuts to London, three weeks later, with Segal under strain, only escaping from his Park Lane hotel room to run in Hyde Park. The story builds to its climax when Segal gets to meet the Beatles in the recording sudio. He is encouraged to play the piano by Ringo, who requests "Rimsky-Korsakov." Segal suggests a Harvard fight song, and soon his piano blends "into a George Martin-arranged sitar version of 'Yo Ho the Good Ship Harvard.'" Segal's two-page "script" is surrounded by four black and white stills from the film, followed by a page with three color frames (shown on the page 74). The magazine came with a removable color poster of the Beatles and a Blue Meanie.

THE LOG OF THE YELLOW SUBMARINE

Charted by Max Wilk
Designed by Heinz Edelman

The irrepressible Beatles are on their way back, this time aboard "The Yellow Submarine," a full-length, animated fantasy film that may rival "The Wizard of Oz," Wonderland, and the adventures of Dr. Dolittle. Defying monsters, the Beatles sail to the rescue of Pepperland, a cartoon Camelot that lives on love and music. The film, now running in London, reaches New York in the fall, preceded by a million-copy paperback-book version, from which McCall's presents this preview.

 nce upon a time,

or maybe twice, there was a paradise called Pepperland. It lay eighty thousand[...] sea. The principal natural resources of Pepperland were—and still are—sun...mu[...] love. You will not find Pepperland by looking for it. It's a country that must be li[...] and smile to each other, and think about the next person. But...

"HARK! What is that ghastly sound that offends my ears? Send me my Glove," cried the Chief Blue Meanie. "Your Blueness called?" replied the dreadful flying Thing. The battle was joined! Over hill and dale it was fought—music, music, music, echoing everywhere—rousing the land. The Meanies were routed! All was once again serene in Pepperland. Love conquered all.

Long live Pepperland. But there are other Pepperlands to be found, here, there, anywhere. When you hear: Lovely day, isn't it? May I help you?—you've found one. Please remember, there are Meanies everywhere that despise friendship, love, music—and will try to stamp them out. They have got to be held back. Who will protect *your* own private Pepperland?...
Only you can say that.

PSSSSSST!

We have a very serious announcement. Newer and Bluer Meanies have been reported in your vicinity. We would like to suggest that you.....start *singing*.

75

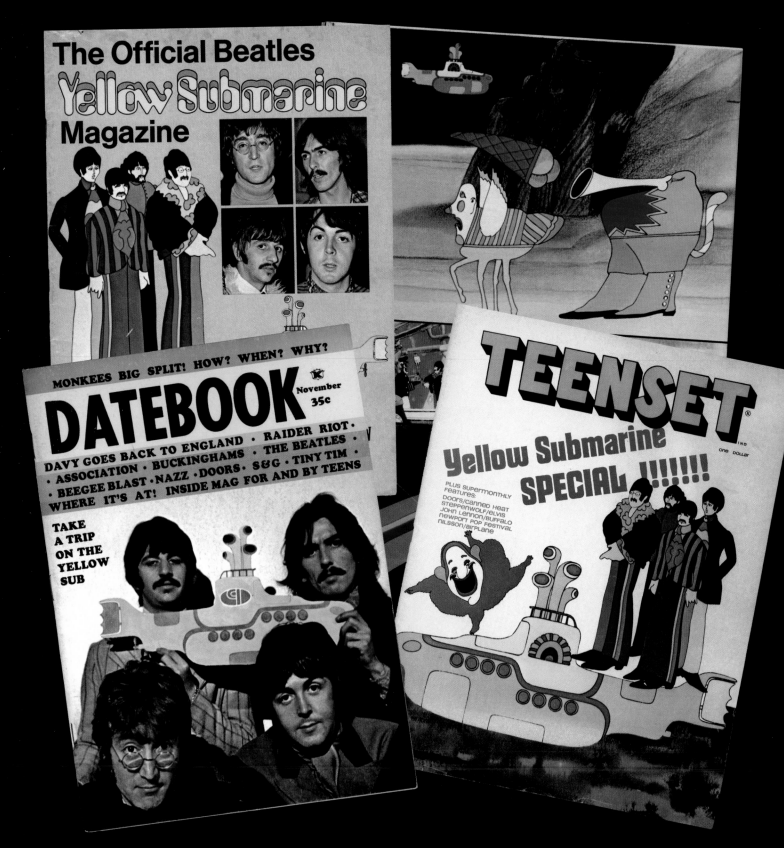

The August 19, 1968 Newsweek reviewed *Yellow Submarine* in an article titled "Framing the Beatles." Although the group had little to do with the film, "such is the continuing power of the Beatles to bestow their blessing on many distinct enterprises that the film turned out all right." The article told of how Beatles manager Brian Epstein rejected the first six treatments of the film and told producer Al Brodax that the film needed "great art."

The October 1968 Teenset ran a two-page spread with five images on "The Incredible Yellow Submarine" by Editor Judith Sims, who attended a preview of the film in September. She saw the British edit of the movie, commenting on an "especially delightful number" that backed a scene featuring a bulldog with several heads. (The "Hey Bulldog" sequence was dropped from the film for its American screenings.) Sims felt that the excellent music, dialog and characterization were overshadowed by the incredible visual trip of brilliant colors. She described the film as "the most enjoyable, happy even meaningful experience to appear on the silver screen." About a month later, Teenset published a *Yellow Submarine* Special issue. It was not limited to the Beatles, but had a 20-page color center section that told the film's plot and contained the lyrics to the four new Beatles songs. Its introduction states: "Yellow Submarine is happy, brilliant and beautiful, and one of the most artistically advanced films in the field of animation. The visual effects alone will give chills, bring tears, and cause smiles of joy. The dialog and whimsical escapades and enchanting characters will delight the senses and expand the mind, and you will find yourself singing along..."

The cover to the November 1968 Datebook shows the real-life Beatles holding a cut-out of an earlier version of the Yellow Submarine as it appears in the film and invites readers to "Take a Trip on the Yellow Sub." Inside, the magazine tells the story of the Yellow Submarine, Pepperland, the Blue Meanies and the Beatles on six pages adorned with a dozen illustrations from film plus head shots of each Beatle posing with his cartoon likeness. Unfortunately the interior pages appear to have been attacked by the Blue Meanies and are devoid of any color.

King Features Syndicate co-published The Official Beatles Yellow Submarine Magazine, which is subtitled "The Beatles—Yesterday, Today and Tomorrow." The 48-page magazine was sold on newsstands and in some theaters showing the film. Its 32-page color center section tells the *Yellow Submarine* story with text and illustrations that differ from both the Signet *Yellow Submarine* book and the film. It also has two pages on the film's London premiere.

American newspapers ran articles on *Yellow Submarine* prior to its U.S. release. Richard Christiansen, writing in the September 8 Chicago Daily News, stated that the imaginative imagery of the Beatles cartoon "has been triumphantly realized in the film's beautiful, stunning art work," which was a "dazzling array of styles," including "art nouveau, op, pop, kinetic and psychedelic." Christiansen predicted that the film had a "long and happy future ahead of it" and added "I look forward to returning to it regularly, as I would with a happy, treasured story from my childhood."

In addition to reading about and seeing illustrations from *Yellow Submarine* for months prior to its U.S. release, some American Beatles fans saw a seven-minute featurette on the film on Saturday night, October 12. *The Beatles' Mod Odyssey* aired after the first American TV broadcast of the group's second film, *Help!*, on the NBC network. It told of animators in a London Soho studio working in an "atmosphere of inspired insanity" on "one of the most unusual motion picture challenges of all time–the visualization and animation of the enormously popular Beatles for their next feature film." *Yellow Submarine* was a "mod odyssey" comparable to the voyages told by Homer and Tolkien. With the "mind-bending sound of the Beatles," the film "brakes new ground in the art of animation."

Yellow Submarine made its American debut at a midnight screening on Friday, October 25, at the San Francisco International Film Festival. Philip Elwood praised the film in the October 28 San Francisco Examiner: "It is the best animated movie anyone has ever produced, seen, or heard. So brilliant, so lively, so magnificently magical that the post-midnight crowd at the Film Festival applauded and cheered intermittently throughout the showing. At the end we all stood up and roared our approval at the distressingly empty screen." He added: "You have never seen colors in motion and conflict the way 'Yellow Submarine' splashes them around. The animation (reputedly the result of over a half-million separately drawn frames) makes the fantastic believable; even the most obscure and involved optical illusions...are so entertaining and vivid that the illogical becomes logical." His favorite bits were the "Time" sequence, the dancing "Holes" portion, the exquisite "Nowhere Man" section and the recoloring of Pepperland that provides the climax. He called *Yellow Submarine* "THE animated cartoon masterpiece, certainly, for this generation– if not the century." In his report on the San Francisco Film Festival for the October 28 Los Angeles Times, Kevin Thomas reported that the festival's program director aptly described the film as "a sort of Beatles-in-Wonderland."

In the November 1 LA Times, Wayne Warga wrote that the animated Beatles film *Yellow Submarine* had "astounding graphics and whimsical plot." It was the "first full-length cartoon to part with the traditional Disney-dominated way of doing things." Warga viewed this complete departure form the Disney technique as an "animation revolution."

The WEST magazine supplement to the Sunday, November 10, Los Angeles Times contained an article on *Yellow Submarine* by Times Entertainment Editor Charles Champlin, complete with several illustrations from the film. Champlin declared that there seems to be "no limit to the magic the Beatles can produce, or inspire others to produce." He found it appropriate that the new Beatles movie would premiere at the County Museum of Art on November 12 because the film was "indubitably a work of art." He noted that the movie had been called a "major breakthrough in the art of animation" and "pop art in motion." Champlin stated it is both. "It is a funny, fascinating, whiz-bang, untiringly inventive tour de force through everything that has mattered and glittered in the op art, pop art, art nouveau, way out, way in, cool, hard-edge, psychedelic, poster-style, mixed media world of graphics over the last decade or so." He went on to call the film "an instant classic, so richly layered with verbal and visual allusions, satiric asides, analogies and throwaway lines, in-jokes and sight-gags and who knows what all else that, as with Swift, Joyce and Peanuts, one viewing only skims the surface."

Champlin singled out prize-winning poster artist and illustrator Heinz Edelmann as the film's "resident genius." After endless study of the Beatles movies, Edelmann "designed the figures of the boys as they are animated in the film." Champlin observed that in the film, the Beatles are "closer in style and feeling to old French posters than to the quite ordinary and cartoon-like Beatles figures on the Saturday morning television series." The film is a "sort of animated collage or palpitating pastiche [whose] graphic richness and variety is a long reach beyond anything we've had on the screen before, and its inspirations lie closer to gallery art than to the cartoon." The film's message appeared to be that "love and singing are the most useful antidotes to the Blue Meanies and other forms of villainy and vile temper." Champlin noted that the Beatles appeared in person at the end of the film and acknowledged it was nice to see them, but added that "after all the artistic splendors that have gone before, seeing them in *photograph* is somehow a crushing anticlimax, which is perhaps as high a compliment as *Yellow Submarine* can have."

United Artists held a screening of *Yellow Submarine* for the New York press on October 16. It opened in a limited number of American cities and theaters on Wednesday, November 13, with additional cinemas added throughout the country a few weeks later. This differed from the U.K., where the film was not given a full general release in London or the British Isles and was pulled out of theaters due to lackluster attendance. The August 19 Newsweek reported that *Yellow Submarine* was "running at periscope depth." It wasn't a flop, but as one distributor put it, it was no James Bond. In the U.S., the film was generally well received by movie-goers, Beatles fans and critics alike.

Renata Adler reviewed the movie the day after its debut in the November 14 New York Times. Adler states that the film is beautifully designed and has "the spirit and conventions of the Sunday comic strip." She addresses the importance of the music, writing that "the rhythm of the movie direction...and the rhythms of the music are meant for each other." The film is "full of enfolded meanings, jokes, puns...that would delight a child, or a head, or anybody who loves or admirers the Beatles," even though they only appear briefly in "one of their worst acted appearances ever." The movie has "completely lovely visual ideas," including a fish with hands swimming the breast stroke, a "consumer creature with a trumpet snout, who ingests the world," "decanting people out of a glass ball," "Dantesque landscapes of other worldly types" and wonderfully-drawn thistles. While not a great film, it is "truly nice" and a "family movie in the truest sense." It has "something for the little kids who watch the same sort of punning stories, infinitely less nonviolent and refined on television; something for the older kids, whose musical contribution to the arts and longings for love and gentleness and color could hardly present a better case; something for the parents who can see the best of what being newly young is all about." While the group's prior films were "more serious, and more truly Beatles saturated," *Yellow Submarine*, with "its memories of Saturday morning at the movies" and lovely graphics makes the Beatles message of "hooking up and otherwise commingling very possible." She closes by noting that when invited, the "entire audience picks up the 'All Together Now' refrain and sings."

Lita Eliscu praised *Yellow Submarine* in the November 15, 1968 edition of the East Village Other, a New York underground newspaper, writing: "It is wonderful, a beautifully realized animation flick, and although the voices are not those of the real Beatles, the sentiments and puns could belong only to them."

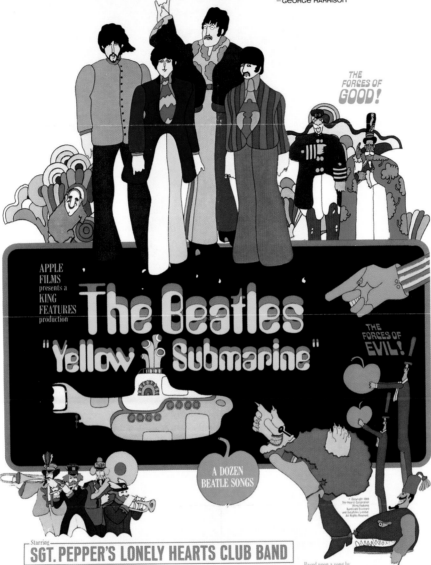

Charles Champlin followed up his WEST feature on *Yellow Submarine* with a review in the November 15 Los Angeles Times, calling the film "further proof of [the Beatles] catalytic powers." He repeated some of his prior comments on the movie and further described it as a "a soaring, sizzling display of graphic whoop-de-do which is as far beyond the animated cartoons we've been used to as 'Help!' and 'A Hard Day's Night' were beyond 'Rock Around the Clock.'" The film has the "unpatronizing charm of a very hip fairy tale, which proceeds by verbal and visual jokes, puns and marvelously imaginative nonsense." Champlin assured readers that the feature-length cartoon was nothing like the "very ordinary Saturday morning cartoons" from the same producer, Al Brodax, with Heinz Edelmann giving the film its "essential and unique look." The movie was written by Lee Minoff and embellished by Eric Segal. Even with the Beatles music, the "impact and pleasure of 'YS' is still more visual than musical."

Champlin's praise of the movie's "explosion of pictures and colors" was echoed and expanded in the newspaper's same section by LA Times Art Editor Henry J. Seldis, who called the film the "most stupendous animation feat in decades." It was a "veritable compendium of styles from Beardsley to Pop" with an "overabundance of visual and verbal puns." Seldis added: "The interpolation of realistic happenings with the over-all dreamlike odyssey undertaken by the Beatles is related closely to the tenets of Dada and Surrealism. Nearly every frame reveals the influence of original or latter-day adherents to these irrational yet sanity-saving ideas as they puncture all pedantic considerations. This phantasmagoric underwater journey, with its resultant sense of euphoria, is consistent with efforts by most 20th-century artists to delve beneath surface realities." This was a film to be seen more than once: "If my first encounter with 'Yellow Submarine' seemed nearly overwhelming to the senses, the second viewing brought out marvelously funny tricks of draftsmanship, spacing and color that add to the total magic of this cinematic marvel."

In the November 15, 1968 Life, Richard Schickel wrote that the Beatles imposed their high standards on an animated film "that may rescue this great art form from the doldrums in which it has so long languished." He praised the film's "wonderous visual freedom," which was "genuinely liberating." While some college kids had told him that the only way to fully appreciate Kubrick's *2001* was to be stoned, "*Yellow Submarine* needs no such artificial flavoring." The film reinforced his "conviction that the great function of the Beatles...is to build a bridge across the generation gap."

Arthur Knight opened his review in the November 16 Saturday Review with high words of praise: "Those astonishing Beatles have done it again! Just as *A Hard Day's Night* kicked holes in all the ordinary ways of presenting musical groups on the screen, their new feature-length animated film, *The Yellow Submarine*, utterly demolishes the slick naturalism of post-Disney cartooning." Animation allows for departure from reality into "realms limited only by the artist's imagination." And in *Yellow Submarine*, "that imagination soars, in fitting counterpoint to the hallucinogenic poetry of the Beatles' songbook" leading into a "fascinating excursion into never-never Pepperland."

In the November 27 San Francisco Examiner, Stanley Eichelbaum wrote that the film was "unquestionably the most imaginatively drawn–the most visually exciting–movie that has been done in the cartoon genre." Its artwork was "a constant delight–so rich in its variety that it never ceases to involve the eye and so astonishingly free in its form and content that it leaps light-years ahead of Disney and even neo-Disney cartooning." Just as the Beatles had revolutionized pop music, the film's sophisticated approach to animation was a breakthrough, a fascinating composite of many styles, including poster art and "serial patterns and vibrant colors of Pop Art and Op Art." Its "optical pleasures are almost infinite and ever-changing." Its humor "stems from the Beatles' affection for self-ribbing, whimsical wisecracks and puns." Conceptually the film is like *Fantasia* with its use of music to paint pictures, "each one illustrated with extraordinary flair." It is a "very trippy film" that "has a lot more to it than meets the ears." John Wasserman of the San Francisco Chronicle added: "an instant classic. There has never been anything like it."

Crawdaddy No. 20 (November 1968) presented two points of view. Bert Lee titled his piece "Lost at Sea." Although he admitted the animation was excellent, he thought the film was "the product of a promomachine that threatens to package the Beatles into a hole in the ground" and was "indicative of the same mentality that gave us paisley toilet paper...and psychedelic deodorant commercials." Eve Adamson thought the film was a magnificent voyage, whose power "lies in its simplicity," with the fantastic presented "as an end, an experience in itself...in which wonders occur as a matter of course." It didn't matter that the plot was simple-minded and the villains were at times overdone and silly. "Ulysses did not stop to question the delights and terrors of his journey, nor did Gilgamesh, Orpheus, or Alice. Nor do John, Paul, George, Ringo, and Old-Young Fred, their navigator. Nor should we."

APPLE FILMS
presents a
KING FEATURES
production

The Beatles

"Yellow Submarine"

Starring
SGT. PEPPER'S LONELY HEARTS CLUB BAND
COLOR by DeLuxe United Artists
Entertainment from
Transamerica Corporation

ELEVEN
BEATLE SONGS

In the November 30 New Yorker, Pauline Kael wrote of the Metamorphosis of the Beatles: "From nursery to the boutique is now a very short path; 'Yellow Submarine' travels it with charm and ease. The Beatles...rescue the people of Pepperland and save them from the Blue Meanies, their weapons being...music and love–but what is so pleasant about 'Yellow Submarine' is its lighthearted, throwaway quality." She noted the film's "giddy flower-childness" and multitude of art sources: "The eclecticism is so open that it is in itself entertaining–we have the fun of a series of recognitions." The movie is full of "visual puns and transformations," but works best when its ingenious animation images "are choreographed to the music," even though they do not always connect with the meaning of the lyrics.

As for the magic of animation, "anything can turn into anything else, and children love it for the illogic that is a visual equivalent of their nursery rhymes and jingles and word games." The film, "with its bright Pop flourish and inventiveness, restores the pleasure of constant surprise, which has always been the fun of good animation." Kael also writes of the Beatles metamorphosis as they appear in the film: "They are no longer the rebellious, anarchistic Pop idols that parents were at first so outraged by; they're no longer threatening. They're hippies as folk heroes, enshrined in our mythology...[as] gentle, harmless Edwardian boys, with one foot in the nursery and the other in the boutique." Although she has issues with the work of director George Dunning and designer Heinz Edelmann, the movie is charming and a nostalgic fantasy. They "have done what hasn't been done before in animation–at least, not on anything like this scale." The film "uses Pop heroes and Pop Art deliberately, and with sophistication." Two of her favorite bits are the "gluttonous consumer with a vacuum snout, who devours the universe," and the "Lucy In The Sky With Diamonds" sequence, with its "stunning use of stylized human figures–an apotheosis of Rogers and Astaire." The magazine's Motion Pictures section provided the following summary: "Brightly colored and ingenious Pop Art animation, so blatantly derivative that it's an entertaining catalogue of twentieth-century graphic design."

Michael Korda of Glamour Magazine called the film "a journey through the mind, the imagination and the soul, a work of almost unbelievable beauty, power and sheer good humor." He saw it so many times that he was an addict. Good Housekeeping gave the film its seal of approval, calling Yellow Submarine "the Beatles' best effort to date."

In a satire on pop art, Ringo leads submarine skipper through a hall of monstrous artifacts.

"Lucy in the Sky with Diamonds" appears in images evanescent as heat lightning.

The Vacuum Flask Monster mindlessly devours anything and everything.

The Blue Meanies, who hate everything gay, launch an attack on happy Pepperland.

YELLOW SUBMARINE: A LATTER-DAY MORALITY TALE

The Chief Meanie instructs his sinister pet, the Ferocious Flying Glove, who smashes things.

Blue Meanies silence Sgt. Pepper's Band with a huge blue bubble. Pepperlanders flee.

The December 27 Time devoted six pages to the film (four with color illustrations) in its Art section in an article titled "New Magic In Animation." This was quite a contrast to the magazine's November 22 review in its Cinema section, titled "Bad Trip," which called the movie a "curious case of artistic schizophrenia" that was "too square for hippies and too hip for squares." Its eclectic art styles included art nouveau, comic strips, Dada and the vibrating poster art of Peter Max, almost becoming a style of its own and occasionally being effective. As for the script, "Flabby punjabs pass for wit" with "the boys' voyage...filled with stilted symbolism." The film's biggest problem was that the Beatles had little to do with it. The review ends with: "All but the most compelled Beatlemaniacs can profit by their example."

Time's art critic saw it differently, describing *Yellow Submarine* as an "87-minute melange of arty art work and allusory sight gags, which has turned into a smash hit, delighting adolescents and esthetes alike." The film "combines every trick and treat of film animation with a dazzle of takeoffs on schools and styles of art. Picassoesque monsters compete with gentle grotesques from Dr. Seussland. Graham Sutherlandish plants burst in and out of bloom. Plump Edwardians wander with suave decadence out of Aubrey Beardsley's world, and creatures consume themselves with Steinbergian detachment. There are silk screens from Warholville and numbers from Indiana. Psychedelia explodes and art nouveau swirls in the most unexpected places. Corridor doors are open on surrealist nightmares, Freudian symbolisms and early movies—all combined in a swiveting, swirling splurge of phantasmagoria, puns, pastiches and visual non sequiturs." Beatles songs "become wildly improbable visualizations," with the Yellow Submarine itself depicted as a "jam-crammed maze of machinery, levers, toggles and buttons that visually mocks every science-fiction film ever made." Time notes that: "The whole surrealistic mix of pictures, words, songs and images is the result of two years of bickering and brainstorming by an international collection of diverse talents." Producer Al Brodax got the *Fantasia*-like idea for a feature-length animated film on the Beatles. Designer Heintz Edelmann ("The future of animation is as limitless as the imagination") studied *A Hard Day's Night* to get the Beatles characteristic walks and watched newsreels of Hitler to model the movements of the Chief Blue Meanie. A team of 40 animators and 140 technical artists made over 500,000 drawings. "If the result seems less a coherent story than a two-hour pot high, *Submarine* is a breakthrough combination of the feature film and art's intimacy with the unconscious."

In November 1967, when Capitol learned of the Beatles plans to issue the six *Magical Mystery Tour* songs on a double-EP set, the company requested and was granted permission to issue an album with the six film songs on one side and five songs from recently released Beatles singles on the other side. By the summer of 1968, the EP format continued its fall from favor in the U.K., leading the Beatles to ponder whether to release the four new songs appearing in *Yellow Submarine* on an EP or LP. Capitol, however, showed no hesitation, assigning an album catalog number for its projected *Yellow Submarine* LP in July. The disc would have the film songs plus "Yellow Submarine" and "All You Need Is Love" on Side One and selections from George Martin's score on Side Two. By October the Beatles had decided to issue a *Yellow Submarine* soundtrack LP and insisted that it not be released until after their next LP, the double-disc set *The Beatles*. During the second half of October, George Martin supervised the mixing of the Beatles film songs and re-recorded selections from his film score at Abbey Road. The album, released in America on January 13, 1969, opens with "Yellow Submarine" followed by the new recordings "Only A Northern Song," "All Together Now," "Hey Bulldog" and "It's All Too Much." The first side closes with "All You Need Is Love," which was also on the *Magical Mystery Tour* LP, but this time in true stereo. The discs were pressed with Apple labels.

Two of the three music trades reviewed the *Yellow Submarine* album in their January 18, 1969 issues. Billboard stuck to the basics, informing readers that the set contained "songs and music from their highly successful cartoon feature" and listing the titles to the new and old Beatles songs. George Martin's score was described as "intoxicating." Cash Box indicated that the main selling point of the album of music from the Beatles cartoon film was the four new songs performed by the group. The set was "filled out by the engaging film music composed by George Martin and an instrumental written by Lennon & McCartney and arranged by Martin ['Yellow Submarine In Pepperland']." The magazine concluded that "The new Beatles cuts make this set a must for Beatles collectors, of whom there are, of course, thousands." Oddly enough, Record World did not review the Beatles soundtrack album.

Yellow Submarine made its debut in the Billboard Top LP's chart on February 8, 1969, at number 86. On March 1, the album peaked at number two behind the two-disc set *The Beatles*, which was in its last of nine weeks at the top. Billboard charted the soundtrack album for 25 weeks, including two weeks at number two and six in the top ten. Record World charted the LP for 17 weeks, including three weeks at number two (blocked from the top by *The Beatles* for all three of those weeks) and six in the top ten. Cash Box showed the album peaking at number three for two weeks during its 16-week run in the Top 100 (plus six more weeks in its second tier listing of the top 101-140 LPs), which also included six weeks in the top ten. The disc was quickly certified gold (signifying sales of one million dollars) by the RIAA, which later certified sales of one million *units* for platinum status on December 26, 1991.

Prior to the album's release, some radio stations obtained tapes of one or more of the new Beatles songs appearing in the film. Indianapolis' WNAP-FM listed the songs "Hey Bulldog" and "You're Too Much" as "Hitbound" on its November 16, 1968 survey. As "Hey Bulldog" was not in the American cut of the film, the two tracks may have come from a British source or may have been taped during a September screening of the film before it was edited for the America market. The song identified as "You're Too Much" was, of course, George Harrison's "It's All Too Much," and may have been the movie edit of the song. In Redwood Falls, Minnesota, KLGR listed "Hey Bulldog" and "You're Too Much" at numbers four and five on its January 1-7, 1969 chart. Such unauthorized air play became moot when Capitol distributed promotional copies of the album to radio stations during the second week of January.

Some radio stations played songs from the *Yellow Submarine* album in steady rotation. New York's WABC listed "Hey Bulldog" and "All Together Now" as album cuts in its January 7, 14 and 21 surveys. WORC in Worcester, Massachusetts charted "All Together Now" at number 9 in its February 1, 1969 survey.

Capitol prepared an eye-catching floor merchandiser for *Yellow Submarine*. Its lower section is adorned with colorful images from the cartoon film, including head shots of each Beatle, Blue Meanies and yellow flowers over a bright reddish-orange background. A 14-inch-square bin sits atop the base to hold copies of the album. Its sides have black holes over a white background representing the Sea of Holes, and either "Yellow Submarine" or "The Beatles" printed in the same style and colors as on the album cover. A yellow cardboard tube runs from the floor through the center of the record bin to attach a large cardboard Yellow Submarine. A three-piece motor mechanism fits inside the top of the tube and, when activated, rotates the submarine. The display is about five feet tall. Capitol also distributed a 20" x 37" two-sided poster for window display. The front of the poster features the Yellow Submarine with each Beatle looking out a separate porthole. The back shows each Beatle looking out a porthole. A variation of the poster (shown right) was included as an insert to the January 25, 1969 Billboard. The New American Library prepared a colorful poster to promote its full-color *Yellow Submarine* Signet paperback book.

Although the December 1969 charity album *No One's Gonna Change Our World* was not issued in America, copies were imported. Some radio stations added the Beatles contribution to the disc, "Across The Universe," to their play lists. The song appears on the February 3, 1970 survey of Milwaukee's WRIT.

Most Americans did not get to see *Magical Mystery Tour* until many years after its British broadcast; however, they were able to purchase the film songs on an album augmented with five songs previously available only on singles. This was not only more convenient, but also a superior listening experience compared to the British EP. *Magical Mystery Tour* was nominated for a Grammy for Album of the Year, but lost out to Glen Campbell's *By The Time I Get To Phoenix*. And while the "Hey Bulldog" segment was edited out of the American release of *Yellow Submarine*, at least the movie was in general distribution in the U.S. for several months. As George said, "It's all in the mind, y'know!"

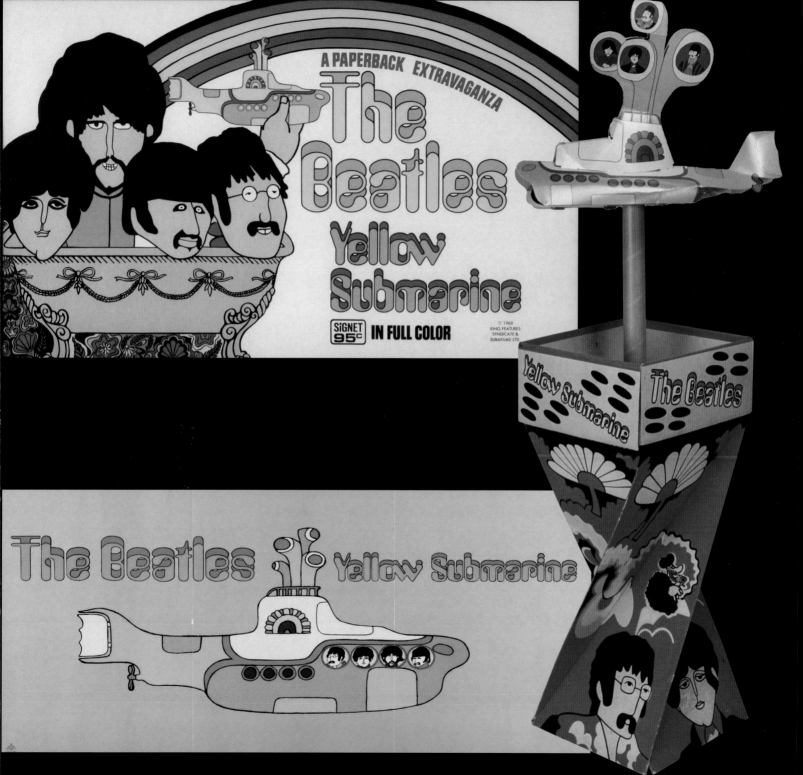

The Beatles in Canada: From Our World to No One's Gonna Change Our World

by Piers Hemmingsen

June 1967 was a terrific month for Beatles fans in Canada, with stereo and mono copies of the Beatles new *Sgt. Pepper* LP spinning on turntables everywhere. But the Beatles weren't done yet. In the June 17 edition of the Vancouver Province newspaper, disc jockey Terry David Mulligan wrote: "The most sensational news in years, concerns, rightly so, the most sensational group in years, the Beatles. 500 million people will watch the Beatles record their next single in a British recording studio on June 25. Sound impossible?" It did sound impossible, but Mulligan explained how it would happen via a worldwide satellite broadcast. The day before the big event the Toronto Daily Star reported: "The Beatles appear on the two-and-a-half-hour $2,250,000 intercontinental TV spectacular Our World tomorrow afternoon." The concept of the program fit in well with Montreal's 1967 International and Universal Exposition (Expo 67), whose motto was "Man and His World." Canada would contribute five live segments to the Our World program, allowing people across the globe to get a view of everyday life in Canada. The broadcast by the Canadian Broadcasting Corporation ("CBC") was preceded by an interview in Toronto with futurist Marshall McLuhan.

Many Beatles fans missed the show because it was aired on a Sunday afternoon during summer break. But even if you missed seeing the Beatles record "All You Need Is Love," it wasn't long before you heard the song on the radio. In the Capitol Sizzle Sheet dated July 7, 1967, Capitol of Canada's Paul White alerted stations and distributors of "Two more astonishing sides from The Beatles...destined for that No. 1 position around the world in double fast time." White wrote that "All You Need Is Love" was composed by John and Paul for the Our World TV spectacular, which was "seen by 400,000,000 people in 24 countries!" Although the single was not released until July 17, Toronto's CHUM was already playing the song by the time it issued its July 10 Top 50 survey, debuting the single at 32.

Within a month of its release, "All You Need Is Love" was number one on Vancouver's CFUN, Ottawa's CFRA, Montreal's CJMS and Toronto's CHUM. The national survey published by RPM Music Weekly charted the song for 10 weeks, including two non-consecutive weeks at number one when it replaced the Monkees' "Pleasant Valley Sunday" (August 26) and the Rascals' "A Girl Like You" (September 9) at the top. By the end of August, "All You Need Is Love" had sold over 80,000 copies, with about 5,000 discs packaged in picture sleeves imported from the U.S. "All You Need Is Love" proved to be THE BRILLIANT ANTHEM for the Summer of Love. Its flip-side, the catchy, psychedelic-sounding "Baby You're A Rich Man," was played almost as frequently by Canadian Top 40 radio stations.

In November 1963, Capitol's Paul White and Ottawa journalist Sandy Gardiner heralded the arrival of Beatlemania in Canada. Four years later the duo were once again delivering the latest Beatles news. In his November 10, 1967 Capitol Sizzle Sheet, White announced that a new Beatles single featuring "Hello Goodbye" and "I Am The Walrus" would be issued on November 27. The following week he wrote that the disc's release date had been moved up to November 13. White also told of a new Beatles album that would be released in the first week of December with seven new songs from their recently completed television special. On November 24, Gardiner wrote in his weekly Ottawa Journal Pop column that Beatles fans in Canada would see the new *Magical Mystery Tour* film in color on their television sets over the 1967 Christmas and New Year holiday period. He also included a recent interview with all four Beatles, who individually answered questions about their new film. It quoted John Lennon on why the Beatles had made a film for television: "So if stage shows were to be out we wanted something to replace them. Television was the obvious answer." RPM ran the Beatles Q&A about the film in its December 16 issue.

The November 23 Toronto Telegram provided details about *Magical Mystery Tour*, informing readers that the Beatles next album was scheduled for a December 10 release and would have the same title as their upcoming Christmas film prepared for English television. The article noted that the album would include both sides of each of their three 1967 Capitol singles, but that it could not include "Paperback Writer" or "Rain" because of the long running times of "I Am The Walrus" and "Hello Goodbye." The film would likely not be screened in the U.S. because of the "tight pre-Christmas television schedules."

By early December, "Hello Goodbye" was getting saturation air play in Canada. CHUM charted the single for three straight weeks at number one starting with its December 4 survey. RPM charted "Hello Goodbye" for ten weeks, including three straight weeks at the top starting on December 23. The disc sold nearly 85,000 copies in Canada.

Capitol of Canada issued the same *Magical Mystery Tour* album in both mono and stereo as that of its parent company in the States. Although the 24-page booklet inserts were supplied by Capitol's U.S. printer, the covers were printed and fabricated in Canada and are essentially the same as the U.S. covers, except for the printing, manufacturing and distribution information and a front cover black oval Capitol dome logo not present on the U.S. covers. The album was officially released in Canada on December 6, 1967, and had sold nearly 100,000 units by year's end.

Ralph Thomas reviewed the *Magical Mystery Tour* LP in the December 9 Toronto Daily Star. He noted that the album contained "great, recent oldies" plus "Hello Goodbye" and six songs from the Beatles new Christmas TV film. To ensure readers didn't get the wrong idea, he warned: "The songs are like no Christmas songs you've ever heard." He also thought the film would be "like no Christmas film you've ever seen," stating that it "concerns the weird, magical and mysterious adventures of a busload of strange characters on a tour of England." He cautioned that the film might not be seen for a while in Canada as CBC had no plans to show it and CTV had only made inquiries. As for the music, it was void of "startling new things," with the Beatles continuing to refine "gold mined last year," which was fine with Thomas: "Musically, every song is a masterpiece—an incredibly clever musical maze of intertwining ideas, all groovy, all intriguing."

Peter Goddard reviewed the *Magical Mystery Tour* album in the December 9 Globe and Mail newspaper, noting that the "bizarre nature of the show has been extended to the album." On its cover, "tour guides-cum-sorcerers Lennon, McCartney, Starr and Harrison are dressed like characters from a nightmare." The 24-page inside booklet shows a "Beatles-in-Wonderland view of the English countryside." Goddard noted that whether the film or LP had any value would have "little relevance to the record's sales." Its success was assured, with six of its songs having previously been hits. Advance sales were large, living up to expectations.

Magical Mystery Tour
The Fool On The Hill   Flying   Blue Jay Way
Your Mother Should Know   I Am The Walrus

Includes 24-page full color picture book

Hello Goodbye   Strawberry Fields Forever
Penny Lane   Baby You're A Rich Man
All You Need Is Love

MAGICAL MYSTERY TOUR
THE BEATLES

1. MAGICAL MYSTERY TOUR (BMI-2:48) John Lennon-Paul McCartney
2. THE FOOL ON THE HILL (BMI-3:00) John Lennon-Paul McCartney

STEREO   SMAL-2835
                          (SMAL-X-1-2835)

3. FLYING (BMI-2:16) Lennon-McCartney-Harrison-Starr
4. BLUE JAY WAY (BMI-3:50) George Harrison
5. YOUR MOTHER SHOULD KNOW (BMI-2:33) John Lennon-Paul McCartney
6. I AM THE WALRUS (BMI-4:35) John Lennon-Paul McCartney

Produced in England by George Martin

(Recorded in England)

MAGICAL MYSTERY TOUR
THE BEATLES

1. HELLO GOODBYE (BMI-3:24) John Lennon-Paul McCartney

STEREO   SMAL-2835
                          (SMAL-X-2-2835)

2. STRAWBERRY FIELDS FOREVER (BMI-4:05) John Lennon-Paul McCartney
3. PENNY LANE (BMI-2:57) John Lennon-Paul McCartney
4. BABY YOU'RE A RICH MAN (BMI-3:07) John Lennon-Paul McCartney
5. ALL YOU NEED IS LOVE (BMI-3:57) John Lennon-Paul McCartney

Produced in England by George Martin

(Recorded in England)

Poster insert from the December 29, 1967 CHUM edition of Go magazine

Goddard added that "if the album looks like a slice out of a Richard Lester movie, it sounds like a travelling vaudeville show." Like *Sgt. Pepper*, the LP is the "epitome of studio rock," although it has little of its predecessor's "acidity or melancholy." While many claimed *Sgt. Pepper* was profound, *Magical Mystery Tour* is "merely allusive and elusive," a "bubbling corollary" to *Sgt. Pepper*. Its music is "an amalgam of many styles and many cultures" and has a "sense of the unreal, of the mystical," with lyrics that touch on the absurd as in "I Am The Walrus," where John uses words with the "outrageous authority of a latter-day Lewis Carroll." As explained by Paul, their new music is an attempt "to create magic. It's all trying to make things happen so that you don't know why they're happening." Goddard describes "The Fool On The Hill" as: "a marvelous little lament, constructed around one of the longest and most well-constructed melodies that McCartney has written. Streaked with melancholy and compassion, it is, in a mild way, the most disturbing song." Goddard wrote that most of the other songs "retain a more joyful inventiveness." "Your Mother Should Know" is a track that "effectively salutes nostalgia while not indulging in it." "Hello Goodbye" is saved by the Beatles "high spirits [that] hold it together." With "Penny Lane," "the medium and the message are in perfect harmony." Although the rest of the songs could be considered insignificant, he concludes that *Magical Mystery Tour* is "frequently outrageous, always wacky and constantly a pleasure."

The February 17, 1968 edition of The Star Weekly Magazine gave a sneak preview of the *Magical Mystery Tour* film. Barrie Hale wrote about it being panned after its BBC broadcast: "Reaction in Britain was so bad, in fact, that no one in North American TV seems to want to run it. Or do they?" Hale quoted from several of the film's disastrous reviews, which led Canadian TV executives to defer their decision to broadcast the film until they had seen it. But strangely, they were unable to obtain a print from the BBC for viewing, leading CBC's John Vance to say: "It's the greatest wall of silence we've ever encountered." CTV's Murray Chercover added: "We're beginning to wonder if they're gonna release it at all." As for the plot, "The Beatles and a random assortment of other English holidayers... take a mysterious bus tour....From time to time, where you go is inside various of the travellers' heads; things get a little surreal and trenchant." Hale noted that TV executives should heed Richard Last's view in the Sun that while the film was just a great big bore for him, "millions of The Beatles' faithful fans might've found it just great." That should be enough of an audience to tempt TV executives to show the film in color. Hale ended with: "Let's see it, guys."

THE

star
weekly
MAGAZINE

FEBRUARY 17, 1968 **20** CENTS

Don't miss
of ! late
Pages 43-47

A sneak preview
of the Beatles film
you may never
be allowed to see

**Magician Ringo Starr
in Magical Mystery Tour**

Another exclusive excerpt from
The Smug Minority
the powerful new book by
PIERRE
BERTON

Despite Hale's plea and the curiosity of Canadian Beatles fans, *Magical Mystery Tour* was not shown on Canadian TV in the sixties. It did, however, receive limited theater screenings in Toronto, Montreal and Ottawa in early 1969. CHUM-FM and promoters John Brower and Kenny Walker staged a premier film event at the O'Keefe Center in Toronto on January 2, 1969, with folk singers Eric Anderson and Bob McBride performing before the film. The sold out event attracted over 2,000 people.

Sandy Gardiner got the scoop for Canadian Beatles fans on the group's first record of 1968. In his Ottawa Journal column on March 1, 1968, Gardiner wrote: "The Beatles, still deep in transcendental meditation in the Himalayas, have a new single set for release. Top side is 'Lady Madonna,' described by Paul McCartney as being 'as close to rock 'n' roll as The Beatles could be in 1968.' Paul is the featured vocalist on the deck which should be out here later this month." Gardiner added that the flip side was George Harrison's "The Inner Light," which "has a backing of Indian instrumentation recorded in Bombay while George was working on the tracks for the movie score of 'Wonderwall.'"

"Lady Madonna" was released in Canada on March 11, 1968. That same day it entered the CHUM chart at number 38. The single moved up to number one on April 8. RPM charted the disc for 11 weeks, including four weeks at two. Although "Lady Madonna" reportedly sold between 125,000 and 150,000 copies in Canada, it was unable to pass "Valerie" by the Monkees, "Young Girl" by the Union Gap or "Honey" by Bobby Goldsboro on the RPM chart.

The first extensive coverage of the Beatles *Yellow Submarine* cartoon appeared in The Globe and Mail's edition of July 27, 1968. The full-page spread featured text by Ritchie Yorke and images of the Beatles, the Yellow Submarine and nine characters from the film. Yorke notes that the movie is "full of strange puns, odd implications and weird characters." He writes that the film's Good-defeats-Evil storyline is "told in the mod-styled, pop-tuned adventures of Sergeant Pepper's Lonely Hearts Club Band," which includes the Beatles "complex, fantastic travels" to Pepperland. The Beatles sing 12 songs, four of which are new. He quotes from favorable reviews by the British press and from remarks made by Paul, Ringo and George about the film. Paul indicated that he liked the film, but emphasized it wasn't made by the Beatles. "I won't take the credit–even if it's a big smash. It's like saying Bambi made Walt Disney."

Yellow Submarine was not released in Canada until December 19, 1968, five months after its U.K. premiere and a month after its opening in the States. The film was directed by George Dunning, who started his career with Canada's National Film Board, oversaw The Beatles cartoon TV series and directed the film *Canada Is My Piano* for Expo 67.

Martin Knelman's review of the film, titled "Yellow Submarine is a delight," ran in the December 14 Toronto Daily Star. He saw the film in a New York theater filled with classes of 8- and 9-year-old school kids, most who were black. They were singing along with the Beatles and knew all the words. Knelman called the film "an enchanting little movie that works on any number of levels" and "the best animation movie" he'd ever seen. It was like "Lewis Carroll gone mod" and was "the most wonderfully frivolous festival of pop since the American pavilion at Expo." Geraldine Michener, the movie critic for the Globe and Mail, reviewed the film in the paper's December 14 edition. She thought the film offered "the best of the Beatles, the best animation and graphic design of the past decade and, most important, 89 minutes of almost continuous delight." The film "rushes across that mean old generation gap, succeeding, where the hippies have so often failed, in seducing you with its vision of birds and babies, flowers, love, music, beauty and the joy of just being alive." It is a "surrealistic classic of our times" that "married pop art to pop music."

The *Yellow Submarine* soundtrack album was released in Canada on January 13, 1969. RPM charted the disc for 16 weeks, including two weeks at number two behind the two-disc set *The Beatles* and two weeks at number one. Although no single was issued from the LP, CHUM played "Hey Bulldog" in heavy rotation as if it were a new single.

The Wildlife Foundation Fund charity album *No One's Gonna Change Our World* was issued in the U.K. on December 12, 1969. The record featured the then-unreleased Beatles song "Across The Universe," which was recorded at the same February 1968 session as "Lady Madonna." While the album was not released in Canada, it was imported by Campus Records and went on sale in Canada in mid-January 1970. Some radio stations played the Beatles track, including Montreal's CFOX, which listed "Across The Universe" as a "British Import" on its January 23 chart. Hearing John sing "Nothing's gonna change my world" brought back magical memories of Expo 67, its motto of Man and His World, the Our World television broadcast, the Summer of Love and the Beatles singing "All You Need Is Love."

The Beatles Were a Part of Our World

by Al Sussman

On Sunday, June 25, 1967, the Beatles were a part of OUR WORLD...

From the vantage point of the 21st century, when we can get pristine live video from the International Space Station at the click of a mouse button, we take communications satellites for granted. But the June 25, 1967, telecast of Our World was a big deal because it was the first live multi-satellite-enabled international television broadcast. It was seen by between 400 and 700 million viewers worldwide, what media observer Marshall McLuhan dubbed a "global village" early in the telecast. Among the figures featured in the numerous short segments in the two and a half-hour program were Franco Zeffirelli in an early rehearsal for his 1969 film adaptation of *Romeo and Juliet*, a piano collaboration between Leonard Bernstein and Van Cliburn and segments featuring Maria Callas and Pablo Picasso. But the memory that endures from that broadcast over half a century later is the Beatles offering the world an anthem for the so-called Summer of Love, "All You Need Is Love."

It's a memory that endures, but not one many American Beatles fans saw live. With little in the way of a rock music press and the teen fan magazines dominated by coverage of the Monkees, a majority of U.S. fans were unaware of this satellite spectacular, particularly since the U.S. feed was carried by National Education Television ("NET"), the non-commercial forerunner to PBS. In contrast, the British press covered Our World in advance, since it would be a joint BBC-European Broadcasting Union production with master control out of the Beeb studios in London. And even though the British music weeklies were saturated that summer with stories and pictures of the Monkees, the Beatles were still big news, so they alerted readers to the Beatles participation in the program. In the U.S., TV Guide ran a full-page Close-Up listing for the program, but it contained only a brief mention of the Beatles appearance: "the Beatles at a recording session in London." To make matters worse, the live broadcast was shown in America on a Sunday afternoon at 3:00 PM Eastern Standard Time, 12:00 noon Pacific.

TV CLOSE-UP GUIDE

12:00, 9:05 ㉘ **OUR WORLD**

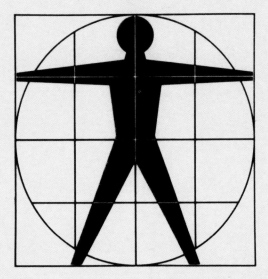

SPECIAL A new chapter in television history begins with the first live, around-the-world telecast. Nations on five continents take part in the program, which is being transmitted to 30 countries through the use of four satellites (three American and one Soviet).

The theme is "Our World"—its problems, achievements and prospects for the future. The major segments . . .

This Moment's World: Cameras circle the globe, showing midnight in Russia, evening in Europe, afternoon in America and morning in Japan.

The Hungry World: Efforts to feed the earth's exploding population are recorded at a Wisconsin farm, an immense greenhouse in Australia and a shrimp farm in Japan.

The Crowded World: Man is seen as a builder of skyscrapers in New York; apartments in Moscow that rotate for natural heat and ventilation; the Habitat complex at Montreal's Expo 67; and a unique new town in Scotland.

Aspiration to Excellence: Physical skills are witnessed in such activities as canoeing in Sweden and "caving" for depth and endurance in Czechoslovakia. Artistic skills are also saluted: Franco Zeffirelli filming in Rome; a rehearsal of Wagner's "Lohengrin" at the Bayreuth Festival in West Germany; painters Joan Miro and Marc Chagall at work in France; pianist Van Cliburn rehearsing with Leonard Bernstein at New York's Lincoln Center; and the Beatles at a recording session in London. (At press time, Soviet ballerina Maya Plisetskaya was scheduled to perform in Odessa.)

The World Beyond: At Cape Kennedy, man reaches for the moon; in Australia, radio signals are received from the farthest known point in the universe.

Live Cameras also visit Austria, East Germany, Hungary, Mexico, Poland, Spain and Tunisia.

Executive producer: Robert Squier. Narrator: Paul Niven. (Live; two hours)

Even after Our World aired, most of the U.S. newspaper reviews were of the wowie-zowie variety, reacting more to the technology that enabled the broadcast than the specifics of what the program contained. The New York Times, for instance, called Our World "a compelling reaffirmation of the potential of the home screen to help unify the peoples of the world." In its July 7, 1967 issue, Time magazine ran a picture of the Beatles taken at the rehearsal for their Our World performance of "All You Need Is Love," but made no mention of the song or the program, merely running the caption "The Beatles in London." The image appeared in the cover story, "The Hippies: Philosophy of a Subculture," which described the Beatles as the "forerunners of psychedelic sound and once again at the forefront with their latest album, *Sgt. Pepper's Lonely Hearts Club Band,*" and as the "major tastemakers in hippiedom."

The lack of coverage for a segment in which the Beatles recorded their next single is bewildering as it had only been three weeks since the release of the group's widely-anticipated and immediately-celebrated *Sgt. Pepper* album. U.S. Beatles fans had spent much of the first half of 1967 waiting, first for the band's first single since the previous August, "Penny Lane"/"Strawberry Fields Forever," and then for the first new Beatles album since the previous summer's *Revolver,* an eternity for fans used to two or more new Beatles LPs and a handful of new singles each year.

In an age long before social media or even fan conventions, the weekend of the release of *Sgt. Pepper* was a communal experience, with fans getting together in groups to listen to the new LP and knowing instinctively that other fans all over our world were savoring this amazing new album, too. But no one could have imagined that the Beatles would follow that up just three weeks later with a live performance and recording via satellite of a new single.

It didn't take long for tapes of the Beatles Our World performance of "All You Need Is Love" to make it to radio, both on AM Top 40 stations and the new breed of FM progressives. Murray the K, the now-cooled-out erstwhile New York AM disc jockey who had proclaimed himself "The Fifth Beatle" three years earlier, played the song on the pioneering New York WOR-FM the night after the telecast, as did Top 40 WMCA. As usual, the Beatles American lawyer, Nat Weiss, issued a short-lived cease-and-desist order until Capitol Records could service radio stations with promotional copies of the actual single, which was in stores less than two weeks after its Our World debut.

JULY 7, 1967

FIFTY CENTS

THE HIPPIES
PHILOSOPHY OF A SUBCULTURE

TIME
THE WEEKLY NEWSMAGAZINE

VOL. 90 NO. 1
(REG. U.S. PAT. OFF.)

ist from Canada through the U.S. to Mexico. There, nature-loving hippie tribesmen can escape the commercialization of the city and attempt to build a society outside of society. At "Drop City," near Trinidad, Colo., 21 hippie dropouts from the Middle West live in nine gaudy geodesic domes, built from old auto tops (20¢ apiece at nearby junkyards), and attempt a hand-to-mouth independent life. An hour's drive north of San Francisco, in apple-growing country near Sebastopol along the Russian River, some 30 to 50 country

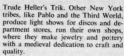

CENTRAL PRESS

THE BEATLES IN LONDON
To Lost Horizons by magic carpet.

hippies live on a 31-acre ranch called Morning Star. Their closest neighbor: Cartoonist Charles Schulz, whose *Peanuts* people are hippie favorites. The ranch is owned by Lew Gottlieb, 43, former arranger, composer and bassist for the folk-singing Limelighters, who has his hippie followers hard at work—rarest of all hippie trips—growing vegetables for the San Francisco Diggers.

Most Morning Star colonists avoid acid. "I'd rather have beautiful children than beautiful visions," says a tanned, clear-eyed hippie girl named Joan. That hippies can actually work becomes evident on a tour of the commune's vegetable gardens. Cabbages and turnips, lettuce and onions march in glossy green rows, neatly mulched with redwood sawdust. Hippie girls lounge in the buffalo grass, sewing colorful dresses or studying Navajo sand painting, clad in nothing but beads, bells and feather headdresses. (Not everyone is a nudist—only when they feel like it.) A shaggy sheepdog named Grass plays with the hippie children, among them a straw-thatched 17-month-old boy named Adam Siddhartha.

Work Trip. The new-found trip of work and responsibility reflected in the Morning Star experiment is perhaps the most hopeful development in the hippie philosophy to date. Other hippie tribes are becoming aware of the work trip as well. New York's Group Image, an aggressive agglomerate of some 50 East Village hippies—many of them from the Middle West—turns out everything from silk-screen prints to psychedelic artifacts and a deadly serious, tidily edited magazine called *Innerspace*. The tribe's seven-man combo plays to packed and palpitating houses at such uptown discothèques as Cheetah and

Trude Heller's Trik. Other New York tribes, like Pablo and the Third World, produce light shows for discos and department stores, run their own shops, where they make jewelry and pottery with a medieval dedication to craft and quality.

The drug scene itself has imposed demands for organization on the hippies. Foremost among the do-gooders are the Diggers; named for a 17th century society of English agricultural altruists, the latter-day Diggers provide free food, shelter and transportation for down-and-out hippies in San Francisco, Los Angeles, Boston and the East Village (where a Digger with the *nom de hip* of Galahad maintains a crowded "crash" pad and returns runaways to their parents). San Francisco alone has such drug-derived service organizations as HALO (Haight-Ashbury Legal Organization), the HIP Job Co-op, with 6,000 names on its part-time employment roster, and Huckleberry's (homes for runaways). In Los Angeles, an outfit called Kerista, founded three months ago by a former heroin addict named John Thomsen, provides pads and proteins for homeless hippies.

Irrelevant Goals. For all the hippies' good works and gentle ways, many Americans find them profoundly unsettling. One reason is that straight society finds it difficult to argue with people who, while condemning virtually every aspect of the American scene, from its foreign policy to its moral values, offer no debatable alternatives. By contrast with the rebels of every previous generation in the U.S.—from the "wobblies" of 50 years ago (*see* BOOKS) to the New Left activists of the early '60s—the hippies have no desire to control the machinery of society or redirect it toward new goals. They have no urge to reform the world, if only because its values seem irrelevant to them.

What offends, perplexes and yet also beguiles the straight sector is hippiedom's total disregard for approbation or disapproval. "Do your own thing," they say, and never mind what anyone else may think or do. Yet this and many hippie attitudes represent only a slight and rather engaging distortion of the Protestant Ethic that they purport to reject.

Indeed, it could be argued that in their independence of material possessions and their emphasis on peacefulness and honesty, hippies lead considerably more virtuous lives than the great majority of their fellow citizens. This, despite their blatant disregard for most of society's accepted mores and many of its laws—most notably those prohibiting the use of drugs—helps explain why so many people in authority, from cops to judges to ministers, tend to treat them gently and with a measure of respect. In the end it may be that the hippies have not so much dropped out of American society as given it something to think about.

In England, the music magazines provided fans with extensive coverage of the Beatles segment in the Our World program, running stories, reviews of the single and pictures from the event. Americans would hear "All You Need Is Love" over and over again, mixed in with tracks from *Sgt. Pepper*, all summer long, but would have no visual reference of the Beatles worldwide celebration of "Love, love, love."

While there were other summer hits in 1967 ("Light My Fire," "Ode To Billie Joe," "To Sir With Love" to name a few), "All You Need Is Love" was nearly without dispute the anthem for what had been dubbed the Summer of Love. From its "La Marseillaise" introduction through the bits of "Greensleeves," "In The Mood" and "She Loves You" on the fadeout, John's straightforward lyrics and the unforgettable sing-along refrain, it was a perfect song for that moment in time for our world and could be heard at youth gatherings and peace rallies throughout that summer and into the fall and beyond, much as Lennon's "Give Peace A Chance" would be two years later.

Unfortunately, that summer in Beatleworld would end badly with the sudden death of the group's manager and guiding force, Brian Epstein. We wouldn't realize the full impact of Brian's passing for some years but, most immediately, it meant that the Beatles would be fending for themselves, both creatively and in their business affairs.

In September, they began work on their next project, a TV special called *Magical Mystery Tour*, which would include six new Beatles songs. The project was the brainchild of Paul and had received Epstein's approval. Much of the fall would be taken up with recording sessions for the show's songs and the final Beatles single of the year, along with the September filming of the largely improvised film and an excruciatingly long editing process.

The last week in November saw the release of the new single, with McCartney's instantly catchy "Hello Goodbye" as the A-side and Lennon's atmospheric and wordplay-dominated "I Am The Walrus," from the film's score, on the flip side. A promotional clip for "Hello Goodbye" was shown on The Ed Sullivan Show on Sunday, November 26. Capitol's *Magical Mystery Tour* LP followed, with the songs from the special on one side and that year's epic Beatles singles on the other.

Despite the annoying reprocessed stereo versions of three of the Side Two singles, the album was a joy to listen to. The show songs on Side One included three delightfully diverse McCartney tunes (the title song, "The Fool On The Hill" and "Your Mother Should Know"), George Harrison's semi-psychedelic and moody "Blue Jay Way," Lennon's epic "I Am The Walrus" and the instrumental "Flying," which would become a staple of FM radio.

The *Magical Mystery Tour* TV special debuted in the U.K. in black-and-white on Boxing Day, December 26, to scathing reviews that caused NBC to cancel plans to broadcast the show in America and scared off the other TV networks. It would be decades before the complete show had its official U.S. debut. But washed-out multi-generational copies of the film began showing up in midnight screenings on college campuses and in theaters as the '60s were winding down and as the closing event at Beatlefest in the '70s and '80s. In the 21st century, fan reaction to *Magical Mystery Tour* is still quite divided, with many loving the song sequences but being bewildered by the amateurish lack of cohesion, causing speculation on whether Epstein would have given the nod to the finished product.

The Beatles exploration of transcendental meditation and the teachings of Maharishi Mahesh Yogi began in the days prior to Brian's death, but was sidelined while the *Magical Mystery Tour* project took shape. After Harrison's January 1968 sessions in India to record music for *Wonderwall* and the early February Beatles recording sessions, the group finally journeyed to India for extended TM education and training. Because of the Beatles involvement, the Maharishi and transcendental meditation received extensive coverage. In the decades since, conventional wisdom has labeled the TM phase a failure, mainly due to Lennon's disenchantment with the Maharishi. But, in fact, the other three Beatles continued to practice TM for decades to come (and from their telling, Ringo and Paul still do). In addition, many Beatles fans were turned on to TM through the Beatles and became TM practitioners as well.

The fruits of the group's February Abbey Road sessions included two songs that made up the first Beatles single of 1968. With a 1950s rock 'n' roll revival sweeping through the U.K., the Beatles reached back to their rock roots for the Fats Domino-influenced "Lady Madonna" as the A-side and Harrison's lovely "The Inner Light" on the flip, once again exposing Beatles fans to Indian music, but this time with a beautiful melody to accompany its unique sound.

On May 11, John and Paul flew to New York for the public launch of the Beatles latest venture, Apple. With a series of interviews and a May 14 press conference, they laid out their concept for a utopian company that would combine music, film, electronics and more. That utopian vision wouldn't be fully realized but, here in the 21st century, these words are being typed on an electronic device that can deliver music, film and video, manufactured by a company, co-founded by a Beatles fan named Steve Jobs, incorporated as Apple Computer, Inc. and now known as Apple.

In late August, our world was introduced to the one successful branch of the Beatles Apple tree, Apple Records. The label got off to a tremendous start with two of its first four singles becoming massive hits. The Paul McCartney-produced disc by Mary Hopkin, "Those Were The Days," topped the charts for several weeks in the U.K. and was a number two hit in America, blocked from the top by the Beatles debut Apple single, "Hey Jude." Although the Beatles disc topped the charts on both sides of the Atlantic, its greatest impact was in the U.S. where it held down the number one spot for nine straight weeks and sold over four million copies, making it the group's most successful American single. "Hey Jude" remains one of the Beatles most-beloved songs. November brought the release of the group's massive 30-track album *The Beatles*, aka *The White Album*. Once again, the weekend following the album's release brought a communal listening experience, with fans digesting the diverse collection of new Beatles music.

November also brought the U.S. premiere of the animated feature *Yellow Submarine*, which had debuted in London in mid-July. While only moderately successful in the U.K., American audiences loved the film. And although it was overshadowed by "Hey Jude" and *The White Album*, the film's psychedelically colorful animation and Beatles soundtrack made for quite a trip. But the ultimate payoff would come years later when *Yellow Submarine* became a Disney-like classic that made Beatles fans out of millions of youngsters who were taken to see the film in theaters or watched it on video with their parents and grandparents. Indeed, *Yellow Submarine* was the vessel through which at least two Beatle offspring, Sean Lennon and Dhani Harrison, found out about their dad's Beatle past. The film is just one example of how multiple generations have been affected by the Beatles and how the group has been woven into the fabric of our lives. From their universal message of "All You Need Is Love" to the joys of families sharing the delightful *Yellow Submarine* cartoon, we are constantly reminded that the Beatles were and are a part of our world.

Why Don't We Sing This Song All Together: The Beatles & the Stones

by Frank Daniels

The Rolling Stones were an important part of a British blues revival movement, being influenced by such greats as T-Bone Walker, Muddy Waters and Bo Diddley. The Beatles had emerged from the skiffle movement and were inspired not only by R&B artists, but also by the likes of the Everly Brothers, the girl groups and Carl Perkins. Although the Beatles and the Stones were thoroughly British and both shared a love of Chuck Berry, Buddy Holly and Arthur Alexander, from the beginning they were quite different from one another.

The rivalry between them emerged on the heels of their great success on the British music scene. From December 1, 1963, through April 4, 1965, only two musical artists topped the British album charts. You guessed it: the Beatles and the Rolling Stones. First holding that spot was *With the Beatles*, an album so popular that not only did New Musical Express chart it on its singles chart, but also it charted higher on that chart than any other album before or since. Replacing it at number one was *The Rolling Stones*, the group's first LP. The Beatles followed with *A Hard Day's Night* and *Beatles For Sale*, but then along came *Rolling Stones No. 2*, which battled with *Beatles For Sale* for the top spot. For 15 months, the readers of British trade magazines wondered whether any other artist could top them.

In the years that followed, the Beatles topped the album charts with *Help!*, *Rubber Soul*, *Revolver* and *Sgt. Pepper*; the Stones did the same with *Aftermath*, and barely missed #1 with *Out Of Our Heads* and *Their Satanic Majesties Request*. Their biggest competitors were Bob Dylan, the Monkees and the soundtrack to *The Sound Of Music*, which spent over 60 nonconsecutive weeks at number one (on every chart) through the end of 1967. The talk of the British music scene were the Beatles, the Rolling Stones and a few others.

With the famous story of Lennon and McCartney having provided the Rolling Stones with their first Top Twenty single ("I Wanna Be Your Man"), it became too easy for commentators to compare and contrast the two groups with one another. The Beatles had traveled to the United States in February 1964, and the Stones toured the U.S.A. that June. The Beatles had recorded a stripped-down acoustic song with strings ("Yesterday") in early 1965; the Rolling Stones released their version of "As Tears Go By" later that year. At this point the arguments begin. Marianne Faithfull actually sang "As Tears Go By" in the middle of 1964. Oh, but wait. Her recording featured a prominent percussive backing; "Yesterday" did not, and the Stones' later recording is more like "Yesterday" in that respect. With *Rubber Soul*, the Beatles became the first British artist in America to release an album that did not mention the artist's name on the front cover; by late 1965, everybody knew who they were. Ah, but the Rolling Stones had released their first two albums in Great Britain by that time and they didn't mention their name on the cover.

The Beatles recovered from having an American album cover withdrawn in June 1966. The Butcher Cover to *Yesterday And Today* became a legendary collectible. One year earlier, London Records edited the liner notes for *The Rolling Stones Now!*, due to Andrew Loog Oldham's advice to American teenagers to steal the money from a blind beggar if they could not afford to buy the album. In several other countries, including the U.K., those notes appeared on the back of *Rolling Stones No. 2*, where also they were banned. The Stones, therefore, had a worldwide album ban. Oh, but that was only the liner notes, right? But then, *Beggar's Banquet* got banned.

Back and forth went the accusations of one group following the other. By 1969, people were observing that the director of the new (as-then-unreleased) Beatles film was going to be Michael Lindsay-Hogg, who had just directed the likewise unreleased *Rock And Roll Circus* for the Rolling Stones. No, that doesn't count. Lindsay-Hogg had previously directed promo films for the Beatles with "Paperback Writer" in 1966 and "Hey Jude" in August 1968.

The comparisons run deep, and while these form similarities between the artists, they do not imply that one group was simply copying the other. For example, Paul reported that in 1963 he woke up from a dream with the melody for "Yesterday." At first thinking it was a song that someone else must have released, he played the tune for others. Once he realized that it was his, he finished the lyric, and the Beatles recorded it. In May 1965, Keith Richards had a similar experience. The driving riff to "Satisfaction" came to him in a dream. He recorded it, mumbled the title and went back to sleep. Once he was sure he hadn't ripped it off, the Rolling Stones turned it into a worldwide hit. The parallels with McCartney are there, but this is a clear case of musical genius following similar paths of inspiration.

George Harrison had introduced the sitar to the consumers of pop/rock music with "Norwegian Wood," but his use of the instrument on that song was somewhat rudimentary. "Love You To," recorded in April 1966, featured an amazing interplay between the sitar and the tabla. The song might have been the first "pop" song with the label "raga rock," but the Folkswingers invented the term – having used it on their June 1966 album of that name. Meanwhile, the Rolling Stones recorded "Paint it Black" in March. It features a prominent sitar part from Brian Jones, but these two songs could hardly be more different from one another in form, in theme and poetically. Reportedly, Jones consulted Harrison about the sitar part, but he was studying independently of the Beatle under Harihar Rao.

As a whole, the Beatles and the Rolling Stones played counterpoint to one another quite frequently, and until 1969, their rivalry was quite the friendly one. John and Paul were each photographed holding a copy of the Rolling Stones' *Aftermath* LP at the April 14, 1966 "Paperback Writer" session. Seven weeks later, Brian Jones attended the June 1 session for "Yellow Submarine," adding crowd noises and singing on the chorus. Jones also contributed the clinking glasses sound effects and played an ocarina (a vessel flute wind instrument).

By 1967, the Beatles and Stones were rather chummy. Mick attended the Beatles May 11 session for "Baby You're A Rich Man" at the Stones' stomping grounds, Olympic Sound Studios, and may have sang on the chorus. Four weeks later, on June 8, Brian Jones was back at Abbey Road to play tenor saxophone on "You Know My Name (Look Up The Number)." When the Beatles put the "live" touches on "All You Need Is Love" during the Our World satellite broadcast on June 25, Mick and Keith were sitting on the studio's floor, singing along on the chorus. The next month, John and Paul joined the Rolling Stones at Olympic to add their high harmony backing vocals to the group's next single, "We Love You." Lennon and McCartney are believed to have added their backing vocals to the single's flip side, "Dandelion." It was rumored that they accepted the Stones' invitation of "Why don't we sing this song all together" by singing on "Sing This All Together," but this was never confirmed. Both sides of the Stones' single feature Brian Jones on Mellotron, the instrument that opened the previously-issued "Strawberry Fields Forever." It was through the Stones that the Beatles were introduced to Glyn Johns, who would serve as engineer and sometimes de facto producer for the Beatles January 1969 *Get Back/Let It Be* sessions. And, of course, John sang "Yer Blues" at the Rolling Stones Rock and Roll Circus in a band dubbed "The Dirty Mac," which included Keith Richards on bass.

John Lennon would later claim that he thought that "We Love You" was ripped off directly from "All You Need is Love." By that time, he had begun claiming that the Stones always copied his band. Paul McCartney more recently heaped more coal on that fire by saying, "That is the truth. Look at the history: The Beatles go to America; a year later they come too. We wrote their...single, 'I Wanna Be Your Man.' We go psychedelic; they go psychedelic. We dress as wizards; they dress as wizards...." However, these accusations prove to be largely untrue under scrutiny.

Backing up to February 1967, on a tip from the tabloid, News of the World, police raided Keith Richards' house in Sussex. Later, they arrested both Keith and Mick on drug possession charges; they pleaded Not Guilty. On June 29, the court sentenced Jagger for the possession of four amphetamine pills (which may have belonged to Marianne Faithfull). He was ordered to pay a £200 fine and serve three months in prison. The same court sentenced Keith Richards for the crime of allowing people to smoke marijuana on his property. He was ordered to pay a £500 fine and was sentenced to one year in prison. While they were appealing their prison sentences, they recorded and released "We Love You." The song thanks their fans for supporting them, features the sound of prison doors, and has a subversive anti-establishment undertone throughout. An honest assessment reveals that the song was vastly different in tone and musical style from "All You Need Is Love." In the United States, it was the other side of the single, "Dandelion," that gathered more attention.

Lennon seemed to object to the title of the Rolling Stones' *Let It Bleed* album being taken (or so he thought) from *Let It Be*, but Ringo had suggested that they title their 1966 album *After Geography* as a pun on the Stones' *Aftermath* album. It was all in good fun. Did the Rolling Stones really copy the Beatles by dressing as wizards? The Beatles started shooting the *Magical Mystery Tour* film on September 11, 1967. During some of the shots in the film, which was not broadcast on British television until December 26, 1967, the Beatles and Mal Evans are dressed in wizard costumes. The wizard sequences seem to have been among the last to be shot, and photos from September 24 depict them dressed as "four or five magicians." As if inspired by an entirely different Merlin (or in today's world, Harry Potter), the Rolling Stones shot the cover for *Their Satanic Majesties Request* on September 14, entirely unaware that the Beatles were in the process of dressing similarly.

For that album cover, the Stones worked with Michael Cooper, fresh from his duties with *Sgt. Pepper*. Michael's son, Adam Cooper, who appears in some of the staging photographs for *Sgt. Pepper*, recalled the Stones' photo session beginning with the *Sgt. Pepper* concept. "So they went to Michael as a friend and said, 'Look, you've done *Sgt. Pepper*. We want to do a similar type of thing with *Satanic Majesties*.' Typical of Michael, he wanted to take it one step further, so he said, 'Okay, let's do a 3-D cover.' One of the only 3-D cameras that existed in the world in those days was in New York, so they went off to Mount Vernon Studios." Adam remembered that the Rolling Stones had to pay for and construct the set. (The cover reportedly cost $25,000.) According to Adam, the Stones didn't want to make something that resembled *Sgt. Pepper*. They wanted to make a fun and colorful album cover, because the Beatles had shown pop musicians what sort of creative things were artistically possible. They copied the Beatles idea of a colorful custom inner sleeve for the record with both sleeves being red and white, but while the *Sgt. Pepper* sleeve is psychedelic, dripping with pink and red colors, the Stones' sleeve is based on their LP cover's cloud patterns. The Stones also returned the favor of the Beatles paying tribute to them. The *Sgt. Pepper* cover has a cloth doll of Shirley Temple wearing a shirt (owned by Adam Cooper) proclaiming "Welcome The Rolling Stones Good Guys." The Stones hid tiny Beatles heads in the flowers on the cover to *Their Satanic Majesties Request*.

What about the music on the albums? The Stones' songs certainly have psychedelic elements. George's "Within You Without You" is followed by laughter, while Bill Wyman's "In Another Land" is followed by snoring. "She's A Rainbow" is somewhat Beatlesque, but songs like "The Lantern" and "2000 Light Years From Home" have no counterpart in the Beatles catalog. The Beatles continued on their psychedelic journey with *Magical Mystery Tour*, which was released within days of *Their Satanic Majesties Request*. The January 1, 1968 Newsweek reviewed both albums, which held down the top two spots (the Beatles at #1) in the Billboard Top LP's chart for the six first weeks of 1968. The Beatles returned to their rock 'n' roll roots with the "Lady Madonna" single in March 1968. Two months later the Stones were rocking again with the bluesy-sounding "Jumping Jack Flash." The Beatles and the Stones inspired one another, goaded one another and occasionally gave ideas to one another. Rarely, though, did they do anything remotely like "copying" one another. They were friends, at least until the Beatles joined up with Allen Klein. That put the Beatles "In Another Land" and was more a case of "Sing This All Together (See What Happens)."

The Saturday Morning Beatles Cartoons

In the sixties in America, Saturday mornings meant one thing for kids: Cartoons! There were animated shows all morning long on TV. For 1964, top attractions included Tennessee Tuxedo, Quick Draw McGraw, Underdog, Mighty Mouse, Casper The Friendly Ghost, Porky Pig, Bugs Bunny and The Jetsons. Fall 1965 brought a handful of new shows: a tiny super hero named Atom Ant; the super spy Secret Squirrel; and the good-natured Milton The Monster. But the new cartoon that had youngsters glued to the TV on Saturday mornings was The Beatles. The show debuted on the ABC television network on September 25, 1965, at 10:30 A.M. The competition for Season One was Linus The Lionhearted on CBS and Underdog on NBC. The Beatles cartoon show was the first animated TV series based on real, living people. And without the "Beatletoons," there would have been no *Yellow Submarine* feature-length cartoon.

The September 25 TV Guide listing for The Beatles cartoon show told fans of what was to come: "This series presents the cartoon adventures of Liverpool's favorite sons in two episodes each week. Today's episodes: 1. 'I Want to Hold Your Hand.' The Beatles, exploring the ocean floor in a diving bell, encounter a lovesick octopus. 2. 'A Hard Day's Night.' John, Paul, Ringo and George rehearse in a haunted house." The five and a half minute episodes, titled after a featured song, opened and closed the show. In between were two sing-alongs, complete with superimposed lyrics (but no bouncing ball). Unlike the episodes, these segments had minimal animation and relied heavily on stills. They were introduced by John, Paul or George, with Ringo butting in to "set the proper mood" with a series of misguided props. In both the episodes and the sing-alongs, the songs were often edited to save time.

TV Guide later ran a two-page spread in its July 30, 1966 issue on how the Beatles were portrayed in their cartoon show. The masterminds behind the program studied the physical characteristics and mannerisms of the Beatles by watching the group's movies. They then provided guidelines for the animators. The TV Guide article features a color drawing of each Beatle, along with extracts on their personalities, appearances, expressions and movements. John "really looks like the leader." Paul is "the most poised and stylish Beatle." Ringo is the "nice, gentle Beatle."

6 COLOR BUGS BUNNY—Cartoon

10:00 3 8 COLOR UNDERDOG
Last show in this time spot. Next week, "Secret Squirrel" will be seen at 10 A.M. and "Underdog" at 10:30 A.M.

6 COLOR BULLWINKLE

10 15 21 43 MIGHTY MOUSE

48 ROLLER DERBY—San Francisco
The New York Chiefs meet the San Francisco Bombers.

10:30 3 8 FIREBALL XL-5—Children
Commander Zero's son accidentally turns on the controls of a Fireball—and the spaceship takes off.

6 27 BEATLES—Cartoon
DEBUT COLOR This series presents the cartoon adventures of Liverpool's favorite sons in two stories each week. Today's episodes: 1. "I Want to Hold Your Hand." The Beatles, exploring the ocean floor in a diving bell, encounter a lovesick octopus. 2. "A Hard Day's Night." John, Paul, Ringo and George rehearse in a haunted house.

10 15 21 43 LINUS—Cartoons

11:00 3 8 DENNIS THE MENACE
Mr. Wilson's brother John, a magazine writer, comes to visit. Dennis: Jay North. John: Gale Gordon.
Last show of the series. Next week, "Top Cat" moves into this time spot.
CASPER

Afternoon

12:00 3 MONTAGE—Documentary
6 NEWS—George Redpath
8 SUPERCAR—Children
When Mike and Dr. Beeker answer an SOS they find themselves menaced by a mad scientist.
10 15 21 SKY KING—Adventure
Sky and Penny go on location with a motion picture company. Sky: Kirby Grant. Penny: Gloria Winters.
48 COLOR AFL HIGHLIGHTS

12:15 6 CARTOONS—Children
12:30 6 FARM AND GARDEN
6 27 COLOR HOPPITY HOOPER
6 27 WELLS FARGO—Western
Outlaw Bob Dawson is paroled for doing a favor for Wells Fargo. Hardie: Dale Robertson. Dawson: Edgar Buchanan.
10 15 21 43 LASSIE—Drama
This long-time network show begins a series of reruns in this time spot. Today: Lassie is accidentally locked inside a moving van. Timmy: Jon Provost. Ruth: June Lockhart. Paul: Hugh Reilly.
29 COMMANDO CODY—Cartoon
48 FOOTBALL HIGHLIGHTS
COLOR The September 18 game between Notre Dame and the University of California played at Memorial Stadium is seen.

1:00 3 CHEYENNE—Western
CLAY DALRYMPLE—Sports
IN MUSIC

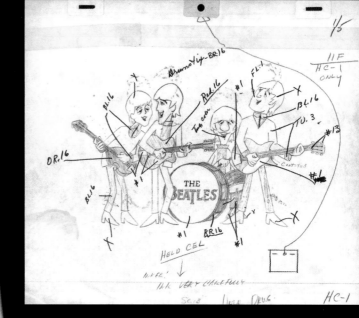

DRAWING A BEAD ON THE BEATLES

The quest for authenticity has driven the masterminds of The Beatles, an ABC Saturday morning cartoon series, to sit gamely through repeated showings of movies starring the real Beatles, to study the physical characteristics and mannerisms of the foursome. The findings of these amateur anthropologists are set forth, in detail, in guide lines for the show's animators. Here are some excerpts.

John, especially when delivering important lines, really looks the leader. . . . He moves with fast, jerky, almost aggressive movements. . . . When facing front, he uses a sly, sideways look to talk to somebody. . . . Gestures: Pulls funny faces, especially after giving orders, which he immediately wipes off. . . . John never sits—he slouches.

George is very loose-limbed and angular. . . . He never stands. He is always leaning against something. . . . Head always tilted forward. . . . Mouth always lopsided. . . . George always gives the impression of frowning. This is because his eyebrows thicken as they reach his nose. . . . He never looks at whom he is talking to.

Paul is the most poised and stylish Beatle. . . . When he is in the background, he stands with his feet together and arms folded. . . . When he talks, he uses his hands, with fingers spread, to express what he's saying. . . . He tends to put his hand to his mouth when he is excited. . . . He doesn't really walk —he skips.

Ringo is the nice, gentle Beatle. He always looks rather sad. . . . When he stands, he always droops forward. His clothes tend to look as though they are a bit too big. . . . Ringo always looks a bit disjointed whether walking or standing. . . . Keep hair at back long and shaggy. Keep Ringo's neck thin to help the disjointed look.

In addition to being gentle, Ringo was often portrayed as a buffoon, particularly when setting the mood for the sing-alongs. For the first two seasons, a dozen mood-setters were in rotation. When John says the next number has a "lot of punch," Ringo produces a kangaroo fitted with boxing gloves. For a "real jump tune," Ringo is outfitted as a paratrooper. A "romantic ballad" has the drummer in a voting booth (for a ballot). When John says the song will "make the folks at home want to join in," Ringo shows up as an Army recruiter to get the folks to "join up." When George introduces a song that "comes on like gangbusters," Ringo turns into a gangster. For a "real swinging, ringer dinger," Ringo produces the liberty bell. For Paul's "romantic love song," Ringo dresses as Cupid and for a "real torch song," he dresses as the Statue of Liberty, complete with torch. Things got even more elaborate for the third season with six new bits. For a "really swinging number," Ringo sets up a trapeze act. For a song that "starts off with a bang," Ringo sets off a cannon. For a song with a really wild rhythm, he decorates the room as a jungle set. For a song that "really takes off," Ringo builds an airplane and flies it around the room. The other Beatles would often look at the audience and encourage the viewers to sing loudly, sometimes calling them out by name.

Although the series ran on ABC for four years, there were only three seasons of new programs. The first season opening sequence featured the Beatles trying to escape from screaming female fans. It opens with the instrumental section of "A Hard Day's Night." After being discovered by the girls, the group jumps out a window and runs down a fire escape to "Can't Buy Me Love" (mimicking a similar scene in the group's first movie). After a few more encounters with crazed fans and close escapes, the group arrives on the stage for their concert. (According to show producer Al Brodax, the screams heard in the sequence are from the Beatles historic 1965 Shea Stadium concert.) The second season opening has the Beatles in disguise trying to hide from their fans. Once discovered, they head to a construction site, but their persistent fans catch up with them. The song "Help!" plays in the background. The third season opening is the most interesting and elaborate. It features the hip-sounding album track "And Your Bird Can Sing" and mixes photos of the Beatles with animated scenes and images of the group. Some of the photos morph into animated versions of the Beatles. The photos include the Beatles in disguise (fake beards and mustaches) from *Help!* and 1967 photos of the Beatles sporting real beards and mustaches. It ends with the group flying away in a hot air balloon. At least for the opening, the Beatles cartoons were maturing along with group and their music.

The same closing sequence was used throughout the series. It opens with "A Hard Day's Night" and shows Paul, John and George unplugging their guitars. When Ringo "unplugs" his drums, they deflate. The boys are then chased by screaming fans until they reach a pier and jump into the water. But even that fails to provide sanctuary as a group of mermaids chase after them.

King Features Syndicate got the rights to produce the cartoons by taking advantage of an unlikely opportunity. In late 1963, the company's editor of cartoons, Sylban Byck, was approached by a man hawking crude caricatures of the Beatles. Sylban, who was not familiar with the Beatles, told the man he was not interested. As fate would have it, Al Brodax, who was head of the company's motion picture television department, saw the disappointed man heading down the hall to the men's room. Brodax followed the man and asked him why he was upset. He learned that the man had obtained the rights to use the Beatles in cartoon form. When Brodax asked him if the rights were limited to print use, the man was not sure. Brodax got the name of the man's attorney, a Mr. Hofer. This was most likely New York entertainment attorney Walter Hofer, who represented Brian Epstein and had lined up the American publishing for the songs written by Lennon and McCartney. Brodax met with Hofer, who helped him secure the rights to do an animated television show based on the Beatles.

The November 11, 1964 issue of Variety, a weekly entertainment magazine first published in 1905, announced that the Beatles were "out to conquer another world—that of cartoons." The article stated that King Features Syndicate had secured the TV animation rights to the group and was preparing a half-hour series for nighttime network broadcast. The cartoon would follow the premise of the group's smash hit movie, *A Hard Day's Night*. Each episode would feature a minimum of two songs, "some of them new, some Beatles classics."

Brodax lined up a toy company sponsor, the A.C. Gilbert Company, whose president, Anson Isaacson, made a deal with ABC to broadcast the show on Saturday mornings during the 1965-1966 television season. The company planned to use the Beatles cartoon show to promote its new line of toys. The other sponsors for the first season were Quaker Oats and the Mars Candy Company.

Now that Brodax had a main sponsor and network for the show, the real work began. He needed to find animation studios to produce the shows, writers to write the scripts, actors to voice the boys and someone to develop the caricatures of the Beatles. The latter task fell to Peter Sanders, a 21-year-old living in Bromley, a town in Greater London in the county of Kent. He designed the basic appearance, gestures and tendencies of each of the Beatles in a simple style (see page 115) to facilitate the work of the animators and bring some semblance of consistency to how the Fab Four looked and acted throughout the series. Brodax hired Dennis Marks, Jack Mendelsohn, Heywood "Woddy" Kling and Bruce Howard as his team of writers. He developed the format for the show and provided the writers with basic story lines and lists of locales and available songs. Everything was done with future syndication of the cartoon show in mind. Brodax recalled: "We did a lot of theme things about subjects such as ghosts, cowboys, ships at sea, Transylvania and things of that nature." ABC had final approval of the scripts and storyboards. Sometimes its Department of Broadcast Standards and Practices would intervene, "suggesting" that a female character not be "too sexy" or rejecting something outright such as an electric chair ("not acceptable for our young audiences").

Brodax hired Paul Frees and Lance Percival to handle most of the voices. Frees, known as "The Man of a Thousand Voices," was an American actor already heard on Saturday mornings as Boris Badenov on Rocky and Bullwinkle and Inspector Fenwick on Dudley Do-Right. He provided the voices of John and George, as well as the incidental male characters in the shows. The female voices were handled by a British woman, Jackie Newman. Brodax brought in British actor, singer and comedian Lance Percival, who recorded a few comedy songs produced by George Martin, to voice Paul and Ringo. (He would later voice Old Fred in the *Yellow Submarine* cartoon.) To ensure that kids could understand what was being said, the decision was made for the actors not to speak with authentic Liverpool accents, but rather provide "Americanized" British accents. While this may have facilitated the enjoyment of the show in America, it contributed to Brian Epstein forbidding the Beatles cartoons from being shown in England.

Brodax selected London's TV Cartoons (TVC) as his production studio. He served as Executive Producer, assisted by Associate Producer Mary Ellen Steward and Production Manager Abe Goodman. The episodes made at TVC were produced by George Dunning with head of production, John Coates. These episodes were directed by Jack Stokes.

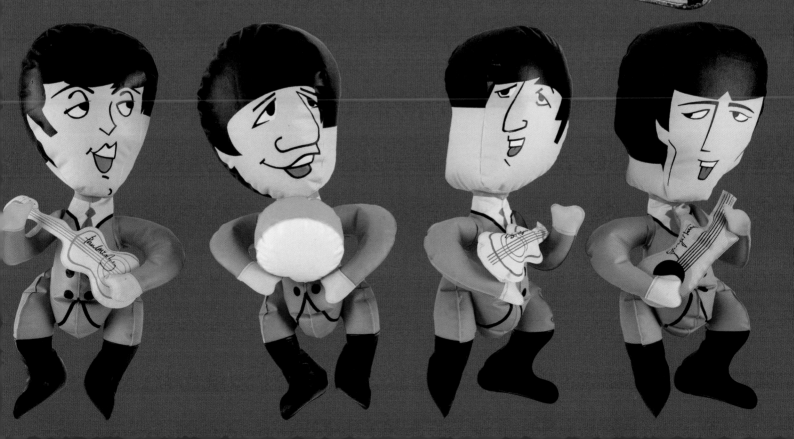

In addition to in-house produced episodes, TVC subcontracted with Group Two Animation in Richmond (in Greater London), Artransa Park TV Studios in Australia, Canawest Studios in Canada and Cine Centrum in Holland.

ABC ordered 17 shows (each with two episodes) for the first season. The debut program attracted an impressive 52 share of the viewing audience in its time slot. The series continued to have excellent ratings through the original shows, but faltered when it went into reruns. The second season consisted of 13 new shows, with reruns mixing episodes from both seasons. The show performed well, but lost its time slot to Space Ghost. This spooked ABC into ordering only nine new programs for the third season, which was moved from 10:30 to noon. The lack of new episodes caused the ratings to crater. ABC moved the series to Sunday mornings for the fourth and final all-rerun season. The TV Guide listing for Sunday, April 20, 1969, told the tale: "BEATLES-Children. Last show of the series."

Although the Beatles cartoon series was gone from network television, it led the way for more music cartoon shows of real groups (The Jackson Five and The Osmonds) and fictitious bands (The Archies and Josie And The Pussycats). The Beatles cartoons went into syndication in 1969, gaining new audiences throughout the years. In 1986 and 1987, MTV (Music Television) aired the cartoons on Saturday and Sunday mornings at 10:00 AM. The Disney Channel began running the shows on Friday at 5:00 PM in 1989. A few years later, the rights to the series were purchased by Apple Corps. Ltd., who has yet to do anything with the shows other than licensing the cartoon images.

Merchandising of the cartoon images in the sixties was fairly limited. One of the more interesting items was a set of 15" inflatable dolls of each of the Beatles (shown on the previous page). The autographed dolls were available as a premium purchase item for those buying certain products. The two deals were: two wrappers of Lux, Dove or Lifebuoy soap plus $2.00; or the code number from a box of Nestle's Quik plus $1.50. The dolls were also available as a coupon redemption item at carnivals and fairs. Colorforms marketed The Beatles Cartoon Kit, which contained plastic pieces of the Beatles, their instruments, fans and music notes to stick onto a background board depicting a stage. World Candies sold sticks of sugar candy in boxes depicting the Beatles. The large box that held 25 small boxes came with a Ringo hand puppet. King Features mailed a generic postcard to those who wrote in to the show.

THE BEATLES, a musical-adventure cartoon program
produced by King Features
and telecast Saturday mornings on ABC-TV

© West. Wld. Mgt. & King Features Syndicate, 1965

Many thanks for your note. We're delighted
that so many viewers of all ages are enjoying
the show. The Beatles themselves are happy
about it too and have approved every aspect of
it. The speaking voices of the cartoons of
course had to be different from the Beatles'
real voices, and they had to be understood
easily by every viewer. The Beatles okay
their cartoon voices in every country and in
every language in which the show plays.

We hope you'll keep watching and singing
along.

Sincerely,

The Producers

Yellow Submarine Merchandise from the Sixties

Unlike the Beatles cartoon show, the *Yellow Submarine* feature film generated a diverse assortment of colorful merchandising items in America, the United Kingdom and other countries, including notebooks, binders, bookmarks, bulletin boards, lunch boxes, buttons, calendars, candles, art work cels, coasters, switch plate covers, water color sets, coloring books, stickers, rub-ons, postcards, plastic models, die-cast metal submarines, hand puppets, Halloween costumes, candy cigarettes, trading cards, greeting cards, coin banks, pen and pencil holders, pennants, photo albums, scrapbooks, planters, posters, puzzles, wall plaques, stationary, snow domes, wrist watches and alarm clocks.

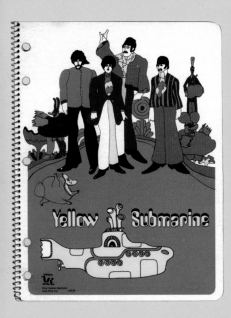

The Beatles

5810

125

The BEATLES
All You Need Is Love
Baby, You're a Rich Man

Capitol
RECORDS
5964

PRINTED IN U.S.A.

126

THE **BEATLES**

Lady Madonna
The Inner Light

2138

The Official Beatles FAN CLUB

FABULOUS POSTER OFFER!

U.S. Branch Director: FRAN FIORINO, BEATLES (U.S.A.) LTD.,
P.O. Box 505, Radio City Station, New York, N.Y. 10019.

HERE'S HOW YOU CAN GET A

NEW GIANT-SIZED FULL-COLOUR BEATLES PHOTO POSTER

THE OFFICIAL BEATLES FAN CLUB is offering to new members AN EXCLUSIVE FULL-COLOUR PHOTO BONUS—FREE OF CHARGE!!! This is an entirely NEW colour picture of THE BEATLES enlarged to G-I-A-N-T POSTER SIZE, the ideal bedroom-wall souvenir for every Beatle Person! THE PHOTOGRAPH WAS TAKEN JUST A FEW WEEKS AGO, THE VERY LATEST THERE IS, AND IT WAS TAKEN EXCLUSIVELY FOR THE FAN CLUB, SO YOU WON'T SEE IT ANYWHERE ELSE!

HERE'S HOW YOU CAN GET YOUR OWN PERSONAL COPY OF THIS MARVELLOUS FAN CLUB SOUVENIR COMPLETELY FREE. JUST COMPLETE AND RETURN THE FAN CLUB MEMBERSHIP APPLICATION FORM PRINTED BELOW. BE SURE TO FOLLOW THE INSTRUCTIONS (SEE OVERLEAF) VERY CAREFULLY.

As soon as you mail off the completed form, together with first year's subscripton fee of TWO DOLLARS, you will become a fully-enrolled Fan Club Beatle Person and your poster will come through the letter-box along with your new membership card and other club material. And there are no hidden extras, nothing more to pay. Your single payment of just TWO DOLLARS will run all the way through until the beginning of May 1969 when there'll be another exclusive free bonus for you before you are asked to pay up your next annual subscription fee. Don't forget that the advantages of club membership include a free gift every Christmas—and for the last few years this has been the Beatles' fan club Christmas record, a specially produced LP-Speed record available only to Members. That record alone is worth your year's subscription!

DON'T DELAY—ACT TODAY. SURPRISE YOUR FRIENDS AND SEND AWAY! ALL YOU HAVE TO DO IS FILL UP THE FORM AND FOLLOW THE INSTRUCTIONS. IT COULDN'T BE EASIER—AND IT COULDN'T BE MORE WORTHWHILE!

- -

APPLICATION FOR MEMBERSHIP OF THE OFFICIAL BEATLES FAN CLUB

FAN CLUB MEMBERSHIP AND SPECIAL POSTER OFFER VALID FOR RESIDENTS OF THE UNITED STATES OF AMERICA ONLY. POSTER OFFER CLOSES ON JULY 31 1968

I WANT TO BECOME AN OFFICIAL BEATLE PERSON AND I WANT MY FREE COPY OF THE SPECIAL 1968 COLOUR PHOTO POSTER!

MY NAME IS...

MY FULL POSTAL ADDRESS IS...

IMPORTANT!: READ INSTRUCTIONS OVERLEAF BEFORE COMPLETING!

FAN RECOLLECTIONS

GARRY

So *Sgt. Pepper* took us by surprise! Fantastic! The Summer of Love was upon us with some incredible music coming out all around us. We wore our Hippy bells to school. So just how could it get any better?

Well, then, the Our World program was broadcast on BBC 1 at 7:55-10:00 P.M., Sunday, 25th June 1967. As a 13-year-old I thought the whole thing incredible, very futuristic, and just as I was getting into reading Science-Fiction too, but even better—it had the Beatles. I watched the whole program with my Dad, then 37, and my Grandmother, aged 71. As far as I recall we all loved

the special feeling that the whole world was watching with us. I really couldn't believe it: The Beatles live in front of us in our sitting room. Wow! The song was fabulous. It was so easy to sing along that we all joined in on the chorus. My Gran was very "with it" because the three of us listened to lots of music together. I was astonished by all the other stars singing along with the Beatles.

Back in school the next day we were all singing "All You Need Is Love" despite us not knowing the words, just the chorus. I had to wait almost two weeks before I could buy the single on Saturday, 7th July. I had clipped out the lyrics from a newspaper, so when I played it at home I could sing along. I was just blown away by the song, and most of my friends loved it too. I thought the B-side was brilliant. It had great weird sounds in there.

The following Thursday I got to see the Our World performance of "All You Need Is Love" again on Top Of The Pops. It really was the Summer of Love and the Beatles sang the best song ever. Although at school we all wore uniforms, hair was beginning to get longer, Granny glasses came in, and out of school our clothes became much more colourful than school grey.

As Christmas approached, the Beatles new single, "Hello, Goodbye," was played on Top Of The Pops on Thursday, 23rd November, the day before it was released. The clip was a bit strange, showing bits and pieces from *A Hard Day's Night*, but I liked what I heard, especially the last bit, the refrain, which seemed to be a whole other song. All my mates at school loved it too; we all thought it very Mod. I bought the single the following Saturday. When I played "I Am The Walrus" for my Dad, he thought it was "a bit weird," but he said he liked it too.

Two weeks later the *Magical Mystery Tour* double EP was out. I had read about it so much; it was great to finally hear it when Radio 1 played some tracks. "I Am The Walrus" caused a bit of a stir over John singing "Boy, you've been a naughty girl, you let your knickers down."

I didn't buy my first copy of the *MMT* EP. It was too expensive, almost a pound. Instead, I borrowed it from my cousin Paul in early January 1968 and still have that mono copy to this day! The package was brilliant: the songs, the cartoon booklet, the words to the songs, but just out of my financial league. Thank you Paul Lowe.

I didn't get to hear the songs in stereo until years later when I bought my first stereo system and purchased a Canadian copy of the *Magical Mystery Tour* album. The stereo sound was mind blowing!

The *Magical Mystery Tour* film aired on BBC 1 in black and white on Boxing Day (very important to us British!), 26 December 1967. I watched it with my Dad and Grandmother. We enjoyed the antics, which were like the Goons, the silly voices and dialogue and, of course, the music. It was, in our case, great family viewing. It was still the Beatles like in their two previous films, but it was different. Despite what the papers said at the time, I didn't know anyone who didn't like it.

The film was shown in color on BBC 2 on 5 January 1968, but for me it was still in black and white. I didn't know anyone who had a color TV set. They were still an unaffordable luxury back then. (It seems to me that the BBC gets a lot of unfair blame for showing *Magical Mystery Tour* in black and white when only people such as the Beatles would have actually had color TV sets.)

In March 1968 I bought the "Lady Madonna" single on the Saturday after seeing the Beatles clip of the song on Top Of The Pops. Rock 'n' Roll was back! It reminded me of Little Richard and Bill Haley. The film on TOTP showed the Beatles enjoying themselves in the studio.

In July 1968 *Yellow Submarine* was in the cinemas. I saw it on a double bill with *Help!* I loved the cartoon film and all the music, especially the new songs. It was an incredible psychedelic experience.

I had to wait until January 1969 to get the *Yellow Submarine* soundtrack LP. (That's me in the mod yellow vest proudly holding my copy!) I loved the four new songs and the George Martin score.

I had to wait even longer to hear "Across The Universe," a song I had read about in February 1968. It was finally issued in December 1969 as the lead track on the *No One's Gonna Change Our World* charity LP. The version of the song on that album is my favorite, perhaps because I heard it there first.

Garry Marsh

I grew up in Kensington, Maryland. The Our World broadcast was hyped in the D.C. area in June 1967 because it was both a technological and music event. At the beginning of the broadcast they showed short bits from around the world of things we would see later in the program, including a short clip of the Beatles singing to a backing track. After an interminable amount of time looking at shrimp farms and the like, the Beatles came on. I was impressed and thought I was watching a real build-up of tracks, but later learned much was pre-taped. I watched on a color television set and was disappointed that the program was in black and white. The only person I recognized in the crowd was Mick Jagger. When the show was broadcast again a couple of days later in the evening, I taped the performance on a reel-to-reel tape recorder, thus becoming the first kid in my neighborhood to have the next Beatles single!

George C. Heon

Our World and the Beatles appearance on the show holds a fond and notable place in my memory. I had just completed the 4th Grade. It was the first Sunday of summer vacation, as well as being just days before my 10th birthday! Adding to the excitement was the Our World special broadcast on New York's WNET. As I watched the show with my parents, we all marveled at how technology allowed us to explore so much of our world. All was of great interest; however, the highlight for me was seeing the Beatles on TV again. Not since their initial appearances on The Ed Sullivan Show (when I was six) had I been so excited! Although in black and white, it was like being there with them (and, in the control room, of which we got a glimpse). "All You Need Is Love" was an instant classic for me! And they looked so cool! 'Twas magical, indeed!

Bob Briar

I was 12 years old on June 25, 1967, and attending the obligatory end of the school year (Grade 7 for me) barbecue. For whatever reason, I got bored and walked home that afternoon. By pure luck, I turned on the TV just in time to catch the Our World broadcast of "All You Need Is Love." I hadn't heard about it in advance. The *Sgt. Pepper* album had been released only a month before, but was already blowing minds and changing everything. Later that summer I fell under the spell of "Baby You're a Rich Man" (alongside "A Whiter Shade of Pale" and "Light My Fire"). Christmas '67 brought *Magical Mystery Tour* and the Stones' *Their Satanic Majesties Request*. God knows how many hours I spent poring over the images on the garish covers of these two albums and listening to every note in the grooves. 1967 was the year that my ears and my mind made the big leap from the 7" single to the 12" LP, and *Magical Mystery Tour* was a big part of that. A lot of sounds have taken up residence in my music collection in the decades since, but it is still a fun record that can still take me back in time to decidedly more innocent days.

Robert Woods (Toronto)

I watched the Beatles sing "All You Need Is Love" on the Our World TV special in June of 1967, the summer before I started high school. It was on Channel 11, WENH, out of Durham, New Hampshire. I may have heard about the broadcast on one of the nearby Boston radio stations or maybe through my listening to the BBC World Service on my shortwave radio. (Yes, I was that big of a Beatles fan!) "All You Need Is Love" was perfect for the special, and what a thrill it was to actually see The Beatles making a record. I was already enthralled by *Sgt. Pepper*, and then, a few weeks after Our World, the song I heard recorded live came out as a single. What a summer!!!

Susan Gagne

"ALL YOU NEED IS LOVE"
(3:57) THE BEATLES

"ALL YOU NEED IS LOVE"- The genius of the Beatles is obviously going to be a never ending source of amazement to the world. This selection and the flip side, "Baby, You're a Rich Man," embody all the best of everything in the recording industry today. Their individual and collective creativity is dominant in every phase of their records -- melody, lyrics, arrangements, production, etc. etc. No more need be said here -- they've said it all over the record.

RECORD NO. 5964   RELEASE NO. 1109
FORMAT: POP, R&B, GOOD MUSIC, C&W   RELEASE DATE: 7/24/67
PREVIOUS RELEASES: #5810, 5715, 5651

I was living in Palo Alto, California, 35 miles south of San Francisco's Summer of Love, but alas I was 12 years old and too young to join in the fun. I kept an eager and envious ear on the scene to the North through our local AM radio stations KYA and KFRC, which that summer played top forty plus album cuts from the Jefferson Airplane, *Sgt. Pepper* and long versions of songs like "Light My Fire."

The Our World live telecast featuring the Beatles was pretty well promoted in the local papers and on San Francisco's NET station, so I made sure to tune in since, like everyone else my age, I was a stone-cold Beatles freak. Obviously I loved the Beatles segment and thought it looked like a great party. The one thing that still sticks in my mind is when John and Paul broke into "She loves you, yeah, yeah, yeah" at the end. It immediately took me back to those glorious first few months in 1964, and those few seconds kind of gave me shivers!

John Place

"I started to call you last night," Dana Greeson informed me at the local A & W drive in. "You did??" My heart skipped a beat. I had a mad crush on the electric organ/rhythm guitar player for our town's resident band, The Square Circle, since the day I'd seen him singing in a navy blue Nehru jacket on the East Natchitoches Junior High School's gymnasium stage. I wondered if it was about him. But then Dana said, "The Beatles were on TV. I started to call and let you know. But I was pretty sure you already knew all about it." "What?!" I had no idea. Everyone always assumed I knew telepathically when the Beatles were on television or radio or anything...and everyone was always wrong. "Yeah, they did this big satellite transmission...One World or Our World or something like that—I can't remember—and it was seen all over the globe, I heard. Like the first time ever.

And John had written this new song for it called 'All You Need Is Love.' And man, it was great! One of his best." "You gotta be kidding me! I missed it?" "Well, if you didn't see it," Dana shrugged, "then yeah, I guess you did." "Dadgummit." I hung my head.

Over the next few days, it seemed that literally everyone else on the planet Earth had seen the Beatles broadcast. Everyone was singing, "All you need is love! (Dum-da-da-da-dum!) All you need is love! (Dum-da-da-da-dum!) All you need is love, love! Love is all you need!" And Everyone was talking about John's song and the set and the stars who'd made Our World into "a happening." Everyone was saying they should have called and let me know. And Everyone was sorry that they'd thought about it, but done nothing, in the end.

And so, on 25 June 1967, while lucky Beatles fans in the know were glued to their TVs watching the Beatles record a song, in Natchitoches, Louisiana, "river rat" Judy Southerland had been out on Cane River, enjoying every ski of the day on a silvered crescent lake. I have great memories of that afternoon: laughing with my friend, Joanna Henry, and her future husband, Neal Reeder. I can still smell the musty river and hear the sound of that ragged outboard motor behind the green fishing boat. But those darned lucky kids heard different sounds, saw something incredible and were a witness to history.

However, because I must (as an unspoken obligation attached to my name) "take a sad song and make it better," I will tell you that just a few short days later, I was the first in my class to actually hear "All You Need is Love" on the Lovable Larry Ryan Show, KEEL radio, Shreveport! And when I was the first one singing the lyrics—loud and strong—on Cane River Lake, everyone (including the Dana Greeson) was jealous!

Jude Southerland Kessler
Author of the John Lennon Series

The very first time I saw and heard the *Magical Mystery Tour* album was in December 1967 or January 1968 when I was the ripe old age of 12. I was at a local teen hangout, the Starlight Skate Center, in North Platte, Nebraska. An employee was taking the cellophane off from the LP jacket and showing it to anyone that had an interest – including Beatles-Fanatic, ME! He put the LP on the Skate Center's turntable and played the entire album (both sides) for the skaters and listeners. Of course, I was completely blown away. Within days that album was the newest addition to my Beatles collection. That memory has stuck with me now for 53 years!

Dennis D. Dailey

When the *Magical Mystery Tour* album came out, I was bedazzled by the colorful album graphics that perfectly matched the experimental music contained within. I was frustrated as a U.S. fan that I couldn't see the film, which I finally saw when I was in college. Adding the singles made the U.S. release a strong album indeed. Fast forwarding to 1999, I was on a vacation to Disney World in Orlando with my family. We rounded a corner and came upon a restored *Magical Mystery Tour* bus. I was like a kid in a candy shop. We explored every inch of the outside, but unfortunately we not able to see the interior. We felt, for that moment, we were part of the original tour and a splendid time was guaranteed for all!

Mike Cooper

Growing up in Puerto Rico in the 1960s my parents made sure that my sister and I had records to listen to. When *Magical Mystery Tour* came out, my parents bought it for us. It totally blew me away. My mother was a seamstress. When I saw the photo of the Beatles with the Neru jackets I begged her to make one for me! She finally agreed, so then we had to find the colorful fab-ric and a pattern to cut it. After several trips to San Juan (Puerto Rico's capital and a large town), we finally found the great looking fabric. My mother spread out the cloth, pinned down the pattern on the fabric and began to cut. Unfortunately, she failed to unfold the fabric and cut two left sides! Even though she promised to go to town again to purchase more fabric, she never had the time. Needless to say, my life has never been the same! LOL.

Henry Ordosgoitia (Henry O)

Although many believe that *Magical Mystery Tour* was not shown in the U.S. until the mid-seventies, that is not true. I saw the film on the campus of the University of Illinois in 1969. I later learned that the film was shown on only a few select U.S. campuses in 1968 and 1969 from a fellow who worked for Beatles attorney Nat Weiss. After the bad reception the film had in England, the Beatles were glad to have any distribution at all in America!

Alan Chrisman

I traveled from Los Angeles to London when I was 17 years old towards the end of summer 1967. After checking into my hotel, I immediately set out to find Carneby Street. While walking through Trafalgar Square I looked inside an expensive car and was surprised to see Ringo and George. I followed the car down the streets into Soho, where it stopped in front of the Raymond Revuebar. I went inside the bar to meet the Beatles and ask for their autographs. I then went back to my hotel to get my 8mm movie camera and returned to the bar to film the Beatles. I was then asked if I wanted to be in the movie. I spent six hours with the group during the filming of the strip club scene, where I sat behind John and George watching stripper Jan Carson perform as the Bonzo Dog Doo Dah Band played "Death Cab For Cutie."

Johnny Walker Kisselburgh

I received the *Magical Mystery Tour* double EP from my cousin Heidi as a gift. Contrary to the U.S., EPs were quite common in Europe, but so far I'd never seen a double EP looking like a small book with 24 pages of a story in comics. I listened to the songs immediately and fell especially in love with "I Am The Walrus," although I didn't understand a single word, living in the German speaking part of Switzerland as a ten-year-old boy.

Years later I found out that the American version of *Magical Mystery Tour* was actually a long playing record with all of the songs that were on the British double EP on Side One, while Side Two was filled with singles A and B sides from the same year. What a great LP after all.

Around the same time I saw the TV movie for the first time. It was shred to pieces in Britain and called absolute nonsense, but I didn't think that way at all. Looking back from today's point of view I think the movie is still worth for another viewing, having all four Beatles fooling around and presenting great songs.

Marcel Reichmuth

In the early 1970's I was taking art class in high school. The instructor had a mono copy of *Magical Mystery Tour* with the Capitol rainbow label. I added the LP to my Christmas wish list and got the stereo copy on the Apple label. When I listened to it I noticed differences in the stereo mix, especially in "Blue Jay Way." That's how I learned of the differences between the mono and stereo mixes with the Beatles music. When I began reading books about the Beatles catalog, I learned of the *MMT* EP. Of course I bought that, but it was a stereo copy. After getting married, my wife and I traveled to Cornwall to visit a relative and we visited the site where *Magical Mystery Tour* was filmed! They had a plaque on the hill overseeing the ocean. Awesome memories!

Tom Drill

My mother took me to Wallich's Music City in Hollywood, California to buy my first copy of the *Magical Mystery Tour* album in early December 1967. It was one of the most beautiful sights I have ever seen. There was a rack of monaural copies and a rack of stereo. I bought a stereo copy I could play on my Heathkit record player. I was all set! I had played *Sgt. Pepper* a million times, but *Magical Mystery Tour* was a step up for me. It is still my second favorite Beatle album after *The White Album*. The whole concept of *MMT* was just what I needed in my life. The songs within the album were all perfect to me.

We moved to Northern California in 1968, and in January 1969, I got my chance to see the film at last! A local FM station that I loved screened the film at the old San Jose Civic Auditorium in San Jose, California for just $2.00. I remember it was a small crowd, but a very nice copy of the entire film. "I Am The Walrus" is my favorite Beatle song. I will defend the quality, spirit and execution of the *Magical Mystery Tour* film until the day I die. It is one of the purist and honest of Beatle creations.

Gary Norris

In 1973 I was listening to my new copy of *Magical Mystery Tour*. The album was a Christmas gift, along with a new record player, and I could not wait to play it. I opened the cover to see the fab gatefold and way-cool booklet, and carefully put the disc on the turntable. As the Apple label spun round and round and the trippy "Blue Jay Way" came through the speakers, my mother ordered sternly, "Turn that off. Turn that off, right now!"

I did not get to see the film until another few years, at a midnight Beatles film fest. How could anyone not love the celluloid performance of "I Am the Walrus"? Some folks dismiss *Magical Mystery Tour* for not being a "real" Beatles album, but Capitol got this one right.

David Persails

In 1967 I was living on campus at Adelphi University for my junior year. By then, I was known as the Beatles guy in the dorm. I had the Richard Avedon Beatles posters and many other Beatles images on my dormitory wall and ceiling. Over Thanksgiving break, I bought the new "Hello Goodbye" single, but it was "I Am The Walrus" that got the most spins. After learning on the radio that the Beatles new LP, *Magical Mystery Tour*, was coming soon, I began calling the Record World store at Roosevelt Field Shopping Center on Long Island on a daily basis to see if the album had arrived. Since I had a car and was obviously going to the record store as soon it was out, several of my friends asked me to buy copies for them.

By the time the store got the album, I had orders for six mono and four stereo albums. When I arrived at Record World, I was surprised and disappointed to learn that they had only received stereo copies. Mono LPs were still popular and cost a dollar less! What do I do?

I only bought stereo copies for those who wanted stereo because we had been told that you couldn't play stereo records on a mono record player. (We found out much later that this was untrue.) But I had to listen to the new Beatles album, so I immediately purchased a small stereo record player at the mall to enable me to play the record as soon as I got back to the dorm.

We knew there was a film because there was a booklet that came with the album that showed us many photos from it! Although the film was shown at nearby Hofstra University the next year, I could not go. I finally saw *Magical Mystery Tour* for the first time at the first Beatlefest, held September 7-8, 1974 in New York City. Thanks to John's personal support and involvement, Apple sent over a bunch of films, including *Magical Mystery Tour*, for us to show. When we played it on Sunday night at 10:30 PM in the Grand Ballroom at the old Commodore Hotel, the room was totally packed.

Nobody went home early as most in attendance had yet to see the film. It was enthusiastically received. The "I Am The Walrus" sequence was a definite highlight for me.

A Fest attendee later arranged for me to meet with Mal Evans. I met him in New York City and invited him to the 1975 Beatlefest. He agreed to come and had a wonderful time. He sat and signed autographs for hours, spoke of his experiences on stage and answered audience questions. On Sunday night, I sat with Mal as we watched *Magical Mystery Tour*, again to a jam packed ballroom. He kept telling me what was going on behind the scenes in real time as the film played on. I only wish I had written them all down after the weekend, but I didn't.

I do remember his story about the filming of "The Fool On The Hill," which very few people knew about in 1975. Paul wanted to shoot this scene in the French Alps and he wanted to go right away! So Mal arranged a camera man to join him and Paul. The problem is when they were leaving the U.K. or arriving in France, neither Paul nor Mal had any money or official identification on them. Apparently details like that never stopped a Beatle! They made it to the mountains and it was very cold outside. They filmed it quite quickly and headed home.

After the convention was over, Mal told me, "Mark, this was the greatest weekend of my life!" This gentle giant of a man was the star of the weekend. Through his Beatles years, he was like wallpaper, always in the background, rarely heard from by the public, but 100% loyal to and protective of the Fab Four.

I spoke to him during Christmas week 1975 and he told me he was very excited about finishing his book on his Beatles days and coming to many future Beatlefests. Sadly, that never happened as he died two weeks later. I will never forget the Magical Mystery Tour he took me and those attending the 1975 Beatlefest on.

Mark Lapidos, Founder of The Fest For Beatles Fans

The crowning achievement of Capitol Records presenting the Beatles music to America might have been turning *Magical Mystery Tour* into a full-length album. Throughout most of the world, it was a deluxe double-EP set. When people discuss which album by the Beatles is the best, they rarely mention *Magical Mystery Tour*. And I would have to agree. However, imagine for a moment that the songs on Side Two had never been released as singles and that you had never heard them before you bought the album. Would you then consider *Magical Mystery Tour* one of their best recording efforts? Possibly!

I don't recall exactly what year it was, but I won two tickets to a screening of the *Magical Mystery Tour* film in Boston long before it was officially shown in the U.S. Fearing that I might not get another chance to see it, I drove 900 miles to Bean Town [Boston]. I was expecting it to be shown in a small theater, but to my surprise the viewing was in a bar with one of those large pull up screens like the ones we used to watch 8mm home movies on. I was probably in my late teens and was enthralled watching it for the first time. Like the movie *Help!*, the story was daft but the song sequences were totally fab.

David R. Rauh

I saw one of the first American screenings of *Magical Mystery Tour* on Thursday, May 16, 1968, in Royce Hall on the UCLA campus. I went with a bunch of my Los Angeles high school buddies. I saved the flier from the movie, which shows that tickets were only $1.50. At 16 years old, I was prepared to have my mind blown. And it was. Like finally having validity in knowing who the Eggman was – amazing!

Stephen M.H. Braitman

Sadly, I was not a first generation fan for the Beatles and not even born when *Magical Mystery Tour* was originally released. However, I remember how exciting it was to see the film for the first time on cable channel USA's Night Flight. I found it amusing how every time it was showed after that (and we watched it many times before finally taping it on one of those VHS tapes), they always stated that it had "never been shown before in America until now!" I loved the film, loved the album, and made sure to buy the version of the album with the booklet as soon as I had the money and opportunity to do so!

Donald Jack

During the time the Beatles were filming *Magical Mystery Tour*, my family was living in the town of West Malling in Kent, England. As children were needed for the film, a casting call took place and my four-year-old sister and I were lucky to be in the chosen group. Being an extra in the film was fun and games for me. At seven years of age, I knew who the Beatles were, but did not understand how big they were.

I recall the scenes we were in because they were redone over and over until they got what they wanted. In the tug-of-war, my sister kept struggling to get up on her feet. The start of the Marathon was re-shot several times because people kept starting off too early. My sister and I were to the right of George. I ended up on the bus with Ringo at the wheel. During some of the shots taken in front of the hanger, I was on John's shoulders. During the filming of "Your Mother Should Know," there was a power cut that caused delays. I remember the nets holding up the balloons, the Beatles coming down the stairs and my clapping and jumping around.

My mother was asked to play the part of Ringo's aunt, but turned the role down because of the way the spaghetti scene was originally going to be filmed. John wanted the spaghetti to be shoved down between my mom's cleavage and then removed with his hands. This idea was dropped when everyone asked turned this down even though they had made a model of woman's breasts for the person to wear.

I now have an extensive *Magical Mystery Tour* collection that includes a rough script for the film and a few crude hand-drawn pie charts, but my prize possession is the bus used in the film. When I purchased this item, I thought I was getting a sister coach, but several experts, including three selected by the British Motor Museum at the Vauxhall Heritage Centre in Luton, Bedfordshire, concluded that mine is the actual bus. Corgi Toys used my bus, which is currently being restored, to design its die-cast metal model of the coach. I plan on writing a book about *Magical Mystery Tour* and my bus.

Simon Mitchell

I became a Beatles fan in 1977. By this time I owned my parents' copies of *Abbey Road* and the "Help!" single, and I had seen *Help!* and *Yellow Submarine* on TV. I wanted to buy another Beatles album, but had no idea which one. The early Beatles albums seemed plain looking, so I opted for *Magical Mystery Tour* as it was very colorful and it had a 24-page booklet. I figured that if the album was terrible, at least I would be getting some nice color photos of the band. I already knew "All You Need Is Love" from *Yellow Submarine*, so I figured at least one tune was good. As it turned out, I loved virtually all of the tunes.

From the booklet, I realized that half of the album was a soundtrack for a Beatles TV special that I learned never aired in the U.S. It made me want to see it even more. Fortunately the local Saratoga Library was having a film night where they were going to play *Magical Mystery Tour* on 16mm film for free. My sister and I were excited, thinking we were going to see another *Help!*-type of movie. We were both in for a shock. While my sister hated the film and found it boring, I was intrigued by it, despite it not making too much sense. It was a very dark print with muddy dialogue, so it was difficult to see and hear the film. As we left the library, I realized that more people sided with her and were disappointed with what they had seen. I, however, wanted to see it again.

About a year later, a local San Francisco TV station, KTSF Channel 26, played a muddy, muffled print of the film. I taped it on my VCR and watched this print for many years until a restored and remastered print was issued in 1993. The difference between the two was like night and day. I suddenly could hear dialogue that was just mumbles before and the film's picture had lush colors and clarity that was dark and washed out in the past. I loved the film even more. Now, I could also see the film's true shortcoming: it really has no ending. Had the Beatles made one more scene at the end with the four of them waking up and saying something like "What a crazy dream" instead of just ending, *Magical Mystery Tour* would have been much more satisfying for all. As it is, it's an excellent document of its time and I agree with what Paul McCartney said on *Anthology*, "Where else can you see The Beatles performing 'I Am The Walrus'?"

Mark Arnold

I was only 15 when the *Magical Mystery Tour* LP was released. Although I owned all the previous U.S. Beatles albums, I delayed buying it for a while. My friends let me hear their copy after school. I later bought the Capitol LP, the British import stereo EP, the German Apple label true stereo version and even the half-speed master LP.

In 1974, when I told my parents I was going to see the *Magical Mystery Tour* film at a local theater, they told me I couldn't go because the film had been "banned." I explained that it wasn't banned, that it just received bad English TV reviews, so American TV didn't pick up the rights, thinking it would not be financially successful. Being 22, I went to see the film with some friends.

Several years later, the film was issued on VHS tape. My video store only had one copy for rent. Since they didn't want anyone failing to return the film for the retail cost of the tape, they required a $100 cash to rent the movie. I paid the deposit and rented the film. When a local TV channel broadcast *Magical Mystery Tour* a few years later in the wee small hours on a weekday, I recorded it on my VCR. It was a poor copy, but it was all I could get. A few years later I bought an import DVD copy (of questionable legal origin) at a local record store, with equally poor picture quality. I was pleased when the official remastered Blu-Ray was released, but thought that the picture quality could have been improved, especially the animated bridge between scenes.

Robert Jakubiec

When I first took the *Magical Mystery Tour* LP out of the shrinkwrap in late 1967 at my home in Kewanee, Illinois, I was immediately impressed with the packaging. There was an album-sleeve-sized booklet with great color photos and the story of the film told in cartoon form. I enjoyed looking through the booklet as I listened to the album the first time. Since then, I've always thought that this album was, in a way, a summation of the Beatles year of 1967. The first side, with songs from the film, was a logical continuation of what was started earlier that year with *Sgt. Pepper's Lonely Hearts Club Band*. And both the A and B sides that year's three outstanding singles filled out the rest of the album. The US Capitol LP holds a special place in the official Beatles catalogue. It's the only Capitol reconfiguration of British Beatles records to become part of the official Beatles album canon, taking its place along with all the original British albums.

My first encounter with the *Yellow Submarine* LP was in January of 1969, on the new releases rack at my favorite place to buy records, Bob Dilts TV in Kewanee, Illinois. It was an unusual Beatles album. After all, *The White Album* had just been released less than two months before. And the record itself was different. Only half of it was actually the Beatles, and only four of those six songs were new. The other half of the disc was George Martin's instrumental score from the film. Although I liked the new Beatles songs, I was somewhat disappointed with the album. However, when I saw the film a few weeks later at the Wanee Theater, I developed a new appreciation for the album as I saw how all the music on the record fit into the film. That album and the movie both became parts of the "*Yellow Submarine* Experience" for me. I also grew to appreciate the George Martin side of the album, especially "Pepperland." The album is a unique part of the Beatles legacy.

Michael Rinella

Yellow... what? Submarine. What is it? That was my first reaction in 1991 when I heard that title for the first time. My brother told me it's a cartoon film and an LP by the Beatles that we became aware of only after the USSR fell. It was so rare and unknown way back then that we didn't even know it existed. That feeling, the excitement of discovering something new from Beatles, was priceless. It still is. I was watching the film three to four times a week, enjoying the new songs. Little did I know that the song "Hey Bulldog" was omitted from that version. I discovered that a year later, when unexpectedly we saw the full version on TV. When "You can talk to me" began with the four-headed dog and twin Beatles, I was blown away.

Getting original U.K. stereo and mono copies of the *Yellow Submarine* album was quite a challenge. And of course, Side Two of the record is a very romantic piece of music. I had to grow older, get married and listen to it again after my wife forced me to truly appreciate it. Every time you listen to a Beatles album, you always hear something new and magical.

The experience of listening to the Beatles in the USSR was a magical mystery tour all its own! After the Union fell, we had a Russian pirate self-made label that released all the Beatles albums, including *Magical Mystery Tour* paired with *Yellow Submarine*, with a completely drawn and altered cover. But we were thankful to have the albums in their complete form for the first time.

As a Beatles collector, I have the original U.S. mono and stereo versions of *Magical Mystery Tour*, along with the U.K. EPs and versions from many other countries.

Yaakov Edisherashvili

I bought the *Yellow Submarine* LP in the eighties, but only played it once. After seeing the movie on DVD in 2019, the album made a lot more sense to me.

Janet Redick

I spotted the Official Yellow Submarine Magazine on a newsstand shelf in Lakeland, Florida in 1968. Its 32-page insert showcased full-page comic book-style color illustrations from the forthcoming *Yellow Submarine* motion picture, whetting my appetite. I was also enamored with the remaining 32 pages covering other things Beatles, including a two-page spread of London's film premiere with ten large photos of the Fabs and entourage in attendance.

October 12, 1968, NBC's Saturday Night at the Movies hosted the television premiere of *Help!* Following the film was a seven-minute documentary called *The Beatles Mod Odyssey*, which explored the inventive techniques animating the Fab Four in the upcoming full-length flick. A close study of the Beatles gaits intrigued me as lending an uncanny reality to their cartoon personae.

Yellow Submarine landed at local area theaters in January 1969. Five months on, Filmland, a drive-in movie theater just up the road from where I lived, paired it with *2001: A Space Odyssey*, with the Beatles film on the top of the bill. Our carload of five sat stunned and captivated. It was quiet until the real Beatles showed up, inspiring a joyous reunion, unleashing our spontaneous, boisterous sing-along and capping the evening's spellbinding double-feature. Blue Meanies be damned!

Bruce Weaver II

I saw *Yellow Submarine* in a theater a month or so after it was released, but it was nothing like the mayhem for *A Hard Days Night* or *Help!* Concerned that it would not be around much longer, I took some of my paperboy money and had my dad drive me, my sister and her friend to the Camelot Theater in Dearborn, Michigan, a movie house with cheesy Medieval decorating that usually showed new movies that had already been at the downtown theaters. We went on a Sunday afternoon.

Based on my previous Beatle movie experiences, I was concerned we might not get in or get a seat. But we were three of only ten ticket holders taking our journey aboard the Yellow Sub through the Sea of Empty Seats.

Fortunately the theater had an excellent sound system and the print was pristine. That was especially nice when the stunning section for "Only a Northern Song" came on. To me, just hearing that new Beatles song was well worth the time and money! But seeing *Yellow Submarine* was a far different experience than watching the Saturday morning cartoons. The movie was dark and very...British. Still being several years away from seeing Monty Python's Flying Circus, that alone made the movie rather confusing. I remember thinking, "Why had the Beatles only made a cartoon for their English fans?" But the colors seemed brighter than we had ever witnessed before! When the film was coming to an end, everyone else had made a hasty exit, so we were the only ones there when the Beatles themselves made an unexpected appearance at the end to warn us about more Blue Meanies being sighted and we had to sing to scare them away! After my dad picked us up at the theater, we headed home and "All You Need Is Love" came on the car radio, which prompted us kids to start singing quite loudly and shouting about Blue Meanies! My dad didn't have a clue what caused this behavior!

Over the years, I saw the film again at a few midnight movies. That was always crazy and fun! But I didn't truly realize how good *Yellow Submarine* was until I showed it to my own children. Hearing my son imitating Ringo and saying that he had "a hole in me pocket" never failed to make us both explode in silly laughter! And my daughter, who never really cared for the Beatles because, you know, I was so in awe of them, liked *Yellow Submarine* for the work of art that it is!

Phil Maq

As a first generation Beatles fan growing up in New York City in the 1960s, I was one of the lucky few who attended the dress rehearsal of The Ed Sullivan Show on February 9, 1964, when the Beatles made their American debut. That made up my mind to try to meet these amazing gentlemen after I graduated high school in 1967. I set my goal to go to England to meet John, Paul, George and Ringo. Although I was told by almost everyone that this would be impossible, I kept my dream and kept saving money. I volunteered at The Beatles Fan Club in New York City and was President of a Fan Club Chapter in NYC.

The sixties were very turbulent times, and many young people (including me) found themselves fighting for Civil Rights or protesting the war in Vietnam. One of the organizations involved in the Civil Rights movement was the Student Non-Violent Coordinating Committee (SNCC). When the Beatles "Yellow Submarine" single premiered in August 1966, SNCC took advantage of this soon-to-be-well-known symbol by making a button with a yellow submarine sprouting poppies instead of a peri-scope and featuring a peace symbol. I took several of the buttons for when I would meet my idols. (Think positive!)

In July 1967, I started living my dream and found myself at the homes of Paul, George, John and Ringo. I had brought a handful of Yellow Submarine peace buttons as gifts for each Beatle. I could not believe I was actually sitting with Paul in his garden in Cavendish, visiting with George at his home, Kinfauns in Esher, meeting John at Kenwood and visiting Ringo's home, Sunny Heights. Each of the Beatles was so cordial to me. They shared stories and answered my questions. John even showed me his psychedelic Rolls Royce he recently had painted and let me sit in it. As I gave each Beatle a Yellow Submarine button, they pinned it on their shirts. George even pinned two on his shirt. I guess they approved of the artwork! How amazed I was when I saw photos of the *Yellow Submarine* World Premiere in London in July 1968 showing George with the Yellow Submarine peace button I gave him on his yellow hat!

Leslie Samuels Healy a/k/a BeatleTripper

I saw the *Yellow Submarine* movie with my friends for my 11th birthday and of course we all loved it! The above photo is me proudly showing off my new copy of the *Yellow Submarine* soundtrack album.

Wayne Olsen

In 1968, I was an editor of my school newspaper at Franklin K. Lane High School in Brooklyn, New York when an invitation arrived from United Artists asking if we would like to be their guests at an advance screening of *Yellow Submarine*. YES! We trekked from Queens to midtown Manhattan and found the United Artists building, where we were seated in a private screening room with other students wide-eyed at the colors before us. The take-away was the catchy, easy-to-learn Beatles song at the conclusion, "All Together Now," which we were able to just about recite on the train ride home with joy.

Cousin Steve Goldmintz

I was in my senior year of high school when the *Yellow Submarine* movie was released at the end of 1968. I remember seeing the movie in downtown Williamsport, Pennsylvania with a couple of my Beatles buddies who had been following the Beatles since we first heard them in 1964. The movie offered some pretty cool new songs and some familiar Beatles classics. The animation was particularly good for the time. There were some good discussions about the film in school the next day. Of course we all bought the LP when it came out in January 1969 so we could listen to the new songs, including "Hey Bulldog," which was not in the movie.

As time passed, when I was a junior in college in the Spring of 1972, *Yellow Submarine* played at the Penn State Ice Pavilion during a three-day Festival of Life event. The event was jam-packed with bands, art exhibits, movies, etc. By that time, *Yellow Submarine* had somewhat of a cult following, and it was great fun watching it again in a concert-like atmosphere among hundreds of Beatles fans.

Rob Foust

In January 1969, while most of my 8th-grade classmates were busy studying for mid-terms, I was busy enjoying the *Yellow Submarine* soundtrack LP with four new Beatle songs and a great score by George Martin. I remember putting together the Yellow Submarine plastic model kit while listening to the LP. Up until then I was pretty much only buying Beatle LPs and 45s. With *Yellow Submarine*, there were neat things like models, books, magazines and comic books. I put a Blue Meanie sticker on my school locker. I still have my Beatles mobile, which is still hanging in my Beatles Room today! It was an exciting time in Beatles history and just like the movie itself, very enjoyable. A splendid time was guaranteed for all.

Robert G. Robbins

I was a fan of the Beatles Saturday morning cartoon show. When *Yellow Submarine* was released in 1968, I was definitely interested in seeing it. The movie was playing at the 8th Street Playhouse in Greenwich Village in New York. I was mesmerized by the colors and music; the Sea of Holes sequence was incredibly trippy. It was my first exposure to the music from the *Sgt. Pepper* album. I went to see the movie several more times during its initial run and at revivals and Beatles conventions. The last time I saw it on the big screen was at the Ziegfeld Theatre in New York with producer Al Brodax in attendance.

Fred Velez

The *Yellow Submarine* film didn't get a wide release in the U.K., so we had to keep an eye on the local press. Eventually it was announced that it was to be shown in Ellesmere Port! We all piled into Ashley's Mini (he was the only one of us students who had a car) and drove off from Liverpool. I still remember the sight of the oil refinery at night with the gas burning off lighting the sky – alien! But boy did we enjoy the film, and the surprise appearance by the boys at the end was a real thrill.

Alan Wright

I saw the *Yellow Submarine* film in November 1968 in Washington, D.C. It was the American version lacking "Hey Bulldog." One of the AM rock stations later played "Hey Bulldog" and said it was a new Beatles song. As *The White Album* had just been released, and the film had three new songs, this was like Beatle overload, as here was yet another great song. I only heard it once, and with the low-fi AM radio I heard it on, I thought the title was "Hey, Hold On." When the LP came out in January 1969, there it was, but I didn't learn that the song had been excised from the film until a few years thereafter.

George C. Heon

I first saw the *Yellow Submarine* movie in late 1968 when I was 17 years old. Me and my best friend were blown away by the animation and colors, so much so that we saw it at least twice a day for the next two to three weeks. Our favorite line was "It's all in the mind!" We used that as a reply for just about everything for the next couple of years. I introduced the film to my kids in the eighties and they both loved it. To this day we still banter back and forth with lines from the movie!

John Giglio

EXCERPT FROM *It's All In The Mind: Inside The Beatles' Yellow Submarine, Volume 2*, by Robert R. Hieronimus, Ph.D., and Laura E. Cortner (Hieronimus & Co. Publications, 2021)

Twenty-four-year-old artist and elementary school art teacher Bob Hieronimus first sat down in the darkened Landmark Theater in Baltimore in November 1968 eager to see what this new Beatles movie was all about. He assumed it was a film created by the four Beatles themselves, and while he hadn't paid much attention to the Beatles music until the release of *Sgt. Pepper* the previous summer, he was interested to see how their more adventurous creative trajectory would be visualized in pictorial form. He described his reaction in a series of articles for a Baltimore newspaper in 1968:

"I can quite distinctly remember that after the movie started, I became hypnotized. It seemed to me that I had actually seen the whole picture before at another time. Everything seemed so familiar. The colors, the patterns, the symbols seemed to be allowing me to travel to a time of the forgotten past, tens of thousands of years back. How could it be? I became aware that several stories were being told, and all of them seemed to relate to one another. I recognized that almost everything in the *Yellow Submarine* had two and three meanings."

My grandma was a librarian, and one of her fun tasks was intercepting discontinued books if she thought someone she knew might want them. When I was 14, I was a Beatles fan, but I hadn't seen *Yellow Submarine* yet. Much to my delight, she rescued and gave me a little hardcover Signet book of the film/story.

Throughout the next months, my little sister and I read that book aloud together until we almost had it memorized. To this day, she can recite Jeremy Hilary's entire introduction speech as it appears on the page. The book even included amusing "footnotes," like a "lost" classified ad for Jeremy, indicating that a reward for his return was circulated.

By the time I saw the movie on a Chicago television station, commercials and all, I knew the story and its characters, enabling me to say things like, "That's great, but it's not exactly like the book!"

Karen Duchaj

I well remember receiving the Signet paperback of *Yellow Submarine* as a surprise Christmas gift from my Mom and Dad in 1968. I was 11 and in 6th grade at the time. I was so happy and excited to receive it! I read it again and again! I remember bringing the book to school with me so some of my classmates could see it, too! The "pop art" incarnation of the Fab Four in such vibrant, dazzling color was just wonderful! It still captures my imagination to this day!

Not long after, on a dark winter Sunday afternoon, my Dad took me to see the film at the Whitney Theater, in Hamden, Connecticut. We both enjoyed it immensely! To see the static pages of the book come to life, as well as the "special appearance" of the Fabs at the conclusion, was not only a "Wow" moment for me at the time, but a very special memory to this day!

Bob Briar

I was five when the Beatles first appeared on The Ed Sullivan Show, so I was a casual fan from that day. But I truly became a serious fan around the age of 10, right around when the *Yellow Submarine* film came out. During her holiday break from college, my oldest sister, Linda, took me to see the film at the ornate Stanley Theatre in our hometown, Utica, New York. I was rapt throughout the film and we left the theatre singing "All Together Now" on the streets of downtown Utica.

I got the album soon after. I know many fans felt shortchanged with only four new Beatles tracks, but I enjoyed, and still enjoy, the George Martin instrumentals on Side 2. The new Beatles songs were a mixed lot, but "Hey Bulldog" was an instant classic. (Even though American film viewers were puzzled by this non-film track being on the soundtrack!) I also loved "It's All Too Much" with its feedback, blaring brass, and Indian-like drone. I was thrilled when the film was released on VHS tape so I could share the joy of the Beatles and the film with my sons.

Michael Cooper

In the fall of 1968 I had recently entered 7th grade as an awkward, nearsighted 12-year-old. Having discovered "Hey Jude," the Beatle bug had taken hold. My older sister informed me that the new Beatles movie, *Yellow Submarine*, was playing at an area theater. Our father, a non-Beatles fan, consented to drop the two of us off for a 4:00 PM weekday matinee, which played to a near-empty auditorium: me, my sister and the elderly theater doorman. The entire picture was baffling from my pre-teen perspective. When our father picked us up at the conclusion of the film, he commented that we "looked like mine mules." The experience did not, however, affect my attitude as a fledgling Beatles fan.

Andrew Caldwell

I was in first grade when I heard of *Yellow Submarine* being released. Blue was one of my favorite colors, and to be truthful, the Blue Meanies (especially the Flying Glove) attracted me! I knew vaguely of the Beatles because of the Saturday morning cartoon show and I had the album *The Chipmunks Sing The Beatles Hits*. So, on a Saturday afternoon, my Mom took me to the Calderone Theater in Hempstead, New York for a showing. I was hooked! I could not take my eyes away from the screen! My Mom got dizzy from the psychedelics; she told me to stay in my seat, she was going to the lobby. I shook my head yes.

Afterward, all I could think of was that movie! I got the soundtrack LP as a gift! I'd come home after school, my friend Danny would come by and we'd go downstairs to the record player. "There it goes!" my Grandfather would say as the LP would begin. I later got the *Yellow Submarine* lunchbox, Corgi die cast toy, model, mobile, cutouts, comic book, etc.

I brought my lunch to school each day in my *Yellow Submarine* lunchbox, which my school bus driver wanted. I would bring my album and cutouts to class. My first grade teacher and I made a big copy of the submarine on posterboard, and at a Nassau Lutheran School concert, me and three classmates sang "Yellow Submarine" holding that giant model. I wish I had photos of that, but I do have a picture of me and Danny, with me holding my Corgi Yellow Submarine.

Robert Koenig

I saw the film *Yellow Submarine* with my parents when it first came out in a movie theater in Greenwich, Connecticut. My favorite moment, of course, was when the boys appeared at the end! My mother then surprised me with both the scrapbook and photo album, which I still have to this day!

Ted Amoruso

Over fifty years later, I still recall the first time I saw *Yellow Submarine* one weekend afternoon in the fall of 1969. At the time, I was an almost 7-year-old Beatlemaniac whose first movie, according to my Mom, was *A Hard Day's Night* in 1964! My main memory is of me holding up the *Yellow Submarine* album cover and waving it back and forth. Why I did that, and whether anyone objected, I can't recall. (I do remember not being a fan of side two of the LP.) I also remember being excited because my Mom let me see the movie with a friend and without adult accompaniment (as opposed to *A Hard Day's Night*). After all these years, I remember the name of the cinema – the Community Theatre in Fairfield, Connecticut – and a little bit of research helped confirm my memories!

Paul Friend

I was in junior high, attending Niles Elementary School in Niles, Illinois, when *Yellow Submarine* was released. Our art class teacher, Terry Gibbons, arranged a field trip for the entire class to walk to the local movie theater, Lawrencewood Theatre, to see a special matinee performance of *Yellow Submarine* screened just for us. Mr. Gibbons was my favorite teacher and the fact that he was a Beatle fan like I was one of the reasons why. I had so much fun that day with my friends laughing and singing along to all of the great Beatle songs. I was happy to see my classmates were Beatle fans just like I was. When I talk to my grade school classmates all these years later about our school days, this always seems to be one of our fondest memories.

Lawrence Gualano

My little brother Mike and I both went to Catholic schools. We were off for the Solemnity of the Immaculate Conception on December 8th, 1968, a cold winter day. I was 17 and Mike had just turned 11 the day before. So with the day to ourselves, and as a birthday present to Mike, we took a few buses from the far south side of Chicago all the way into the downtown Loop theater district to see the first run of *Yellow Submarine*. It was a big old ornate Chicago movie palace with a very large screen and good sound system. We settled down with our popcorn in a fairly cold theater as the heat was likely just turned up. We most likely kept our coats on. The movie played with all its glorious animation and great music that we both loved. After the film concluded with the surprise appearance of the real Beatles at the end, Mike and I waited for a while, thought about it and decided to sit through a second showing. After round two of this glorious film we headed home back to 115th Street. Mike and I remain good friends and Beatle buddies to this day.

Tom Dziedzic

I remember KJR radio in Seattle playing the entire *Yellow Submarine* album when it was released in 1969. A few days later I called in to request "Hey Bullfrog," but the DJ didn't recall a song by that name and hung up.

My family had an old 1950's phonograph in the basement that we played our records on, so we heard everything in mono. But one day my older brother invited us over to his apartment. I noticed he had the new *Yellow Submarine* album and asked to listen to it. He said OK, but thru his headphones. I had never worn headphones before. Listening to the Beatles in stereo for the first time was incredible. It changed my life. But it wasn't until I went to college in 1973 that I bought my first stereo and really enjoyed the Beatles sound in stereo. Fun days!

Bill Hansen

My first memory of the Beatles cartoon movie was in first grade when I saw a *Yellow Submarine* lunchbox at my table. Next I was flipping channels on my new B&W TV and found the film. It scared me and I turned it off! I attended my first Beatlefest in Chicago in 1979, where I saw the movie again, bravely watching the whole thing. The cartoons looked so strange. But once I boarded the *Yellow Submarine*, I was hooked. I got my first vinyl album on the orange Capitol label from my aunt for Christmas. In 1987, I got the CD in a longbox.

The movie's re-release in 1999 was exciting, especially the "Hey Bulldog" segment. The *Yellow Submarine Songtrack* release added a new CD and amazing yellow vinyl to my collection. I gave up trying to get all the related memorabilia as "it's all too much." I treasure my inflatable chair, promo mylar sub-balloon, Hot Wheels and bubble gum cards (including one signed by Al Brodax). My Beatles collection and love for the band would not be the same without the advent of *Yellow Submarine*.

Dr. Jennifer Sandi

Yellow Submarine was a strange phenomenon. Initially, the Beatles did not seem to have as much interest in the film as previous film efforts. However, once they realized the film under Heinz Edelmann's guidance was becoming a groundbreaking and innovative enterprise, they seemingly regretted not having more to do with its creation and finally agreed to do a cameo to end the film. When the film was issued, hardcore Beatle fans were upset that the UK version of the film differed from the US version. The US version had the "Hey Bulldog" sequence cut from the film. I remember being very pleased that so soon after the release of *The White Album*, we were getting more released Beatles music. Unlike the Beatles US *Help!* album where I did not appreciate the additional Ken Thorne music score, I loved the George Martin material that appeared on the *Yellow Submarine* soundtrack. I also remember being fascinated with the marketing campaign of *Yellow Submarine* characters like Jeremy Hillary Boob, Max and the Chief Blue Meanie. I loved the magazines that followed as well. I am probably in the minority by being disappointed that the planned Disney sponsored Robert Zemeckis sequel or remake to *Yellow Submarine* was never attempted, but "It's all in the mind, y'know!"

John Bezzini

I was probably 14 or 15 in 1977 when I biked to a public library in my hometown in Ottawa, which had a good collection of albums. I didn't have a job then, so I wanted to find albums that I could borrow and transfer to tape. When I got there, I saw the *Yellow Submarine* soundtrack LP, which I didn't know existed. I had all the Beatles albums from my older siblings' collections or taped from friends. These were new Beatles songs to me! I couldn't wait to get home and listen to these four tracks. Outside of "Hey Bulldog," which I loved immediately, the others left me a bit disappointed. I did put them to tape and rapidly grew to love these odd tunes. When I hear them today, I still feel like they are "new" songs; I still remember the excitement of bringing these home.

André Poirier

I was born in 1967 and was the youngest of eight. When I was a toddler in 1969-1970, my oldest brother frequently played Beatles music on his record player, and from the *Yellow Submarine* LP he often played "All Together Now" and "Hey Bulldog." After he left for college in the fall of 1970, I did not hear these songs again until I bought my own copy of the album a decade later.

Terence Moore

Three months after "The Ballad Of Bonnie And Clyde" by Georgie Fame hit the charts, "Lady Madonna" was released. Both songs share a classic '50s Fats Domino rock 'n' roll sound. "Lady Madonna" was so different from the previous half dozen or so Beatle singles, it sounded revelatory. Fats was immediately signed to Reprise and had his cover version out five months later, his second release on his new label.

The Beatles contributed mightily to the late '60s rock 'n' roll revival with "Lady Madonna." As trendsetters, many followed the Beatles. Soon after, Creedence Clearwater Revival was unstoppable with their classic rock 'n' roll sound. This was after ten failed original releases as the Golliwogs and Creedence. NRBQ, the Flaming Groovies, Dave Edmunds and others hit the stores. The revival was on for six or seven years. Grease, American Graffiti and the TV show Happy Days appeared. It all ended for the most part when Disco exploded in 1975. That said, "Lady Madonna" and the Beatles made early rock 'n' roll cool once again.

Maury Mollo

A Fan's Notes: When All We Needed Was Love

by Bill King (portions of these notes were previously published in Beatlefan magazine)

With the newly released *Sgt. Pepper* LP spinning on my suitcase-style turntable, the Beatles were a big part of my summer of 1967. It was a great time to be a fan of the Fabs. I'm not sure whether the "Summer of Love" tag coined in San Francisco's Haight-Ashbury district had come into use in Georgia by then, but the editors of the daily papers in Atlanta seemed fascinated by the newly emerged hippies. They kept running bemused stories written as if about some curious primitive tribe discovered on the far side of the globe. Much to my delight, I found that the media fascination with the hippie world and psychedelia meant that hardly a week went by without a report on the Beatles, who became the Summer of Love's ultimate icons.

The second week of June saw an item in The Atlanta Journal on the psychedelic paint job given to John Lennon's Roll Royce, and on Monday, June 19, there was a story about Paul McCartney admitting he'd used LSD (which he'd already admitted the week before in Life magazine). Two days later, loyal Beatles manager Brian Epstein jumped into the fray to deflect some of this negative attention from Paul, saying he, too, had taken LSD. All four Beatles and Epstein would follow up a month later by taking out a full-page ad in the Times of London advocating the legalization of marijuana.

Also in the paper was news of that Sunday's first global satellite TV broadcast which would feature the Beatles. Our World was telecast to 26 countries on five continents at 3 p.m. EDT on June 25, with NET (the precursor to PBS) carrying it live. The segment on artistic excellence included, among others, Van Cliburn, Leonard Bernstein, and Franco Zeffirelli on the set of *Romeo And Juliet* in Rome, directing 17-year-old Leonard Whiting and 15-year-old Olivia Hussey (with whom I would fall in love from my cinema seat a year later). But the main attraction was the segment from London's Abbey Road Studios: the Beatles, backed by an orchestra, recording a new song in a flower-bedecked studio before an all-star assemblage of friends and family.

I only recently had gotten my own television in my bedroom. This was long before VCRs, so I nervously set up in front of the TV with my little audio tape recorder, which used 3-inch reels, and made my first home Beatles recording as "All You Need Is Love" blared out of the television set. I remember loving the song immediately and being thrilled that I actually was getting to witness its recording. That little tape I'd made would get quite a workout between then and the release of the single three weeks later. Nobody else had recorded it, so I was the only kid in the neighborhood with the Beatles next single! Once the actual 45 was released and I'd bought my copy at Woolworth's, I think I stuck that little reel in a box of tapes that probably got thrown out by my parents years later.

That summer wound up memorably. My family moved to a bigger house across town, and, on Monday, August 28, the TV news and papers reported Brian Epstein had been found dead the day before. That next week, the day after I'd started 10th grade, the Journal had an article about how the Beatles, shaking off Brian's death, were planning a Christmas TV special. It also told of their newfound fascination with an Indian guru, the Maharishi Mahesh Yogi. The following Tuesday, there was a story about a London bobby making Paul McCartney and his entire entourage clear the sidewalk near the Baker Street underground station in London while they waited for the psychedelic bus that would carry them on their "Magical Mystery Tour."

During Thanksgiving break I turned on the radio to my favorite Top 40 station playing a song I'd never heard before. It only took a few seconds for me to recognize the Beatles. The song was their new single, "Hello Goodbye." On November 26, The Ed Sullivan Show ran a promo film featuring the band miming the song in their Sgt. Pepper band uniforms.

The single's A-side, with its simple yes-no, high-low, hello-goodbye lyrics, was the antithesis of the B-side, "I Am The Walrus," with its Lewis Carroll-inspired nonsense lyrics. Its line, "Boy you've been a naughty girl, you let your knickers down" became even more provocative to my friends and me after my British mom explained that, in the U.K., "knickers" were what we called "panties." Both songs were included on the Beatles new *Magical Mystery Tour* LP, which I wasn't going to get until Christmas (it was on my gift wish list). I first heard the *Magical Mystery Tour* album at school when our hip world history teacher (who was in her early 20s and on whom I had a hopeless crush) played it in class.

After retrieving my copy from under the tree on Christmas morning, I spent the rest of the day playing the album and poring over its illustrated storybook of the film. I was eagerly awaiting the future NBC airing I'd read about in TV Guide, but then came word in the paper that the film had been a big flop with the U.K. viewing audience when it first aired there on the night after Christmas, so it likely wasn't going to be shown on American television after all. I fretted that I might never get to see it.

Next up for U.S. Beatles fans was a new single, "Lady Madonna." This time the promo film aired on The Hollywood Palace on March 30. While it always was fun to see the Beatles on TV, I didn't think much of the clip, since, in the shots of the Fab Four performing, it was obvious they weren't even singing that song. (31 years later, when the clip was re-cut with the song they actually were filmed recording, "Hey Bulldog," it became one of my favorite Beatles promo films.)

We learned through news reports that the Beatles were in India. After their return, we heard they would be releasing an animated feature film. I recall seeing a photo of the Beatles attending the July 17, 1968, London premiere of the movie *Yellow Submarine*. For those of us in the States, we would have to wait four to five months to see the film. We did, however, get a taste of what the cartoon would be like when NBC aired *The Beatles' Mod Odyssey*, a featurette on the making of the film, after the October 12 TV debut of *Help!*

Although *Yellow Submarine* opened in New York and LA on November 13, 1968, it would not arrive in my hometown until January 1969 when it played on an incongruous double-bill with the violent Clint Eastwood Western *Hang 'Em High*. I was charmed by the film's good vs. evil storyline and colorful psychedelic and op art images. Later that month I bought the *Yellow Submarine* soundtrack LP even though it had only four new Beatles songs. Fortunately, they proved to be of surprisingly high quality, especially "Hey Bulldog."

I finally got to see *Magical Mystery Tour* in 1974 and thought it was imaginative, with much to offer. The "Fool On The Hill" sequence is lovely, with McCartney prancing about in slow motion. The "I Am The Walrus" sequence could stand alone as a very fine music video. Considering they didn't know what they were doing, the Beatles showed a lot of promise as filmmakers.

The Third Film & EP That Never Came To Be

When United Artists entered into a three-film deal with the Beatles in October 1963, its primary motivation was to obtain the rights to the film soundtracks for its American record division, United Artists Records. As part of the three-film agreement, UA obtained the rights to two soundtrack LPs for the American market. The first film, *A Hard Day's Night*, provided the company with both a hit movie and a soundtrack album that sold over two million units in 1964. The group's second film, *Help!*, was also a box office hit; however, the soundtrack album was conceived, manufactured and distributed by Capitol Records rather than United Artists Records. The LP sold over three million units.

After completing their first two motion pictures in two years, the Beatles had difficulty coming up with an appropriate vehicle for their third film. In February 1965, it was announced that the group's next movie would be a Western titled *A Talent For Loving*, which would be made for Pickfair Films, a company co-owned by Brian Epstein. The Beatles met with their manager on June 20 to discuss the project, but apparently were not satisfied with the script. By this time, the group had decided that they did not want to portray themselves and did not want to do a period piece.

United Artists planned to shoot its third Beatles film in the autumn of 1965, even though it had no script or title. These plans were put on hold as the Beatles concentrated on recording and touring. In April 1966, Walter Shenson, producer of the first two Beatles films, confirmed that there would be no motion picture from the group in 1966. Richard Lester, who directed the group's first two films, unsuccessfully pitched a remake of *The Three Musketeers* to the group.

In summer 1966, Shenson hired Owen Holder to script the group's next film, dubbed *Beatles 3*, with production tentatively set for January 1967. The film would be about a man, played by John, who suffered from a personality disorder giving him three different personalities in addition to his own. The other personalities would be played by Paul, George and Ringo. In June 1967, it was announced that the film, *Shades Of A Personality*, would be directed by Michelangelo Antonioni of *Blow Up* fame. The group, however, was too busy working on *Magical Mystery Tour* to do the film.

Meanwhile, *Shades Of A Personality* was reworked by Joe Orton and re-titled *Up Against It*. The group turned down the script as it was essentially a gay film featuring political assassination, guerrilla warfare and transvestism. Paul explained, "It wasn't that we were anti-gay; just that we, the Beatles, weren't gay."

The idea of producing an animated feature-length movie starring the Beatles was successfully pitched to Brian Epstein in 1966 by Al Brodax, who produced the group's cartoon show for ABC-TV. Unable to find the time to shoot or find an appropriate vehicle for a major motion picture, the Beatles attempted to fulfill their three-film contractual obligation to United Artists by giving the company their animated film, *Yellow Submarine*. While producer Al Brodax thought that the cartoon film counted, former UA executive David Picker indicated that the company refused to accept the cartoon as the third Beatles movie, but agreed to distribute the feature for Apple Films. As the cartoon was not considered the third film under the contract, Capitol was able to release the *Yellow Submarine* soundtrack album.

Realizing that the Beatles were still in need of a third movie, Denis O'Dell, head of Apple Films, met with United Artists to discuss the group starring in J.R.R. Tolkien's fantasy masterpiece, *The Lord Of The Rings*. United Artists was excited by the idea and suggested that the film have a star director such as David Lean, Stanley Kubrick or Michelangelo Antonioni. O'Dell, bringing copies of the Tolkien books with him, met with the Beatles in India while they were studying TM with the Maharishi in February 1968. John was excited about the project and the prospect of working with Kubrick, but when O'Dell met with Kubrick, the director declined because he thought the books were "unfilmable." The plan came to an end when Tolkien objected to the Beatles involvement.

In Spring 1969, George Harrison indicated that the Beatles had agreed on the script for a third film. "It will be at least as big as *2001* visually, with full stereo sound and Cinerama." He stated that they had the idea a year ago and that it was fantastic. "We agreed to let each other do exactly what he wants to do with it. By allowing each other to be each other we can become the Beatles again." It is not known what film George was talking about, as it never came to be.

Realizing that there would not be another *A Hard Day's Night* or *Help!*, UA accepted the Beatles documentary film, *Let It Be*, as the third movie owed under the agreement. United Artists Records was given the American distribution rights to the *Let It Be* album.

It all worked out for the best, with director Peter Jackson utilizing technology unavailable in the sixties to make *The Lord Of The Rings* into an epic film trilogy released from 2001 to 2003. On January 30, 2019, Apple announced that Jackson had been hired to create a new film, *The Beatles: Get Back*, of the group's January 1969 sessions previously shown in *Let It Be*.

According to George Martin, the Beatles initial plan for the *Yellow Submarine* songs was to issue an EP containing the four new songs from the film. Martin was going to produce an album mixing his background score with narration and voices from the movie, done in the same style as *Peter And The Wolf*. Prior to Martin beginning his album project, Capitol Records objected to the proposed EP and requested permission to issue an album with Beatles music on one side and selections from George Martin's score on the other. The Beatles and EMI then decided on issuing the same LP in the U.K. and throughout the world.

In mid-January 1969, the Beatles began questioning their decision to issue the songs recorded for *Yellow Submarine* on an album rather than an EP. Because the LP contained only four new Beatles songs, the group was concerned they were not giving their fans good value for their money. This prompted John and Paul to program an EP featuring the four new songs from the cartoon film plus the previously unreleased "Across The Universe." Due to the six-minute plus length of "It's All Too Much" and the addition of the bonus track, the EP would run at 33⅓-rpm rather than the standard 45-rpm speed for extended play discs.

A mono master tape for the EP was compiled at Abbey Road on March 13, 1969, by Edward Gadsby-Toni. Although the mono *Yellow Submarine* LP was a fold-down mix of the stereo album, the tape for the EP used mono mixes: "Only A Northern Song (April 21, 1967); "All Together Now" (May 12, 1967); "Hey Bulldog" (February 11, 1968); "It's All Too Much" (October 16, 1968); and "Across The Universe" (February 8, 1968). For reasons unknown, the *Yellow Submarine* EP was aborted at this preliminary stage. The mono mixes were finally released in 2009 on the *Mono Masters* disc included in *The Beatles In Mono* box set.

No One's Gonna Change Our World

Although recorded in February 1968, "Across The Universe" was not released until nearly two years later on December 12, 1969. The song was recorded during the same sessions that yielded "Lady Madonna," "The Inner Light" and "Hey Bulldog." And while those who heard the song thought it was great and deserved to be the single, John was not happy with the recording. As fate would have it, comedian Spike Milligan was at Abbey Road on the evening that overdubs were added to the track on February 8. At the time he was organizing a charity album that would benefit the World Wildlife Fund. While visiting George Martin and the boys in the control room of Studio Two, he was told that the Beatles did not plan to release "Across The Universe" on their next single. Milligan boldly asked if the group would contribute the song to the World Wildlife Fund charity album. Much to his delight and surprise, the Beatles agreed to donate the track to the project.

During the mono mixing of the song at the end of the session, the engineers added 20 seconds of sound effects of chirping birds and flying birds landing on water to the beginning of the track and the sound of flying birds for a few moments during the song's fade-out ending. Because these wildlife sounds fit with the charity benefiting from the album, it is likely that they were added at the suggestion of George Martin or Spike Milligan rather than being part of John's vision of the song.

Although conceived in early 1968, the charity album took longer to organize and compile than anticipated. Finally, in the fall of 1969, the album began to take shape. The decision was made to highlight the inclusion of the unreleased Beatles song by having "Across The Universe" open the album and by modifying a line from the song to serve as the album's title. The refrain "Nothing's gonna change my world" was altered to *No One's Gonna Change Our World*.

Because the album was to be issued in stereo, George Martin needed to mix the song for stereo. On October 2, assisted by engineers Jeff Jarratt and Alan Parsons, Martin prepared a stereo mix of the song. He sped up the tape of Take 8, shifting the song up a half step from D major to E flat, reducing the running time of the song and raising the pitch of John's voice. He also added the same bird sound effects that had been used for the mono mix. The next day Martin banded the album, which contained the following songs:

"Across The Universe" by the Beatles; "What The World Needs Now Is Love" by Cilla Black; "Cuddly Old Koala" by Rolf Harris; "Wings" by the Hollies (also making its debut); "Ning Nang Nong" and "The Python" by Spike Milligan; "Marley Purt Drive" by the Bee Gees; "I'm A Tiger" by Lulu; "Bend It" by Dave Dee, Dozy, Beaky, Mick & Tich; "In The Country" by Cliff Richard; "When I See An Elephant Fly" by Bruce Forsyth; and "Land Of My Fathers" by Harry Secombe.

The album was released on EMI's budget Regal Starline label as SRS 5013 on December 12, 1969. The front cover was drawn by Michael Grimshaw and features sketches of the recording artists and a panda bear. The back cover has a picture of and a personal message from Prince Philip, H.R.H. the Duke of Edinburgh, and a thank you from Spike Milligan. The artists, composers, publishers and recording companies waived all fees. Royalties were donated to the World Wildlife Fund for the preservation of rare animals in danger of extinction. The album was not well promoted and did not chart. Although the LP was not issued in America, copies were imported.

The Magical Mystery Tour Package, a Journey on a Yellow Submarine and a Return to Their Roots

In the fall of 1967 the Beatles realized that they were facing a problem of what to do with the seven new songs they had recorded. Six of the songs would be part of the soundtrack to their *Magical Mystery Tour* TV film and one, "Hello Goodbye," would be the group's next single. This was a change from the initial plan of issuing the film's title song as a single and four film tracks on an extended play (EP) disc.

The November 1967 issue (No. 52) of The Beatles Book summed up their dilemma. The group could not issue a one-sided LP and did not have the time to write enough additional songs to fill an album. The group considered "all sorts of other solutions" including: a four-track EP plus a single with one track on one side and two on the other; or three singles, one of which would have an added track on one side. Another idea was to prepare an EP to be played at 33⅓-rpm, but this was rejected over concern of loss of volume and fidelity. The magazine stated that the current plan was to issue a single by the end of November and follow it with an EP "accompanied by a picture story of the Mystery Tour in December."

Ultimately, it was decided to release a single with "Hello Goodbye" and "I Am The Walrus" on November 24, and follow it two weeks later on December 8 with a two-EP set, with each disc having two songs on one side and one on the other. (Although "Hello Goodbye" had been recorded specifically for single release and was brimming with commercial appeal, John unsuccessfully lobbied to have his "I Am The Walrus" as the A-side.)

The two discs are packaged in an elaborate 32-page book, whose page count includes the front and back covers as four pages plus a 24-page interior booklet plus four pages containing song lyrics. The lyrics are on a center spread insert originally printed on light blue paper.

The front cover has a star-covered blue background with the Beatles appearing in the center wearing their animal costumes from the "I Am The Walrus" sequence. The group's name is spelled out in yellow stars at the top and the *Magical Mystery Tour* rainbow logo is at the bottom. The back cover has a kaleidoscope of images of the staircase finale of "Your Mother Should Know" with the Beatles dancing in their white formal wear.

The discs were housed in white center-die-cut inner sleeves, either with a slightly-rounded tab top or a wavy top. The Side 1 and 2 disc was placed in a flap inside the front cover, while the Side 3 and 4 disc was in a flap inside the back cover. The books, printed by Garrod & Lofthouse, measure 7½" x 7½".

The inside cover flap features a colorful caricature of the Beatles in their magician costumes drawn by Bob Gibson. Below the drawing is a message: "Away in the sky, beyond the clouds, live 4 or 5 Magicians. By casting Wonderful Spells they turn the Most Ordinary Coach Trip into a Magical Mystery Tour. If you let yourself go, the Magicians will take you away to marvelous places. Maybe you've been on a Magical Mystery Tour without even realizing it. Are you ready to go? Splendid! The story begins on Page 7... or 8..."

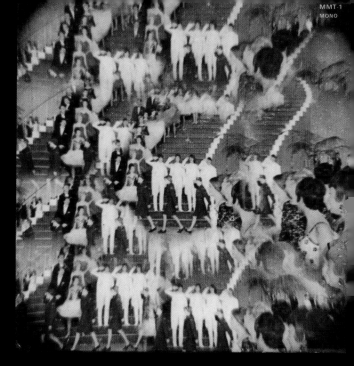

MMT 1
MONO

AWAY IN THE SKY, beyond the clouds, live 4 or 5 Magicians.
By casting WONDERFUL SPELLS they turn the Most
Ordinary Coach Trip into a MAGICAL MYSTERY TOUR.
If you let yourself go, the Magicians will take you away to
marvellous places.
Maybe YOU'VE been on a MAGICAL MYSTERY TOUR
without even realising it.
Are you ready to go?
SPLENDID! The story begins on Page 7 . . . or 8 . . . .

A COLOUR FILM FOR TELEVISION

with

GEORGE CLAYDON
as Little George The Photographer

JESSIE ROBINS
as Ringo's Auntie

IVOR CUTLER
as Mr. Buster Bloodvessel

DEREK ROYLE
as Jolly Jimmy Johnson The Courier

SHIRLEY EVANS
as The Accordionist

VICTOR SPINETTI
as The Recruiting Sergeant

NAT JACKLEY
as Happy Nat The Rubber Man

MANDY WEET
as Miss Wendy Winters The Hostess

NICOLA
as The Little Girl

MAGGIE WRIGHT
as The Lovely Starlet

MADE IN ENGLAND BY THE BEATLES
"Magical Mystery Tour" Book Edited by Tony Barrow
Editorial Consultants (for Apple): Neil Aspinall & Mal Evans
Photographs: John Kelly   Drawings: Bob Gibson
(c) 1967, NEMS ENTERPRISES LTD.

1

The inner booklet has color and black and white photos taken by John Kelly during filming. It also has six pages featuring a color cartoon depicting the film's storyline drawn by Bob Gibson and written by Tony Barrow. Because the cartoon was prepared prior to completion of the editing of the film, it contains scenes not present in the film (particularly panels 14-20 depicting a "marvelous lunch," Happy Nat's dream about pretty girls by the seaside and Ringo's Aunt Jessie playing the drums). The story is also out-of-sequence, with the Magical Mystery Tour Marathon Race, striptease club scene, mountains of spaghetti dream and squeezing into the tiny tent scene appearing in different places.

The back inside cover flap has an early rendition of the Apple logo with "apple presents The Beatles in Songs and Music from a Colour Television Film called 'Magical Mystery Tour,'" followed by the list of songs with the songwriters credit and "Produced by Big George Martin."

The listing for "I Am The Walrus" is followed by a parenthetical notation of "('No you're not!' said Little Nicola)." The words "No you're not!" are hand written. This has caused some people to incorrectly believe that the Nicola notation is the song's subtitle even though it does not appear on the record label. Its origin is from a scene in the film where a little girl named Nicola Hale is sitting on John's lap. The film does not contain a verbal exchange where Nicola says "No you're not!" after hearing John say "I am the Walrus." This imaginary conversation may have been concocted by Tony Barrow for insertion into the booklet.

There is also a plug for the Official Beatles Fan Club and The Beatles Monthly Book in a box under the heading "Hurry now! Don't delay! Amaze your friends and write today." The Beatles next single, "Lady Madonna," came with a flier plugging the Fan Club and magazine.

Capitol Records balked at the idea of issuing the Magical Mystery Tour songs on two EP discs because the format had never really caught on in America. Instead, Capitol requested and obtained permission from the Beatles to issue the Magical Mystery Tour songs on an album. With the six film songs taking up only one side of the disc, Capitol came up with the perfect solution for the other side. While the Beatles had been reluctant to place singles on their LPs under the belief that fans should not be expected to pay twice for the same songs, Capitol took the opposite approach for its version of the Beatles album catalog, adding singles because "hit singles make hit albums."

For its Magical Mystery Tour album, Capitol placed the non-film A-side of the group's latest single, "Hello Goodbye," along with both sides of the Beatles other 1967 singles on Side Two. None of these songs had previously been issued on an album.

Capitol packaged the album in a gatefold cover designed by the head of its art department, John Van Hamersveld, using the artwork from the British EP. The front cover features an 8½" x 8½" enlargement of the 7½" x 7½" colorful front cover of the EP surrounded by a pointillist representation of clouds, with yellow, orange, red and blue as the dominant colors. The titles to the songs from the film appear in red at the top in a series of white curved banners. The non-film song titles are in red in white rectangular banners at the bottom. A white banner directly below the EP cover states "Includes 24-page full color picture book" in brown. The back cover is the same as that of the EP.

The left inner gatefold sleeve combines the art work and text of the two inner flaps from the British release. The right inner sleeve has the lyrics to the film songs. The Capitol package has the advantage of having the booklet expanded from 7½" x 7½" to 12" x 12".

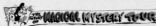

1. RINGO AND AUNTIE JESSIE are *always* quarrelling about one thing or another. But they both agree it would be exciting to go on a Mystery Tour. "Your Uncle Jack always liked a Charabanc Trip" says Auntie Jessie. "And this is a MAGIC trip" adds Ringo.

2. A few days later, VERY early in the morning, they set off to start the tour. Auntie Jessie looks at the B-I-G bus and smiles: "It's all yellow and blue! My favourite colours!" When everyone is ready JOLLY JIMMY JOHNSON (THE COURIER) climbs aboard.

3. "Good Morning Ladies And Gentlemen, Boys And Girls! WELCOME TO MAGICAL MYSTERY TOUR! I am your Courier. All my friends call me Jolly Jimmy and YOU are ALL my friends! Everyone comfy? SPLENDID!"

4. Then Jolly Jimmy introduces the Tour Hostess, THE DELIGHTFUL WENDY WINTERS. "And over HERE . . ." he goes on "is our driver for the trip, a wonderful driver (WE HOPE!) whose name is ALF. Away-way-way we go, Alf! SPLENDID!"

5. Needless to say Auntie Jessie finds something to argue about. "You ain't coming with me anymore" she tells Ringo. "Who bought the tickets? I DID, DIDN'T I!" replies Ringo. "Yes, YOU bought the tickets" agrees Auntie Jessie "BUT I GAVE YOU THE MONEY!"

6. At the front of the bus sits a Sad Little Man in a funny old uniform. "Who *IS* that man?" whispers Wendy Winters. "That's Mr. Buster Bloodvessel" answers Jolly Jimmy "He's quite harmless. He thinks HE'S THE COURIER! Last trip he thought he was THE DRIVER!"

Continued on Page 9

 apple presents

THE BEATLES
in Songs and Music from a
Colour Television Film called
"MAGICAL MYSTERY TOUR"

RECORD ONE: Side One .. MAGICAL MYSTERY TOUR
(Lennon-McCartney)

YOUR MOTHER SHOULD KNOW
(Lennon-McCartney)

Side Two .. I AM THE WALRUS
(Lennon-McCartney)
(*"No You're not!"* said Little Nicola)

RECORD TWO: Side One .. THE FOOL ON THE HILL
(Lennon-McCartney)

FLYING
(Harrison-Lennon-McCartney-Starkey)
instrumental

Side Two .. BLUE JAY WAY
(Harrison)

℗ 1967

PRODUCED by BIG GEORGE MARTIN

 PARLOPHONE   E.M.I. RECORDS
(The Gramophone Company Ltd.)
HAYES · MIDDLESEX
ENGLAND

MADE & PRINTED
IN GREAT BRITAIN

Printed and made by Garrod & Lofthouse Ltd.

Magical Mystery Tour

The Fool On The Hill Flying Blue Jay Way
Your Mother Should Know I Am The Walrus

BEATLES

MAGICAL MYSTERY TOUR

Includes 24-page full color picture book

Hello Goodbye Strawberry Fields Forever
Penny Lane Baby You're A Rich Man
All You Need Is Love

apple presents

THE BEATLES in
Songs and Music from a
Color Television Film called
"MAGICAL MYSTERY TOUR"

Side One

Magical Mystery Tour
John Lennon-Paul McCartney 2:48

The Fool on the Hill
John Lennon-Paul McCartney 3:00

Flying
Lennon-McCartney-Harrison-Starr 2:16

Blue Jay Way
George Harrison 3:50

Your Mother Should Know
John Lennon-Paul McCartney 2:33

I Am the Walrus
("*No you're not!*" said Little Nicola)
John Lennon-Paul McCartney 4:35
All side-one selections are
published by Comet Music Corp, ASCAP

...plus these other selections

Side Two

Hello Goodbye
John Lennon-Paul McCartney 3:24

Strawberry Fields Forever
John Lennon-Paul McCartney 4:05

Penny Lane
John Lennon-Paul McCartney 2:57

Baby You're a Rich Man
John Lennon-Paul McCartney 3:07

All You Need Is Love
John Lennon-Paul McCartney 3:57
All side-two selections are
published by Maclen Music, Inc., BMI.
Produced by Big George Martin

AWAY IN THE SKY, beyond the clouds, live 4 or 5 Magicians.
By casting WONDERFUL SPELLS they turn the Most
Ordinary Coach Trip into a MAGICAL MYSTERY TOUR.
If you let yourself go, the Magicians will take you away to
marvellous places.
Maybe YOU'VE been on a MAGICAL MYSTERY TOUR
without even realising it.
Are you ready to go?
SPLENDID! The story begins on Page 7 . . . or 8 . . . .

2835

A COLOUR FILM FOR TELEVISION

with

GEORGE CLAYDON	**JESSIE ROBINS**
as Little George The Photographer	*as* Ringo's Auntie
IVOR CUTLER	**DEREK ROYLE**
as Mr. Buster Bloodvessel	*as* Jolly Jimmy Johnson The Courier
SHIRLEY EVANS	**VICTOR SPINETTI**
as The Accordionist	*as* The Recruiting Sergeant
NAT JACKLEY	**MANDY WEET**
as Happy Nat The Rubber Man	*as* Miss Wendy Winters The Hostess
NICOLA	**MAGGIE WRIGHT**
as The Little Girl	*as* The Lovely Starlet

MADE IN ENGLAND BY THE BEATLES
"Magical Mystery Tour" Book Edited by Tony Barrow
Editorial Consultants (for Apple): Neil Aspinall & Mal Evans
Photographs: John Kelly   Drawings: Bob Gibson
(c) 1967, NEMS ENTERPRISES LTD.

1

With *Yellow Submarine*, the Beatles were once again faced with the problem of how to issue a set of new recordings from a film. Once again, the obvious options were an EP or an album. Because there were only four new songs, the EP option seemed to make sense. But there was a problem with "It's All Too Much," whose long running time would need to be drastically edited down unless the disc's speed was reduced to 33⅓-rpm, which would result in a loss of fidelity. There also were concerns regarding the viability of the EP format, which was fading fast in the U.K.

Capitol did not even consider an EP and decided to issue an album with the four new film songs on Side One surrounded by "Yellow Submarine" and "All You Need Is Love." The other side would contain George Martin orchestrations from the film soundtrack. EMI and the Beatles decided to issue the same album.

The album's colorful front cover features images of the characters and foliage from the cartoon, and, of course, the Yellow Submarine. The white background front cover shows the Beatles standing on top of a gray mountain, with Old Fred and Jeremy Hilary Boob to the left of their image and the Lord Mayor of Pepperland to the right. The right side of the cover pictures, from top to bottom, the following forces of evil: a Butterfly Stomper, the Flying Glove, Apple Bonkers, the Chief Blue Meanie, a Snapping Turtle Turk and Blue Meanies. The lower portion of the cover has the Yellow Submarine to the left and Sgt. Pepper's Lonely Hearts Club Band to the right. "THE BEATLES" appears above the submarine in the same yellow and orange stylized font used on the movie poster. The submarine's periscope is surrounded by the words "YELLOW" and "SUBMARINE" in the same font. The phrase "Nothing is Real" appears in green above the right side of the submarine on the U.K. cover, but not on the U.S. cover.

The upper portions of the British and American back covers are similar, with both featuring the Beatles and the Yellow Submarine surrounded by the list of the Side One selections to the left and the Side Two selections to the right. The lower sections of the U.S. cover (shown above) contain bits of world history from *Beowulf* to the *Magna Carta* to the *Declaration of Independence* followed by a brief summary of the film's plot mixed with images of Sgt. Pepper's Lonely Hearts Club Band and other characters from the film. The liner notes were written by Capitol employee Dan Davis.

The lower portion of the U.K. album contains Derek Taylor's explanation of why he decided against writing the liner notes for the album ("nothing new to say about the Beatles") and instead presented Tony Palmer's entire review of the Beatles last album from the London Observer. Taylor urged people to "buy and enjoy the really wonderful *The Beatles* album."

You've PLEASED PLEASED us!

Thank You, Folks

Paul
John
George
Ringo

The Beatles February 1968 single, "Lady Madonna," marked a return to rock 'n' roll for the Beatles. After the psychedelic leanings and exploration of other genres of music found on the "Strawberry Fields Forever"/"Penny Lane" single, *Sgt. Pepper's Lonely Hearts Club Band* and *Magical Mystery Tour*, the song was unlike anything the Beatles had issued during the past 12 months. Paul, who wrote and sang lead on the track, told NME: "It is not outright rock, but it's that kind of thing–we think the time is right."

The time was right for two reasons. First, the song fit in comfortably with England's latest music trend. In an article on Britain's recent Rock 'n' Roll Revival appearing in the March 2, 1968 edition of Disc, the writer noted that the Beatles had lent their name to the rock revival with "Lady Madonna," which had a blatant rock feel and marked a "swing away from Flowerpower and back to the big beat." The magazine added, "what the Beatles do, everybody does." Record Retailer commented in its March 13 issue that the Beatles "switch styles from complex to simple with complete ease," describing the new single "instantly distinctive, almost frighteningly."

The March 9 NME observed that the Beatles had turned full circle, "back to square one again with a rocker!" The track had "clanking barrel house piano," guttural sax passages and an infectious beat.

For the Beatles, it must have seemed quite natural to return to their roots. But, of course, the Beatles gave the recording "their very own special touch" as so aptly described in the March 9 Disc by Penny Valentine, who loved the "thumping, raving piano and drum combination" and went on to say: "Instead of sounding like tired old baggy eyed rock given a new face lift, it sounds fresh and new without losing any of the brassy urgency we associate with Little Richard...Jerry Lee... Fats and Bill Haley."

The time was also right for another reason as put forth by Chris Welch in the March 9 Melody Maker: "After all that progression, the best thing they could have done was go backwards." British disc jockey Alan Freeman expressed similar sentiments in the magazine's March 16 edition: "After *Sgt. Pepper*, I don't feel they could have progressed any further and still made contact with their fans, and I do believe that, above all else, keeping contact with their fans is what they want to do."

EMI's advertisement for the single appearing in the March 16 music magazines (see page 38) contained a series of slanted lower case letters with no spacing. Those able to decipher the text discovered that the ad, in keeping with the record's return to rock 'n' roll, was describing the Beatles as they were back in 1962 and early 1963: "A new rock and roll combo direct from Hamburg with the Mersey beat now on EMI." This was followed by a bit of the song's lyrics: "Lady Madonna, children at your feet/Wonder how you manage to make ends meet/See how they run." After listing the song titles in a clear bold font, the slanted text concludes with: "A fab new release out now on Parlophone R5675."

The 1968 promotional photo taken for the "Lady Madonna" single appearing in the ad is a mirror image of a 1963 photo of the group (both shown on the preceding page) that was used in an EMI ad appearing in the March 1, 1963 New Musical Express at a time when the Beatles truly were a new rock and roll combo direct from Hamburg with the Mersey beat. A comparison of the two photos shows how much the Beatles had changed their appearance in just five years time.

Capitol ran the same ad in the March music trade magazines substituting its catalog number, Capitol 2138 (see page 66). It also used the color version of the photo for its "Lady Madonna" picture sleeve (see page 128).

The Magical Mystery Tour & Yellow Sub Sessions

On April 1, 1967, the Beatles entered Abbey Road Studio 1 to record the last song needed to complete *Sgt. Pepper's Lonely Hearts Club Band*, the reprise of the title track. Two days later, Paul, accompanied by Mal Evans, flew to America for a ten-day vacation to spend time with his girlfriend, Jane Asher, on her 21st birthday. It was during this visit that Paul began putting together ideas for a Beatles TV special based on a magical mystery trip aboard a coach. According to Paul, "the idea tumbled together that we'd hire a bus, take a bunch of people out and start trying to make up something about a magical mystery tour." During the plane ride home on April 11, Paul began writing lyrics for the title song and sketching out details about the film. Upon his arrival in London, Paul pitched his idea to Brian Epstein, who became excited about the project. Paul then met with John to go over the details, and the two began work on the film's title song, *Magical Mystery Tour*.

The Beatles convened at Abbey Road Studio 3 on April 25 to begin recording the title track. Additional sessions were held the following two evenings and on May 3, with a rough mono mix made the next night. The group recorded an instrumental jam on May 9.

Two nights later, on May 11, the group changed locations and projects, gathering at Olympic Studios to record the first new song specifically slated for their cartoon cinema film, *Yellow Submarine*. The Beatles were skeptical about the full-length cartoon and had no intention of wasting their best new songs on the venture when tunes were needed for their *Magical Mystery Tour* show, as well as upcoming singles and albums. *Yellow Submarine* would get leftovers and throwaways. By this time, they had already decided that a *Sgt. Pepper* reject, George's "Only A Northern Song," would be relegated to the cartoon. On this evening, they completed "Baby You're A Rich Man," although the song would soon be issued as a B-side.

The next night it was back to the familiar surroundings of Abbey Road Studio 2 to knock out another cartoon tune, the sing-along "All Together Now." This was followed by a May 17 session to record the first part of "You Know My Name (Look Up The Number)." On May 25 and 26, the group continued their magical mystery tour of London's recording studios with a session for another song for the cartoon, "It's All Too Much," at De Lane Lea Music Recording Studios.

The group returned to De Lane Lea for sessions on June 1 and 2. The first was an unproductive evening of jamming on the day *Sgt. Pepper* was released. This was followed by a brass and woodwind overdub session for "It's All Too Much" and more wasted jamming. Then it was back to Abbey Road on June 7 for three nights of work completing the instrumental track for "You Know My Name."

On June 14, the Beatles returned to Olympic Studios to record the initial backing track for their contribution to the Our World TV show, "All You Need Is Love." The song was completed during Abbey Road sessions held on June 19 and 23-25.

The Beatles came back to the *Magical Mystery Tour* project on August 22 with a two-evening session at Chappell Studios to record "Your Mother Should Know." This was followed by several sessions at Abbey Road, starting with September 5-8 to work on "I Am The Walrus," "Blue Jay Way" and "Flying." On September 16, the group did a re-make of "Your Mother Should Know" followed by the recording of "The Fool On The Hill" and overdub sessions for "I Am The Walrus," "Flying" and "Your Mother Should Know" on September 25-29. The group began work on their next single, "Hello Goodbye," on October 2 and completed "Blue Jay Way" on October 6.

After a one-nighter on October 12 at De Lane Lea for mixing and editing and the recording of an instrumental by accordion player Shirley Evans, the group returned to Abbey Road for overdub sessions for "Hello Goodbye" and "The Fool On The Hill" on October 19, 20 and 25 and November 2. Final mixing sessions were held on November 6, 7, 15 and 17.

Prior to leaving for India to study transcendental meditation with Maharishi Mahesh Yogi, the Beatles attended a session at Abbey Road during the first half of February 1968 to record their next single. On February 3, the group began work on Paul's "Lady Madonna." The following day they turned to John's "Across The Universe." On February 6, George added his vocals to an instrumental track he had recorded in India called "The Inner Light." The group then completed its overdubs to "Lady Madonna." Additional work was done on "The Inner Light" and "Across The Universe" on February 8. Finally, on February 11, the group knocked out the fourth and final song for the *Yellow Submarine* cartoon, "Hey Bulldog."

Magical Mystery Tour

Recorded: April 25-27 and May 3, 1967 (Abbey Road Studio 3);
November 7, 1967 (Studio 2)
Mixed: November 7 (mono and stereo)

Producer: George Martin
Engineers: Geoff Emerick (April 25-27 & November 7) and
Malcolm Addey (May 3); Richard Lush (April 25-27 & May 3) and
Graham Kirby (November 7)

Paul: Lead and backing vocals; piano; bass guitar (Rickenbacker)
John: Backing vocals; acoustic guitar (Gibson Jumbo); percussion
George: Backing vocals; lead guitar (Stratocaster); percussion
Ringo: Drums; percussion
Mal Evans and Neil Aspinall: Percussion
Embellishments: Maracas; cow bells; tambourines; bus sounds
Outside Musicians: David Mason, Elgar "Gary" Howarth, Roy
Copestake and John Wilbraham (trumpets)

Paul came up with the idea of basing a TV show on a magical
mystery tour in April 1967. He, assisted by John, wrote the title
track, *Magical Mystery Tour*. On April 25, the group entered Abbey
Road Studio 3 to begin recording the song. Additional sessions were
held the following two evenings and on May 3, with a mono mixing session the next night. Since Paul and John had yet to complete
the song, much time was spent rehearsing and fleshing out ideas.
Eventually, a backing track with Paul on piano, John and George on
guitars and Ringo on drums was recorded and mixed down to one
track. The group also raided the Abbey Road archives to make a tape
loop containing the sound effect of a cruising bus.

The next evening, Paul overdubbed his bass. All of the group,
along with Neil Aspinall and Mal Evans, added percussion, including maracas, cow bells and tambourines. Paul, John and George
contributed backing vocals, which were treated with heavy echo.
The following night, Paul recorded his lead vocal, backed by John
and George. The brass overdubs for the song were added on May
3, including David Mason of "Penny Lane" fame on trumpet. Mono
mixes were made the next night, and the tape remained on the shelf
for six months.

When a stereo mix was made on November 6, 1967, the
group realized that the song needed tweaking. During the mixing
session the following evening, sound effects and an additional vocal
by Paul were added to the stereo and mono mixes. The finished
master is a charming rocker that effectively opens the TV film, British
EP and Capitol LP.

The Fool On The Hill

Recorded: September 25-27, 1967 (Abbey Road Studio 2);
October 20, 1967 (Studio 3); Demo (Sept 6 in Studio 2)
Mixed: October 25 (mono); November 1 (stereo)

Producer: George Martin
Engineers: Ken Scott; Richard Lush (Sept 25-27) and Phil
McDonald; Demo (Geoff Emerick; Ken Scott)

Paul: Lead vocals; piano; bass guitar; recorder
John: Acoustic guitar; harmonica; Jew's harp
George: Acoustic 12-string guitar; maracas; harmonica
Ringo: Drums; finger cymbals
Embellishments: Sped-up chattering bird-sounding effects
Outside Musicians: Christopher Taylor, Richard Taylor and Jack
Ellory (flutes)

Although "The Fool On The Hill" was not recorded until
September 1967, Paul had the basic idea for the song several months
earlier. He played the unfinished tune for John in March 1967 while
the two were writing "With A Little Help From My Friends." Paul's
original April 11 notes about the film include the notation "SONG
(Fool on the Hill?)," indicating that from the very start he envisioned
the song being part of *Magical Mystery Tour*.

On September 6, Paul cut a live piano and vocal solo demo of
the song at Abbey Road. This interesting early version of the ballad,
complete with a campy ending, is on *Anthology 2*.

The group first attempted the song on September 25. The
backing track included Paul's piano and John and George on acoustic
guitars, with overdubbed harmonica by John and George. The third
take was mixed down to a single track to allow the addition of Paul's
lead vocal, Ringo's drums and a recorder solo played by Paul. This
version, Take 4, also appears on *Anthology 2*.

The next evening, the Beatles returned to the song and re-recorded many of the instruments, including piano, acoustic guitar
and drums. Paul also redid his vocal, changing some of the lyrics
along the way. The next night, he added another vocal to the song.

On October 20, the song was completed by the addition of
three flutes played by outside musicians. The song was mixed for
mono and edited down from 4:25 to 2:57 on October 25. The stereo
mix and edit were made a week later.

Paul's dreamy ballad appears early in the film during a
sequence in which Paul is shown standing atop a hill near Nice,
France, during sunrise. The scene also contains ad-libs of Paul
spinning, running and dancing, and close-ups of Paul's moving eyes.

Koh Hasebe/Shinko Music

Flying

Recorded: Sept 8 (Abbey Road Studio 3) and 28 (Studio 2), 1967
Mixed and edited: September 28 (mono); November 7 (stereo)

Producer: George Martin
Engineers: Geoff Emerick (Sept 8) and Ken Scott (Sept 28); Richard Lush

John: Chanting; organ; Mellotron (strings)
Paul: Chanting; bass guitar; lead guitar; Mellotron (trombone)
George: Chanting; acoustic guitar
Ringo: Chanting; drums; maracas; percussion
Embellishments: tape loops; sound effects; backwards tapes

The instrumental tune, "Flying," was recorded to provide incidental background music for the film. All four band members share the writer's credit (Harrison/Lennon/McCartney/Starkey) for the tune, which was originally titled "Aerial Tour Instrumental." According to Paul, the track was a simple 12-bar blues made up in the studio, with him providing the melody.

The Beatles began recording the song on September 8, 1967. Its basic rhythm track included organ, guitar, bass and drums. For Take 6, three separate organ parts were taped and played backwards. Overdubs on Take 8 added a Mellotron part by John and "Tra La La La La" chanting vocals by all four Beatles. The song ended with a Dixieland jazz segment from a tape on the Mellotron known as Rhythms & Fills-Dixie Trombone, which also featured banjo. This ending was later edited out.

On September 28, additional overdubs took place, including guitar, a second Mellotron part and various percussion instruments by Ringo. The track was then embellished by various sound effects and tape loops compiled by John and Ringo. The song, still known as "Aerial Tour Instrumental," had a running time of 9:36. After completion of the overdubs, the track was mixed for mono and edited down to 2:14. The finished master is dominated by keyboards, Ringo's drumming and chanting vocals.

In the film, the song provides the musical backdrop to scenes of landscapes and clouds photographed from the air. A significant number of these images are color-tinted outtakes of aerial shots from Stanley Kubrick's *Dr. Strangelove*. Denis O'Dell, who produced the *Magical Mystery Tour* film, had worked on *Dr. Strangelove*. He was allowed to use the leftover aerial footage, which had been shot over the Arctic for the scene featuring the American B-52 bombers heading over the Polar region on their way to drop nuclear bombs on Russia.

Blue Jay Way

Recorded: Sept 6 & 7 and Oct 6, 1967 (Abbey Road Studio 2)
Mixed: November 7 (mono and stereo)

Producer: George Martin
Engineers: Geoff Emerick (Sept 6 & Oct 6) and Peter Vince (Sept 7); Ken Scott (Sept 6 & 7) and Richard Lush (Oct 6)

George: Lead and backing vocals; Hammond Organ
Paul: Backing vocal; bass guitar (Rickenbacker)
John: Backing vocal; tambourine; organ
Ringo: Drums
Outside musician: Peter Willison (Cello)

George Harrison's contribution to the project was "Blue Jay Way," a psychedelic dirge written on the evening of August 1, 1967, while on vacation. According to George:

"I'd rented a house in Los Angeles on—Blue Jay Way, and I'd arrived there from England. I was waiting around for Derek and Joan Taylor who were then living in L.A. I was very tired after the flight and the time change and I started writing, playing a little electric organ that was in the house. It had gotten foggy and they couldn't find the house for some time. The mood is also slightly Indian."

On September 6, the Beatles recorded the backing track to the song in one take. It featured George on Hammond organ (two parts on separate tracks), Paul on bass, John on tambourine and Ringo on drums. The next evening the Beatles made full use of the studio tricks they had previously mastered. During the organ reduction to a single track, the parts were treated with extensive ADT. George's vocals were given full ADT treatment, creating an eerie phasing effect. George, John and Paul supplied the backing vocals, which were sent through a Leslie speaker. One month later, on October 6, cello and tambourine parts were overdubbed onto the tape.

Mono and stereo mixes were completed the following month on November 7. On the stereo mix, a backwards version of the song is faded into the mix between vocal lines. The mono mix does not have this embellishment. The textured sound of the finished master, with its swirling vocals, organ and strings, conveys the feeling of fog rolling into the listener's room through the speakers.

The film sequence for "Blue Jay Way" opens with a kaleidoscope effect of images depicting George sitting in a fog. It mixes in scenes of various activities filmed in Ringo's back yard, including each of the Beatles taking turns playing a white cello and the group tossing a soccer ball. The video's heavily filtered psychedelic images effectively capture the mood of the song.

Your Mother Should Know

Recorded: Aug 22 & 23 (Chappell Recording Studios), Sept 16 (Abbey Road Studio 3) and Sept 29 (Studio 2), 1967
Mixed: October 2 (mono); November 6 (stereo)

Producer: George Martin
Engineers: John Timperly & John Iles (Aug 22 & 23); Ken Scott (Sept 16 & 29); Jeff Jarratt (Sept 16) and Graham Kirby (Sept 29)

Paul: Lead and backing vocals; piano; bass guitar
John: Backing vocal; organ
George: Backing vocal; acoustic guitar
Ringo: Drums; tambourine (possibly Paul)

"Your Mother Should Know" was written by Paul on his harmonium at his Cavendish Avenue home in London. McCartney recalls that he dreamed up the song as a production number, "a very music-hall kind of thing." The song is similar in style to "When I'm Sixty-Four." Although it does not contain clarinets, brass or strings, it just feels like it does. According to Paul, he was "advocating peace between the generations." The song's message is: "your mother might know more than you think she does. Give her credit."

The first session for the song took place on August 22 and 23, 1967, at Chappell Recording Studios. The Beatles went through eight takes on the first evening before completing a satisfactory backing track featuring Paul on piano and Ringo on drums. The second evening was spent on overdubs, including Paul's lead vocal and backing vocals by Paul, John and George and probably George on acoustic guitar. The session was significant in that it was the last time the Beatles saw Brian Epstein, who died four days later on August 27.

Paul was not satisfied with the Chappell recordings, so he ran the band through a remake of the song at Abbey Road on September 16, 1967. These takes were assigned numbers 20-30. On the Abbey Road version of the song, the sound and style of Ringo's snare drum is similar to that of a drummer in a military marching band. This version also features Paul's lead vocal, backed by harmonium and piano, the latter recorded to sound like a harpsichord. Paul didn't get the sound he was looking for, so the remake was not used. Take 27 appears on *Anthology 2*, giving listeners the opportunity to hear the previously unissued alternate arrangement of the song.

After further review, Paul decided that the Chappell version of the song could be salvaged with overdubs. On September 29, he and John entered Abbey Road to provide the finishing touches: Paul on bass and John on organ.

"Your Mother Should Know" is given a grand Hollywood send-up at the end of the film. Paul explains:

"The big prop was that great big staircase that we danced down, that was where all the money went, in that particular shot on that big staircase. I said, 'Sod it, you've got to have the Busby Berkeley ending,' and it is a good sequence. Just the fact of John dancing, which he did readily. You can see by the fun expression on his face that he wasn't forced into anything."

I Am The Walrus

Recorded: Sept 5, 6 & 27, 1967 (Abbey Road Studios 1 and 2)
Mixed: September 29 (mono); November 6 & 17 (stereo)

Producer: George Martin
Engineers: Geoff Emerick (Sept 5 & 6) and Ken Scott (Sept 27); Richard Lush (Sept 5 & 29) and Ken Scott (Sept 5)

John: Lead vocals; electric piano (Hohner Pianet)
Paul: Tambourine; bass guitar
George: Guitar
Ringo: Drums
Outside musicians: Sidney Sax, Jack Rothstein, Ralph Elman, Andrew McGee, Jack Green, Louis Stevens, John Jezzard and Jack Richards (violins); Lionel Ross, Eldon Fox, Bram Martin and Terry Weil (cellos); Gordon Lewin (clarinet); Neil Sanders, Tony Tunstall and Morris "Mo" Miller (horns); The Mike Sammes Singers: Peggie Allen, Wendy Horan, Pat Whitmore, Jill Utting, June Day, Sylvia King, Irene King, G. Mallen, Fred Lucas, Mike Redway, John O'Neill, F. Dachtler, Allan Grant, D. Griffiths, J. Smith and J. Fraser

John's "I Am The Walrus" is one of the more interesting and complicated songs ever recorded by the Beatles. Its title was inspired by the Walrus and the Carpenter from Lewis Carroll's *Through the Looking Glass* (the sequel to *Alice's Adventures In Wonderland*). In his September 1980 interview with Playboy magazine, John recalled:

"In those days I was writing obscurely, a la Dylan, never saying what you mean, but giving the impression of something. Where more or less can be read into it. It's a good game. I thought, 'They get away with this artsy-fartsy crap.' There has been more said about Dylan's wonderful lyrics than was ever in the lyrics at all. Mine, too. But it was the intellectuals who read all this into Dylan or the Beatles. Dylan got away with murder. I thought, 'well I can write this crap, too.' You know, you just stick a few images together, thread them together, and you call it poetry. Well, maybe it is poetry. But I was just using the mind that wrote *In His Own Write* [John's first book] to write that song."

Although the Beatles had recorded the title track and "Your Mother Should Know" earlier, the recording sessions for *Magical Mystery Tour* did not really get underway until September 5, 1967. That evening, the group went through 16 takes of "I Am The Walrus" before obtaining an acceptable backing. Although the finished version of the song was an incredible texture of sound, the basic rhythm track is quite stark by comparison, consisting of John's electric piano, George on lead guitar, Paul on tambourine and Ringo on drums. The following evening, Take 16 was mixed down to one track to enable the recording of Paul's bass, a snare overdub by Ringo and John's lead vocal. This stripped down version of the song is on *Anthology 2*.

The song began to evolve towards its finished form on September 27. That afternoon, a group of 16 classical musicians entered Abbey Road's Studio One to add George Martin's score to the song. The instruments consisted of eight violins, four cellos, a contra bass clarinet and three horns. After another reduction mix, the song was ready for the addition of vocals. But rather than just use the group, the decision was made to bring in a choir of eight male and eight female singers. George Martin recalls: "We got in the Mike Sammes Singers, very commercial people and so alien to John that it wasn't true. But in the score I simply orchestrated the laughs and noises, the whoooooooah kind of thing. John was delighted with it."

The unique vocal session took place in Studio Two that evening. In addition to adding lines such as "Ho ho ho, hee hee hee, ha ha ha," the singers provided the chants appearing towards the end of the song. Although people claim to hear various messages in the chanting (including "Smoke pot, smoke pot, everybody smoke pot"), the score consisted of the males singing "Oompah, oompah, stick it up your jumper!" (borrowed from a 1940s recording by the Two Leslies) and the females contributing "Everybody's got one, everybody's got one." Great fun indeed.

The initial remix session for the song was held on September 28, but none of these mixes were used. The following evening, John participated in the most creative mixing session ever held for a Beatles recording. Seventeen remixes (numbered 6-22) were attempted, but only two were completed. The finished mono master is an edit of two. Remix 10 is fairly conventional and is used until the song changes tempo at the two-minute mark before the line "Sitting in an English garden." The song continues with Remix 22, which was done with a live radio feed into the console. After being scanned through various frequencies and programs, the radio stops on the BBC Third Programme, which was broadcasting a reading of William

Shakespeare's *The Tragedy Of King Lear*. Parts of Act IV Scene vi of the play are effectively mixed into the song, appearing first after John sings "I am the Eggman." By a stroke of good luck, Gloucester "responds" to Lennon's line with "Now, good sir, what are you?" After John sings "They are the Eggmen," Edgar can be heard saying "A most poor man, made tame to fortune's blows." Towards the end of the song, the radio is once again brought towards the front of the mix, providing the listener with a bit more of Shakespeare's prose:

Oswald: Slave, thou hast slain me. Villain, take my purse. If ever thou wilt thrive, bury my body. And give the letters which thou find'st about me to Edmund Earl of Gloucester. Seek him out upon the British party. O, untimely death. [Dies.]

Edgar: I know thee well: a serviceable villain; as duteous to the vices of thy mistress as badness would desire.

Gloucester: What, is he dead?

Edgar: Sit you down, father; rest you.

"I Am The Walrus" was first mixed for stereo on November 6. Creating a true stereo mix posed a problem since the live BBC radio feed had been mixed directly into the song during mono mixing session. Because there was no way to isolate the radio feed, the mono mix was used for the last part of the song containing the King Lear performance. The first part of the song was mixed for stereo and then edited to mono Remix 22 for the conclusion. The switch from stereo to mono occurs at the two-minute mark when the song changes tempo just before the line "Sitting in an English garden." Capitol's *Magical Mystery Tour* LP uses this November 6 stereo mix.

A new stereo mix of the first part of "I Am The Walrus" was made on November 17. It opens with six sets of the two-note pattern, while the original stereo mix only has four sets (as does the mono mix). The new mix has more clarity, particularly in the keyboards and John's lead vocal. The stereo EP uses this later mix.

The blending of the Beatles, the Mike Sammes singers, a 16-piece orchestra and Shakespeare results in a bizarre and thought-provoking ending suitable for a truly remarkable studio creation. George Martin described it best, stating that the song was a result of "organized chaos."

The film's presentation of "I Am The Walrus" is relatively straightforward. It starts off as a performance video with John on piano, Paul on his Rickenbacker bass, George on a psychedelic-painted Fender Stratocaster guitar and Ringo on drums. It then mixes in shots of the group dressed in either their psychedelic mod clothing or animal costumes, with John, not Paul, in the walrus suit.

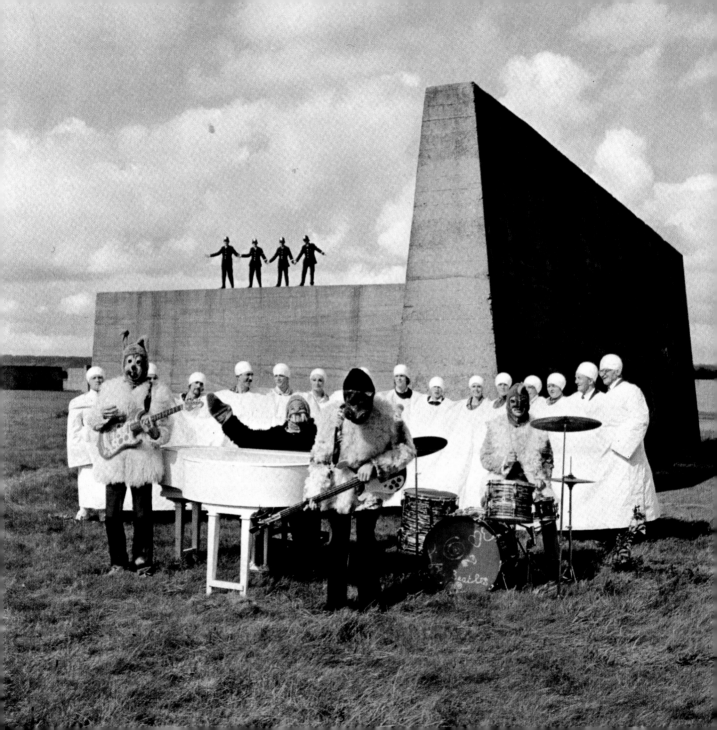

Hello Goodbye

Recorded: October 2, 19, 20 & 25 and November 2, 1967 (Abbey Road Studios 1, 2 and 3)
Mixed: November 2 (mono); November 6 (stereo)

Producer: George Martin
Engineers: Ken Scott (Oct sessions) and Geoff Emerick (Nov 2); Graham Kirby (Oct 2 & 25), Richard Lush (Oct 19), Phil McDonald (Oct 20) and Jeff Jarratt (Nov 2)

Paul: Lead vocal; piano; bass guitar
John: Backing vocal; organ; guitar
George: Backing vocal; tambourine; lead guitar (through Leslie)
Ringo: Drums; maracas
Embellishments: Bongos; conga; handclaps
Outside musicians: Kenneth Essex and Leo Birncaum (violas)

Although recorded during the *Magical Mystery Tour* sessions, "Hello Goodbye" was planned as a single for release concurrent with, but not included in, the project.

Beatles confidant Alistair Taylor was present during the creation of the song at Paul's Cavendish Avenue home. According to Taylor, he asked McCartney to explain how he wrote songs. Paul led him into the dining room and sat down behind an old harmonium. He asked Taylor to shout the opposite of what he said and then told Taylor that he would make up a tune. They ran through "black"/"white," "yes"/"no," "good"/"bad," "hello"/"goodbye" before degenerating into a series of curse words and uncontrollable laughter. McCartney then fashioned opposite pairings into a song.

In Barry Miles' *Many Years From Now*, Paul noted that duality was a deep theme in the universe, and that the song was easy to write. "You say goodbye, I say hello. You say stop, I say go. I was advocating the more positive side of the duality."

Originally titled "Hello Hello," the song's basic rhythm track, consisting of Paul on piano, John on organ, Ringo on drums and George on tambourine, plus overdubbed maracas, bongos and conga, was completed in 14 takes on October 2, 1967. The following embellishments were added to the tape on October 19: Paul's sped-up lead vocals; backing vocals by Paul, John and George; Harrison's guitar played through a Leslie speaker cabinet; and handclaps. The next evening, Kenneth Essex and Leo Birncaum contributed viola. Paul added bass parts on October 25 and November 2.

The finished master is a catchy, moderate tempo rocker with beautifully textured vocals and instrumentation. After the song appears to come to a halt, there is a tempo shift for a unique end bit known as the "Maori finale." This catchy bit of music was used behind the ending credits to the *Magical Mystery Tour* film. *Anthology Two* contains Take 16 of the song, with vocal and guitar enhancements from the October 19 session. There are subtle differences between this *Anthology* mix and the finished master.

The Beatles prepared three promotional color film clips for "Hello Goodbye." These were edited from lip-synced performances of the song filmed on November 10, 1967, at the Saville Theatre in London. Paul served as producer. In the first clip, the Beatles wear their *Sgt. Pepper* uniforms and mime their way through the song in front of a psychedelic backdrop. Paul plays his Rickenbacker bass, John plays his acoustic guitar, George plays his sunburst Epiphone Casino guitar and Ringo plays the drums (minus the Beatles drop-T logo drumhead). The film also contains a salute to the old days with cut-aways of the group wearing their collarless gray suits from 1963. During the Maori finale, the group is joined on stage by dancing girls wearing Hawaiian tops and grass skirts. The second clip is similar, but the Beatles wear casual clothes and mime the song in front of a pastoral image backdrop. Ringo's bass drum has the Beatles drop-T logo in place. The third clip has outtakes and shots from the first two edited with another performance with a different background image, including shots of the group frantically twisting the night away.

On November 15, George Martin prepared a new mono mix of "Hello Goodbye" without the violas. This was done to accompany the promotional clips because no viola players are seen in the films.

The Beatles arranged for the BBC to feature one of the "Hello Goodbye" promos on its November 23 broadcast of Top Of The Pops, but the BBC refused to show the clip as it violated the Musician Union's mid-1966-enacted ban on mimed television performances by singers and musicians. BBC producer Johnnie Stewart explained, "The first two films were absolutely out of the question. They were mimed from start to finish." The third film was considered a possibility, but Stewart realized that it would require so many cuts that the production would be spoiled. Instead, the BBC played the song over footage from the film *A Hard Day's Night* supplied by United Artists. Later broadcasts of the song on Top Of The Pops combined footage shot by the BBC of the group editing *Magical Mystery Tour* with unrelated BBC footage of four young people around a car in the snow who keep appearing and disappearing.

In America, The Ed Sullivan Show ran the first version of the "Hello Goodbye" promo on November 26. The clip was not shown on The Hollywood Palace as is often reported.

Strawberry Fields Forever

Recorded: November 24, 28 & 29 & December 8, 9, 15, 21 & 22, 1966 (Abbey Road Studio 2)
Mixed: December 22, 1966 (mono); December 29, 1966 (stereo)

Producer: George Martin
Engineers: Geoff Emerick & Phil McDonald

Note: For the first part of the December 8 session, Dave Harries served as producer and engineer until Martin and Emerick arrived

John: Lead vocal; guitar; Mellotron
Paul: Mellotron; bass guitar; piano; guitar; bongos
George: Guitar; swarmandal; timpani; maracas
Ringo: Drums; percussion
Mal Evans: Tambourine
Outside Musicians: Tony Fisher, Greg Brown, Derek Watkins and Stanley Roderick (trumpets); John Hall, Derek Simpson and Norman Jones (cellos)

John wrote "Strawberry Fields Forever" while in Almeria, Spain, for the film *How I Won The War*. The song's title comes from Strawberry Field, a Salvation Army home for orphans located near John's childhood home. John recalled going to parties there and took the name as an image. The song, with its childhood references, is in many ways an extension of his reflective "In My Life," but more thought provoking. In a little over three years, Beatles singles had grown from "Yeah you, got that something, I think you understand" to "Living is easy with eyes closed, misunderstanding all you see." In his 1980 Playboy interview, John explained some of the song's lyrics:

"So the line says, 'No one I think is in my tree, I mean it must be high or low.' What I'm saying, in my insecure way, is 'Nobody seems to understand where I'm coming from. I seem to see things in a different way than most people." Not only was John seeing things differently than most people, but now he was expressing it in his songs. The line "It's nothing to get hung about" comes from a childhood expression used by John. When his aunt Mimi criticized his behavior, John would respond, "It's nothing to get hung about," meaning his conduct didn't merit the death penalty.

Upon returning to England, John recorded demos of the song at his Weybridge home. An edited sequence of these demos with guitar and vocals is on *Anthology 2*. The intimate recordings allow the listener to envision how the song sounded when John auditioned it for George Martin at Abbey Road on November 24, 1966.

The Beatles first attempt at "Strawberry Fields Forever" sounded totally different from anything the group had ever recorded. The song opens with John's dreamy lead vocal and Paul on Mellotron, a new electronic instrument capable of duplicating the sounds of various instruments. The finished recording is an exquisite blend of Mellotron, guitar, slide guitar and creative drumming topped with John's double-tracked lead vocal and beautiful backing harmony vocals by John, Paul and George. Although Take 1 is a truly remarkable performance, John was not satisfied, and this early version of the song remained unreleased until its legitimate debut on *Anthology 2*.

The Beatles returned to "Strawberry Fields Forever" on November 28 to record a totally different arrangement. In its second incarnation, the song opens with a Mellotron introduction (on the flute setting) and the order of the lyrics is different. The melody for the Mellotron opening had been in John's head for years. In *The First U.S. Visit*, filmed in February 1964, John can be heard playing a brief segment of the melody on a melodica. This equally compelling and fascinating version of the song, featuring Mellotron, guitars, pianos, bass, drums and maracas, was completed on November 29, with Take 7 being mixed and used to cut four mono acetates. *Anthology 2* contains the mono mix of Take 7, along with an expanded instrumental edit piece tacked on the end.

About a week later, John decided the group should have another go at the song. On December 8, the band started on the new version's backing track, which was considerably faster than the previous arrangements and full of additional percussion, including timpani, bongos and tambourine. Takes 15 and 24 were edited to form Take 25, which was mixed down to one track and subjected to considerable overdubbing the following night. Ringo added percussion parts, while George contributed a swarmandal (an Indian harp-like instrument with 21 to 36 strings). Backwards-recorded cymbals were also superimposed.

On December 15, four trumpets and three cellos played by outside musicians were added, and the four-track tape was mixed down into Take 26. John then added two separate lead vocals. Additional vocals and piano were overdubbed on December 21. The completed Take 26 is a fast-paced heavy-sounding extravaganza, light years beyond the delicate original version of the song.

The following day John informed George Martin that he liked parts of the two most recently completed versions of the song. George Martin recalls: "He said 'Why don't you join the beginning of the first one to the end of the second one?' 'There are two things against it,' I replied. 'They are in different keys and different tempos. Apart from that, fine.' 'Well,' he said, 'you can fix it!'"

Miraculously, Martin and Geoff Emerick solved the problem by speeding up Take 7 and slowing down Take 26. This resulted in both versions running at approximately the same speed and having the same pitch. The first minute of Take 7 was then edited to Take 26 (minus its instrumental introduction) to form the finished master.

Remix sessions for "Strawberry Fields Forever" took place on December 29 and 30, 1966, with a mono tape copy of the finished master made on January 2, 1967, along with a mono tape copy of "When I'm Sixty-Four," supporting reports that "When I'm Sixty-Four" was originally slated to be the flip side of "Strawberry Fields Forever." The *Sgt. Pepper 50th Anniversary Edition* contains Takes 1, 4, 7 and 26.

In the fall of 1969, the song's fade-out ending caught the attention of those looking for clues of Paul McCartney's rumored death. John supposedly could be heard saying "I buried Paul," but his actual words are "cranberry sauce."

"Strawberry Fields Forever" was originally released as a single paired with "Penny Lane" in the U.K. (Parlophone R 5570) on February 17, 1967, and in America (Capitol 5810) on February 13, 1967. In England, the single failed to top the Record Retailer, Disc, NME and BBC charts, blocked by Engelbert Humperdinck's ballad "Release Me," although Melody Maker did chart the single at number one for three weeks. In the U.S., both sides of the single charted separately, with "Strawberry Fields Forever" peaking at eight in Billboard, ten in Cash Box and nine in Record World.

The Beatles prepared elaborate promotional films for the songs. Rather than being mere performance clips, the color films show images of the band and various locations meant to portray the feeling and mood of the songs. This was the forerunner of the concept videos that dominate music today. The films were produced by Tony Bramwell and directed by Peter Goldmann. The films were first shown in their entirety in England on the February 16 Top Of The Pops. They made their American debut on ABC's Hollywood Palace on February 25, and were repeated March 11 on American Bandstand and March 14 on Where The Action Is.

The scenes for "Strawberry Fields Forever" were shot on January 30 and 31 in Knole Park, near Sevenoaks, Kent, 20 miles from London. Several close-ups of the group's faces are intercut with scenes of the Beatles romping past kettle drums in a field, playing around a large dead oak tree and pouring and brushing brightly colored paint on a piano. The final result is best described as surrealistic psychedelica.

Penny Lane

Recorded: December 29 & 30, 1966 & January 4, 5, 6, 9, 10, 12 & 17, 1967 (Abbey Road Studio 2 except January 10 & 12, Studio 3)
Mixed: January 25, 1967 (mono); duophonic mix for Capitol LP

Producer: George Martin
Engineers: Geoff Emerick & Phil McDonald

Paul: Lead vocal; piano; bass; harmonium; chimes
John: Backing vocal; piano; guitar; congas; handclaps
George: Backing vocal; guitar; handclaps
Ringo: Drums; tambourine; hand-bell; handclaps
George Martin: Piano
Outside Musicians: David Mason (piccolo trumpet); Ray Swinfield, P. Goody, Manny Winters, Dennis Walton (flutes and piccolos); Leon Calvert, Freddy Clayton, Bert Courtley and Duncan Campbell (trumpets and flugelhorn); Dick Morgan and Mike Winfield (oboes and cor anglais); Frank Clarke (double-bass)

Paul's "Penny Lane" was the perfect song to link with John's "Strawberry Fields Forever." Like John's contribution to the single, "Penny Lane" was named after a real place in Liverpool. In Barry Miles' *Paul McCartney Many Years From Now,* Paul recalls:

"It was childhood reminiscences: there is a bus stop called Penny Lane. There was a barber shop called Bioletti's with head shots of the haircuts you can have in the window and I just took it all and altered it up a little bit to make it sound like he was having a picture exhibition in his window. It was all based on real things.... John came over and helped me with the third verse, as was often the case. We were writing childhood memories...."

Although "Penny Lane" did not generate three separate versions, it still took the band nearly three weeks to complete. Paul began work on the song on December 29, 1966, recording six takes of the basic piano track until he was satisfied. Two additional piano tracks (one played through a Vox guitar amplifier with reverb and the other played at half-speed and then played back at a faster speed to obtain a different sounding texture), a harmonium (also played through a Vox guitar amplifier), tambourine and percussion were added to fill out the four-track tape, which was then mixed down to one track the following evening to accommodate the addition of Paul's lead and John's backing vocals. On January 4, 1967, John added another piano part and George recorded his lead guitar. The next evening, Paul added another vocal track. On January 6, Paul's bass, John's rhythm guitar and Ringo's drums were recorded, along with John on conga drums. After another reduction mix, John and George Martin added additional piano. The group supplied hand-claps and Paul, John and George added background vocals. The *Sgt. Pepper 50th Anniversary Edition* contains Take 6 and vocal overdubs.

On January 9, outside musicians added four flutes, two trumpets, two piccolos and a flugelhorn. The next evening scat harmony vocals and a hand-bell were added to the tape. On January 12, outside musicians added two trumpets, two oboes, two cor anglais and a double-bass.

The final crowning touch was added on January 17 by David Mason, who was brought in by Paul to play the song's distinctive lead trumpet parts in the middle eight and at the end of the song. Paul had seen Mason's performance of Bach's Brandenburg Concerto No. 2 in F major on the BBC2 television series Masterworks on January 11. Mason recalls: "I took nine trumpets along and we tried various things, by a process of elimination settling on the B-flat piccolo trumpet. We spent three hours working it out. Paul sang the parts he wanted, George Martin wrote them out, I tried them. But the actual recording was done quite quickly. They were jolly high notes, quite taxing, but with the tapes rolling we did two takes as overdubs on top of the existing song."

At the end of the January 17 session, three mono mixes were completed, with the final mix, Remix 11, being considered the best. A tape copy of Remix 11 was made and sent to Capitol for use as the master tape for the single. After further review, it was decided that the song could be improved, so additional mixes were made on the evening of January 25. The third and final mix, Remix 14, was copied to tape for use as the finished master for the single.

The primary difference between Remix 11 and 14 is that Remix 11 has Mason's seven-note B-flat piccolo trumpet solo at the end of the song, whereas Remix 14 does not. The tape of the new finished master was sent to Capitol, but not before the label had pressed promotional copies of the upcoming single using Remix 11 and sent them to distributors, radio stations and reviewers. Thus, when the song received its pre-release air play in America, listeners heard the version with the trumpet solo at the end. The trumpet solo ending was not commercially released until Capitol's 1980 *Rarities* album (Capitol SHAL-12060), which edited the ending solo onto a stereo mix of the song. The complete mono mix with the trumpet solo used for the original Capitol promo record is included on the *Sgt. Pepper 50th Anniversary Edition*, but unfortunately in poor sound quality.

Anthology 2 contains a new edit and mix of the song combining and highlighting various elements of the many overdub sessions. Of particular interest is Paul's single-tracked vocal, the cor anglais and trumpets on the bridge and the extended B-flat piccolo trumpet solo at the end. At the song's conclusion, Paul can be heard saying, "A suitable ending, I think." And who are we to argue?

In America, disc jockeys and listeners preferred the more upbeat "Penny Lane" to its heavier flip side, "Strawberry Fields Forever." The two sides of the single were charted separately, with "Strawberry Fields Forever" making the top ten in Billboard, Cash Box and Record World, while "Penny Lane" topped all three charts.

The promotional clip for "Penny Lane" was filmed at Angel Lane, Stratford, London on February 5, and at Knole Park on February 7. Liverpool references in the song, including the Penny Lane sign, the barber shop and the shelter in the middle of the roundabout, as well as green double-decker buses with Penny Lane route signs, were filmed without the Beatles participation and edited into the film. The Beatles are shown riding horses. During the verse about the nurse who feels she's in a play, the Beatles, on horseback, symbolically ride past their instruments and equipment set up on risers for a performance that never takes place. It's as if the group is saying, "we've gone past that."

Baby You're A Rich Man

Recorded: May 11, 1967 (Olympic Sound Studios)
Mixed: May 11 (mono); duophonic mix for Capitol LP

Producer: George Martin
Engineers: Keith Grant; Eddie Kramer

John: Lead vocals; clavioline; piano
Paul: Backing vocals; bass; piano; guitar; tambourine
George: Backing vocals; guitar; maracas; handclaps
Ringo: Drums; handclaps
Eddie Kramer: Vibraphone
Mick Jagger: Backing vocals?

"Baby You're A Rich Man" was the first song specifically recorded for the *Yellow Submarine* cartoon. When the Beatles rush-released "All You Need Is Love" as their summer of 1967 single, the song was placed on the single's flip side. Because it was released as a B-side, "Baby You're A Rich Man" was not featured in the film (although its beginning is briefly heard).

The track began life as two separate songs: John's "One Of The Beautiful People" and Paul's "Baby, You're A Rich Man." Its lyrics may have, in part, been intended to poke fun of the Beatles manager, Brian Epstein. The song was recorded and mixed during a single productive session at Olympic Sound Studios on May 11, 1967.

As was typical of the group's recordings at the time, a wide variety of instruments was used. John played piano and clavioline, a three-octave electronic keyboard instrument that can only play one note at a time. It can produce guitar, strings, brass, winds and organ effects, which can be modified by knee-swell, reverb and tremelo. For the session, it was played with a double-reed setting. Paul gave the song its distinctive thumping bass sound and also played piano. George was on lead guitar with Ringo on drums. The engineers gave various instruments a backwards effect by overdriving the compressor. Engineer Eddie Kramer played a bit of vibraphone. John, Paul and George supplied the vocals, with Paul doing the high falsetto bits. George and Ringo added handclaps. Mick Jagger was one of several friends who dropped by that night to watch and may have participated in the backing vocals at the end of the song. (One of the session's two tape boxes contains the following notation: "The Beatles + Mick Jagger?")

The American music trade magazines charted "Baby You're A Rich Man" separately. The song peaked at 34 in Billboard and at 60 in Cash Box and Record World.

All You Need Is Love

Recorded: June 14 (Olympic), 19 (Abbey Road Studio 3), 23-25 (Studio 1), 1967
Mixed: June 26, 1967 (mono); duophonic; Oct 29, 1968 (stereo)

Producer: George Martin
Engineers: Eddie Kramer; George Chkiantz (June 14) and Geoff Emerick; Richard Lush (June 19, 23-25); Martin Benge (June 25)

John: Lead vocals; harpsichord; banjo
Paul: Backing vocals; double bass; bass
George: Backing vocals; violin; lead guitar
Ringo: Drums
George Martin: Piano
Outside musicians (conducted by Mike Vickers): Sidney Sax, Patrick Halling, Eric Bowie and John Ronayne (violins); Lionel Ross and Jack Holmes (cellos); Rex Morris and Don Honeywill (tenor saxophones); Stanley Woods and David Mason (trumpets); Evan Watkins and Harry Spain (trombones); Jack Emblow (accordion)

The Beatles began recording the backing track for "All You Need Is Love" on June 14, 1967, at Olympic Sound Studios, London. From the very start, the French national anthem, "La Marseillaise," opened the song in recognition of the international aspects of the upcoming television broadcast. Thirty-three takes were recorded, with John on harpsichord, Paul on double-bass, George on violin and Ringo on drums. George Martin played piano. Take 10 was considered the best and was given a reduction mixdown.

On June 19, the Beatles returned to Abbey Road's Studio Three to overdub vocals, piano, banjo and drums onto Take 10. Two days later, a mono acetate of the song was made and delivered to the BBC. On June 23, the first orchestral sessions took place, with the takes being designated numbers 34 through 43.

The following morning, just one day before the June 25th broadcast, the Beatles switched to Abbey Road's cavernous Studio One. Over one hundred journalists and photographers were invited into the studio for interview and photo opportunities. That afternoon, the Beatles and thirteen classical musicians went through a camera rehearsal for the BBC. Additional work on the song's backing track, assigned Takes 44-47, took place during the evening.

On the day of the broadcast, Studio One was a scene of mixed emotions. Although George Martin, the studio engineers and John Lennon were nervous about the upcoming live transmission, Abbey Road took on a party atmosphere. The guests of the Beatles, including Mick Jagger and Keith Richards of the Rolling Stones, Keith Moon of the Who, Eric Clapton, Marianne Faithfull, Donovan, Pattie

Harrison and Jane Asher, wore colorful mod clothing. The thirteen orchestra members dressed in formal evening attire. The Beatles wore custom-designed psychedelic costumes adorned with beading. John wore a blue flower in his hair while Paul had a red flower held in place by his headphones. The studio was full of streamers, balloons, placards, puppets, palm leaves, plants and flowers.

After additional work on the song's rhythm track and a few rehearsals for the BBC, the big moment was rapidly approaching. The backing track was mixed down and ready to roll on track one of the four-track tape machine. The plan was to record Paul's bass, George's lead guitar solo in the middle eight and Ringo's drums live during the television broadcast onto track two, the orchestra live on track three, and the vocals live on the remaining track. Ringo sat behind his drum kit while John, Paul and George sat on stools surrounded by their friends sitting crossed-legged on the floor.

As the broadcast begins, the Beatles are shown rehearsing the song, singing "Love is all you need" and "Love, love, love" before the BBC announcer breaks in with:

"This is Steve Race in the Beatles recording studio in London where the latest Beatles record is at this moment being built up. Not just a single performance, but a whole month's worth of performances. With some friends in to help the atmosphere, this is quite an occasion."

The group continues its rehearsal of the vocal parts over the backing track, which has the harpsichord and piano sounding more up-front than in the finished master. George Martin then interrupts and speaks to engineer/tape operator Richard Lush, "OK Richard, that'll do. Kill it." After the tape is stopped, Martin continues, "I think that was very good. Thank you John, that's fine. I think that will do for the vocal backing, very nicely. We'll get the musicians in now." After John responds, "Great, oh great, great," Martin says, "Thank you. Run back the tape please, Richard." With the sound of the tape being rewound in the background, BBC announcer Steve Race continues with his narration:

"There are several days work on that tape. For perhaps the hundredth time, the engineer runs it back to the start for yet another stage in the making of an almost certain hit record. The supervisor is George Martin, the musical brain behind all the Beatles records. There's the orchestra coming into the studio now, and you'll notice that the musicians are not rock 'n' roll youngsters. The Beatles get on best with symphony men. The boys began by making a basic instrumental track on their own. Then they added on top

of that a second track of vocal backgrounds, and they just added a third track. Now comes the final stage. It brings in a solo vocal from John Lennon, and, for the first time, the orchestra. Here then is final mixed track, take one of a song which we offer to the whole world, 'All You Need Is Love.'"

As the announcer concludes, John can be heard singing "She loves you, yeah, yeah, yeah, she loves you, yeah." George Martin then gives out final instructions over sounds of the group ad-libbing, which continue until the tape rolls with its "one, two, three" count-in. The horns open the song with the introduction to the French national anthem, followed by the "Love, love, love" vocal refrain and the string instruments. John then sings the lead vocal over the backing track, joined live by Paul and George on backing vocals, Paul on bass, George on the song's guitar solo and Ringo on drums.

The protracted fade out of the song featuring the group singing the refrain "Love is all you need" is mixed with many interesting sounds, starting with a trumpet solo by David Mason, who played the distinctive piccolo trumpet part on "Penny Lane." This is followed by the saxophones playing part of the melody of Glenn Miller's "In The Mood." After John says "Yesterday," the string instruments contribute strands of "Greensleeves" over which John (joined by Paul) ad-libs, "Oh, yeah, she loves you, yeah, yeah, yeah, she loves you, yeah, yeah, yeah." The song then ends in a mixture of the vocal refrain, David Mason's trumpet, "In The Mood" and "Greensleeves." As the music stops, someone calls out "Happy New Year, everybody."

And that's the way it was transmitted to approximately 400 million people around the globe. The Beatles would have had an even greater audience had the Soviet Union and other Communist bloc countries not pulled out of the project a week before the broadcast.

After their guests left the studio, the Beatles made minor overdubs to the tape of the live broadcast (Take 58). Ringo added a snare drum roll to the introduction of the song, and John re-recorded part of his vocal. The song was mixed for mono the following day.

Although the Our World television program was broadcast in black and white, the *Anthology* video effectively switches to a computer-enhanced colorized version of the film at the point where John begins his lead vocal. The *Anthology* video soundtrack uses the finished master of the song in place of the audio from the original BBC broadcast of June 25, 1967. The *Beatles 1* video collection contains a full-length colorized version of the performance, with new stereo and 5.1 mixes available.

Banding and Mastering of the Capitol LP

The stereo *Magical Mystery Tour* album was mastered by Maurice Long on November 10, 1967. Capitol placed the six songs from the *Magical Mystery Tour* British EP on Side One, although it changed the running order of the songs. All but one of the stereo mixes matched those on the EP. Capitol used an earlier mix for "I Am The Walrus." Five songs from singles were placed on Side Two. "Hello Goodbye" and "Strawberry Fields Forever" were true stereo mixes, while "Penny Lane," "Baby You're A Rich Man" and "All You Need Is Love" were Capitol-created fake stereo duophonic mixes. When EMI finally issued the album in 1976, it used the Capitol stereo master tape even though all songs had stereo mixes by then.

The mono album was also mastered on November 10. It uses the same mono mixes found on the mono EP and the mono mixes used on the singles. The mix of "I Am The Walrus" on the LP varies slightly from that of the Capitol single, which is missing an edit.

Yellow Submarine

Recorded: May 26 (Abbey Road Studio 3) and June 1, 1966 (Studio 2)
Mixed: June 3 (mono); June 22 (stereo)

Producer: George Martin (June 1 only)
Engineers: Geoff Emerick; Phil McDonald

Ringo: Lead vocal; drums
John: Backing vocals and effects; acoustic guitar ("Jumbo")
Paul: Backing vocals and effects; bass guitar
George: Backing vocals and effects; tambourine
Mal Evans: Backing vocals; bass drum
Outside musicians: Brass band instruments (names unknown)
Sound effects: John Skinner and Terry Condon (swirling chains in a water-filled metal bathtub); Brian Jones (clinking glasses and playing an ocarina, a vessel flute wind instrument); John Lennon (blowing bubbles in a bucket of water); George Harrison (swirling water in a metal bathtub); ships' bells; whistles; mechanical sounds (engines and gears); shouts, party chatter and more
Other voices on the chorus: Brian Jones, Marianne Faithfull, Pattie Harrison, George Martin, Geoff Emerick, Neil Aspinall, Alf Bicknell

"Yellow Submarine" was recorded during the sessions for the *Revolver* album. It was released simultaneously as an album track and single, paired as a double A-side with "Eleanor Rigby," on August 5 in the U.K. (Parlophone R 5493) and on August 8 in America (Capitol 5715). The song was number one on all of the British charts. In the U.S., the song topped the Cash Box and Record World charts, but

stalled at number two in Billboard, most likely a result of competing with "Eleanor Rigby," which received significant air play and was charted separately in the American trade magazines.

"Yellow Submarine" was a joyous sing-along written by Paul and John for Ringo (with an assist on the lyrics from Donovan: "sky of blue, sea of green"). Like many of the tracks recorded during the sessions for *Revolver*, it was totally different from anything previously released by the group. The finished song is highlighted by sound effects, clever improvisations and backing vocals, a catchy chorus and an overall party atmosphere. It's a song that sounds like it was as much fun to make as it is to hear.

The basic rhythm track was recorded on May 26, 1966, with Judy Martin sitting at the console in place of husband George Martin, who was suffering from food poisoning. The backing track, featuring John on acoustic guitar, Paul on bass, George on tambourine and Ringo on drums, was completed in four takes, all of which had an extended instrumental introduction that was later edited out. Ringo's lead vocal, along with backing vocals by John, Paul and George, were then recorded (as Take 5) at 47½ cycles per second (cps) iso that the vocals would be sped up when played back at 50 cps.

Recording resumed six days later on June 1, with George Martin back in the recording booth. The 12-hour session superimposed the numerous sound effects (bells, whistles, engines, gears, bubbles, crashing waves, clinking glasses and more), John's shouting ("Full speed ahead Mister Boatswain, full speed ahead") and response vocals (on the third verse), brass instruments (by outside session musicians) and backing vocals on the chorus (including Brian Jones of the Rolling Stones, George's wife Pattie Harrison, Beatle assistants Neil Aspinall and Mal Evans, George Martin and the Beatles themselves). The Abbey Road studio log indicates that the party ended at 2:30 a.m.

The "Real Love" EP single, issued on CD and vinyl at the same time as *Anthology 2*, contains a newly created and interesting mix of "Yellow Submarine." It begins with a previously unheard introduction with Ringo (briefly joined by John, Paul and George) reciting over the sound of marching feet (simulated by shaking a cardboard box full of coals) the following passage: "And we will march 'til three the day to see them gathered there, from Land O'Groats to John O'Green, from Stepney do we tread, to see his yellow submarine, we love it." The mix contains more sound effects than the released version of the song. The 1996 mix of the 1966 song reveals how creative the band could be when turned loose in the studio.

YELLOW SUBMARINE
(John Lennon-Paul McCartney)

Capitol
RECORDS

Maclen
Music, Inc.
BMI-2:40
5715
(45-X45619)
Produced in
England by
George Martin

THE BEATLES

MFD BY CAPITOL RECORDS INC., U.S.A. • TM Capitol MARCA REG

THE GRAMOPHONE CO LTD: ALL RIGHTS OF THE MANUFACTURER AND OF THE OWNER OF THE RECORDED WORK RESERVED · UNAUTHORISED PUBLIC PERFORMANCE BROADCASTING AND COPYING OF THIS RECORD PROHIBITED

TRADE MARK
PARLOPHONE

45 R.P.M.

NORTHERN
SONGS, NCB

7XCE 18396

℗ 1966

SOLD IN U.K. SUBJECT TO
RESALE PRICE CONDITIONS
SEE PRICE LISTS

R 5493

YELLOW SUBMARINE
(Lennon—McCartney)
THE BEATLES

MADE IN GT. BRITAIN

b/w Eleanor Rigby

 5715

Only A Northern Song

Recorded: February 13 & 14 & April 20, 1967
(Abbey Road Studio 2)
Mixed: April 21, 1967 (mono); October 29, 1968 (fake stereo)

Producer: George Martin
Engineers: Geoff Emerick; Richard Lush

George: Lead vocal; organ
John: Tambourine; piano
Paul: Bass guitar; trumpet
Ringo: Drums
Group: Tape effects; noises; percussion; glockenspiel

Although initially recorded for the *Sgt. Pepper* album, George's psychedelic-sounding "Only A Northern Song" did not make the cut. The band and George Martin preferred his "Within You Without You," so the *Pepper* reject was relegated to the *Yellow Submarine* cartoon film and soundtrack album.

"Only A Northern Song" is a humorous jab at Northern Songs, a publishing company that was partially owned by John and Paul, although George's target was majority owner Dick James. According to George's lyrics, "It doesn't really matter what chords I play, what words I say...as it's only a Northern song." As George was under contract to the company, his tune truly was only a Northern song.

The band recorded nine takes of backing tracks on February 13, 1967. Instruments included George on organ, John on tambourine, Paul on bass, Ringo on drums and all sorts of weird sound effects. The next evening, Take 3 was mixed down three separate times forming Takes 10-12. Two George Harrison lead vocals were added to Take 12, and the song was mixed for mono for demo purposes. Apparently not satisfied with the Valentine's Day mix, the group came back to the song on April 20, wiping out previous overdubs on Take 3 and adding bass, trumpet (reportedly played by Paul) and glockenspiel. Vocals were then added to Take 11, which was a Take 3 reduction mix from February 14. On April 21, the revised Take 3 and the revised Take 11 were mixed together in sync to form a very strange discordant-sounding mono master. As it was not then possible to make a stereo mix, the soundtrack LP version is fake stereo.

For *Anthology 2*, producer George Martin and engineer Geoff Emerick created a stereo mix that features vocals with different lyrics from the February 14 session. The *Yellow Submarine Songtrack* album from 1999 contains a true stereo mix of the master recording made possible by state-of-the-art digital technology.

All Together Now

Recorded: May 12, 1967 (Abbey Road Studio 2)
Mixed: May 12, 1967 (mono); October 29, 1968 (stereo)

Producer: (George Martin was not present; Paul ran the session)
Engineers: Geoff Emerick; Richard Lush

Paul: Lead vocal; acoustic guitar; bass guitar
John: Lead vocal (middle eight); harmonica; banjo; plastic sax
George: Backing vocal; acoustic guitar
Ringo: Backing vocal; drums
Embellishments: Handclaps; triangle; horn; percussion & effects

The Beatles knocked off another song for the movie, Paul's "All Together Now," at Abbey Road on May 12, the night after the session for "Baby You're A Rich Man." The simple sing-along was recorded in nine takes and subjected to numerous overdubs. Instruments included two acoustic guitars (probably Paul and George), bass guitar (Paul), drums (Ringo), harmonica (John), banjo (John), plastic sax, triangle, handclaps and a Harpo Marx-sounding horn. Paul sang lead and was joined by John, George and others present at the studio. The song's overall innocent feeling covers up its suggestive lyrics. ("Black, white, green, red, can I take my friend to bed?") Although not one of the group's more sophisticated efforts, the song is effectively used twice in the film, including the grand finale during which the phrase "All Together Now" appears in numerous languages.

Hey Bulldog

Recorded: February 11, 1968 (Abbey Road Studio 3)
Mixed: February 11, 1968 (mono); October 29, 1968 (stereo)

Producer: George Martin
Engineers: Geoff Emerick; Phil McDonald

John: Lead vocal; piano; lead guitar (Epiphone Casino)
Paul: Backing vocal; bass guitar (Rickenbacker); tambourines
George: Lead guitars (Gibson SG)
Ringo: Drums

In February 1968, the Beatles were told that they were one song short of the promised four new songs for the film. The shortage resulted from the release of "Baby You're A Rich Man" as the flip side to "All You Need Is Love" the previous summer. According to John, "They wanted another song, so I knocked off "Hey Bulldog." It's a good sounding record that means nothing." John's demo tapes of the tune contain him playing the basic piano riff and singing "She can talk to me, if she's lonely she can talk to me." By the time John was ready to record the song with the group, he switched to a more personal approach singing "You can talk to me, if you're lonely you can talk to me."

"Hey Bulldog" was recorded and mixed in mono during a ten-hour session on February 11, 1968. The basic rhythm track consisted of John on piano, George on guitar, Ringo on drums and Paul tapping two tambourines. Overdubs onto Take 10 included Paul's bass, a distorted lead guitar solo by John, additional distorted guitar by George, fuzz bass, additional drums, John's double-tracked lead vocal and Paul's backing vocal. The finished master has a bass-dominated heavy sound. Towards the end of the song, John and Paul ad lib barks, howls, shouts, gurgles and other vocal effects. And yes, John was right—it is a good sounding record.

The session was originally scheduled for the purpose of filming the group working in the studio to use in a promotional video for "Lady Madonna." However, the Beatles decided to record another song for the *Yellow Submarine* film, "Hey Bulldog," which features John on piano. This explains why the "Lady Madonna" promo clip shows John on piano rather than Paul, who played piano on the single. This footage was later re-edited to form a performance video for "Hey Bulldog," which is on *The Beatles 1+* video.

It's All Too Much

Recorded: May 25 & 26 and June 2, 1967 (De Lane Lea Studios)
Mixed and edited: October 16, 1968 (mono and stereo)

Producer: George Martin (June 2)
Engineers: Dave Siddle; Mike Weighell

George: Lead vocals; Hammond organ
John: Backing vocals; lead guitar
Paul: Backing vocals; bass guitar
Ringo: Drums; tambourine
Embellishments: Handclaps; cowbell; woodblock
Outside musicians: David Mason and three others (trumpets); Paul Harvey (clarinet)

George's "It's All Too Much" was another song relegated to the *Yellow Submarine* film. According to Harrison, the song "was written in a childlike manner from realizations that appeared during and after some LSD experiences and which were later confirmed in meditation." Recording took place on May 25 and 26, 1967, at De Lane Lea Music Recording Studios in London. Neither George Martin nor any of the usual Abbey Road engineers were present at the session,

which was engineered by Dave Siddle and Mike Weighell. The first evening was spent rehearsing and perfecting the backing track of Lennon on guitar (including the song's soaring feedback opening), Harrison on organ, McCartney on bass and Ringo on drums. The group recorded four takes. John starts things off by shouting what sounds like, "Too You're Much!," an apparent reordering of the title. The next night, a reduction mixdown of Take 4 was overdubbed with George's lead vocal, John and Paul's backing vocals, handclaps and percussion, including cowbell, woodblock and tambourine.

The song is full of all sorts of vocal shenanigans. Towards the end, the group sneaks in the opening line from "Sorrow": "With your long blonde hair and your eyes of blue." The tune was originally recorded in 1965 by the American garage band the McCoys (of "Hang On Sloopy" fame) and became a number four hit in England in 1966 by the Merseys. As "It's All Too Much" rolls towards its finish, John and Paul begin chanting "too much, too much" until they switch to "tuba, tuba" and then to "Cuba, Cuba."

On June 2, the group returned to the song and De Lane Lea Studios, this time with George Martin, a bass clarinetist (Paul Harvey) and four trumpeters, including David Mason who played the piccolo trumpet solo on "Penny Lane." The riffs added by the outside musicians included bits of Jeremiah Clarke's "Prince Of Denmark March."

"It's All Too Much" was not mixed until October 12, 1967, when George Martin, assisted by engineer Dave Siddle, mixed the song for mono at De Lane Lea Studios, where the track had been recorded four months earlier. The song ran for over eight minutes.

Both King Features and Martin thought the song was literally too much; however, the edits of the song in the movie and on the *Yellow Submarine* album are totally different except for the first part of the song. The version of the song appearing in the film features a verse that is edited out of the longer album version: "Nice to have the time to take this opportunity/Time for me to look at you and you to look at me." The song fades out 45 seconds after those lines for a total running time of 2:30. The album version of the song is considerably longer.

Following Martin's instructions, EMI engineers Ken Scott and Dave Harries made mono and stereo mixes and edits of "It's All Too Much" on October 16, 1968. The song was shortened to 6:27 by removing the early verse heard in the film and fading out during the lunacy at the end of the song. This explains why the movie version of the song has a verse not present on the album version even though it runs for less than half the time of the finished stereo master.

Lady Madonna

Recorded: February 3 (Studio 3) and 6 (Studio 1), 1968
Mixed: February 15, 1968 (mono); December 2, 1969 (stereo)

Producer: George Martin
Engineers: Ken Scott and Richard Lush (Feb 3); Geoff Emerick and Jerry Boys (Feb 6)

Paul: Lead and backing vocals; piano; bass; handclaps
John: Backing vocals; electric guitar (Casino); handclaps
George: Backing vocals; electric guitar (Gibson SG); handclaps
Ringo: Drums; tambourine; handclaps
Outside musicians: Harry Klein and Bill Jackman (baritone saxophone); Ronnie Scott and Bill Povey (tenor saxophone)

In order to complete the filming of, recording of songs for and editing of their *Magical Mystery Tour* TV spectacular, the Beatles were forced to postpone their planned autumn 1967 visit to India to study transcendental meditation with Maharishi Mahesh Yogi. Now that the project was completed, the group was finally headed for India in mid-February 1968. Prior to their departure, the group gathered at Abbey Road Studios in early February to record songs for their next single, which would be issued in March while the group was away. The first song recorded was one written by Paul.

McCartney recalls getting the idea for "Lady Madonna" from a photo in a magazine depicting a woman and baby with the caption "Mountain madonna." The magazine that Paul saw was the January 1965 issue of National Geographic, which contained the photo of a woman and her children along with the following caption: "Mountain madonna, with one child at her breast and another laughing into her face, sees her way of life threatened. Her people, of Malayo-Polynesian origin, took refuge in the hills centuries ago. Now they live among thousands of newly settled Vietnamese, who clear tribal areas for themselves, while Viet Cong guerrillas make the highlands a battleground."

Paul changed "Mountain madonna, with one child at her breast" to "Lady Madonna, baby at your breast" and wrote the song about motherhood. In a 1986 interview with Musician magazine he asked: "Baby at your breast—how do they get the time to feed them? Where do they get the money? How do you do this thing that women do?"

The rhythm for the song's piano part was inspired by Johnny Parker's piano on the traditional jazz tune "Bad Penny Blues," a 1956 British top twenty hit on Parlophone R 4184 written and recorded by jazz trumpeter Humphrey Lyttelton.

The Beatles began work on the song on February 3, 1968. To further capture the feel of "Bad Penny Blues," George Martin suggested that Ringo use brushes. Three takes were recorded with Paul on piano and Ringo on drums with brushes. The 50th Anniversary Deluxe Edition of *The White Album* contains Take 2. Later that night, Take 3 was enhanced by Paul's bass, John and George on fuzz-sounding guitars and Ringo on drums, this time with sticks, and then Paul's lead vocal and John and George's backing vocals.

The group completed the song on February 6. Paul added a second lead vocal and a second piano part. John and George joined Paul on the "See how they run" vocal refrain and a vocalized brass imitation bit in the middle eight of the song. After the addition of handclaps, four saxophone players (Harry Klein and Bill Jackman on baritone, and Ronnie Scott and Bill Povey on tenor) were brought in to provide a real brass instrumental break. The song was mixed for mono on February 15. The finished master is highlighted by Paul's rollicking piano and powerful Elvis-influenced lead vocal.

Anthology 2 contains a special remix of the song comprised of portions of Takes 3 and 4, along with saxophone overdubs. This stripped-down version of the song contains Paul's vocal and piano before double-tracking, as well as Ringo's brush drumming prior to the addition of his stick drumming. There is also a unique saxophone solo in the middle eight. After the line "Listen to the music playing in your head," handclaps are followed by the brass imitation vocals inaudible on the finished master. At the end of the song, there is a brief saxophone ad lib.

KODACHROMES © NATIONAL GEOGRAPHIC SOCIETY

Mountain madonna, with one child at her breast and another laughing into her face, sees her way of life threatened. Her people, of Malayo-Polynesian origin, took refuge in the hills centuries ago. Now they live among thousands of newly settled Vietnamese, who clear tribal areas for themselves, while Viet Cong guerrillas make the highlands a battleground. Thus thrust into the 20th century, the montagnard strives to find his footing in the tides of change.

Stilted, thatched huts shelter some 25 families near the protected hamlet of Gia Vuc (page 61).

59

The Inner Light

Recorded: January 12 and 13, 1968 (HMV Studios, Bombay);
February 6 (Abbey Road Studio 1) and 8 (Studio 2), 1968
Mixed: February 8, 1968 (mono); January 27, 1970 (stereo)

Producer: George Harrison (Jan 1968); George Martin (Feb 1968)
Engineers: Geoff Emerick and Jerry Boys (Feb 6); Ken Scott and
Richard Lush (Feb 8)

George: Lead vocals
Paul and John: Backing vocals
Indian musicians: Sharad Kumar and Hanuman Jadev (shehnai);
SR Kencare (flute); Ashish Kahn (sarod); Mahapurush Misra (tabla,
pakhawaj); Rijram Desad (harmonium)

George's "The Inner Light" was recorded on two continents. The instrumental backing track, which includes harmonium, flute, shehnai (a quadruple-reed Indian oboe), sarod (a multiple-stringed instrument of the lute family) and various Indian percussion instruments (pakhawaj, tabla and tabla tarang), was recorded on January 12 and 13, 1968, with local Indian musicians under George's supervision at EMI's HMV Studios in Bombay (now known as Mumbai). The session took place towards the end of George's trip to India to record music for the soundtrack to the *Wonderwall* film. The film's soundtrack album, *Wonderwall Music*, was released in the U.K. on November 1, 1968, and in America on December 2, 1968.

The song's lyrics were derived from the poem "The Inner Light," which was a Juan Mascaró translation of "The Tao Te Ching XLVII." Mascaró, a Sanskrit professor at Cambridge University, wrote George a letter suggesting he put a few words of "Tao" into music. George was captivated by the poem and expanded it into his song.

The 50th Anniversary Deluxe Edition of *The White Album* contains the Bombay, India instrumental track over which George added his vocals on February 6 at EMI Studios in London. Paul and John overdubbed backing vocals two days later, after which the song was mixed for mono. An alternate backing track from the Bombay session is on the 2014 remastered edition of *Wonderwall Music*.

During the February 1968 session the Beatles recorded two additional songs, both written by John. "Across The Universe" was a beautiful song, but John was not satisfied with the recording, so it was withdrawn from consideration as the group's next single. "Hey Bulldog," which was recorded specifically for inclusion in the cartoon film *Yellow Submarine*, was never in the running for single release. This left George's "The Inner Light" as the B-side by default, although it was certainly worthy.

Across The Universe (Wildlife Version)

Recorded: February 4 and 8, 1968 (Abbey Road Studios 3 & 2)
Mixed: February 8, 1968

Producer: George Martin
Engineers: Martin Benge and Phil McDonald (Feb 4); Ken Scott and
Richard Lush (Feb 8)

John: Lead vocal; acoustic guitar (Martin D-28); organ
Paul: Backing vocal; piano; bass guitar; acoustic guitar (Take 2)
George: Tamboura; wah-wah guitar
Ringo: Tom-toms; svaramandal (Take 2)
George Martin: piano
Backing vocals: Lizzie Bravo; Gayleen Pease

John considered "Across The Universe" one of his best lyrics. According to Lennon, the song wrote itself. One evening his wife Cynthia had been "going on and on about something and she'd gone to sleep." John "kept hearing these words over and over, flowing like an endless stream." Knowing that he couldn't get to sleep until he put it on paper, Lennon got out of bed and went downstairs to write. The song's verses contain beautiful and somewhat trippy imagery. The chorus mixes the Sanskrit words "Jai Guru Deva" (victory to the Guru-God) and "Om" (Hindu's most sacred mantra or holy sound) with the phrase "Nothing's gonna change my world."

"Across The Universe" was recorded at the same session that produced "Lady Madonna," "The Inner Light" and "Hey Bulldog." On February 4, 1968, the Beatles recorded six takes of "Across The Universe." The first take was an instrumental track consisting of John on his Martin D-28 acoustic guitar, George on tamboura and Ringo on tom-toms. Take 2 features a beautiful Lennon vocal, John and Paul on Martin D-28 acoustic guitars, George on tamboura and Ringo on svaramandal. This pure unadulterated recording is on *Anthology 2*.

The Beatles experimented with different arrangements for Takes 4 through 7 (there was no Take 3). The deluxe *White Album* anniversary edition contains Take 6, which is a recording with John on vocal and acoustic guitar accompanied by Ringo on tom-toms. Take 7 has the same basic arrangement as 6, but adds George on tamboura. All instruments were run through a Leslie speaker and subjected to artificial double tracking. John's lead vocal was then recorded with the tape running slower than normal to give it a sped-up effect upon playback.

John and Paul wanted to add falsetto vocals, but realized that the desired high harmonies were out of their range. Rather than attempt to round up professional singers on a Sunday evening, Paul asked if any of the female fans hanging out in Abbey Road's corridor could hold a high note. When 16-year-old Lizzie Bravo said she could, she and 17-year-old Gayleen Pease were brought to Studio 3 to sing "Nothing's gonna change my world" over the song's backing track.

After the girls completed their parts, Take 7 was given a reduction mix (designated Take 8) to allow for additional overdubs. One of the newly vacated tracks was filled with backwards recordings of Paul's bass and Ringo's drums. The Beatles then recorded three takes of sound effects, which included multi-layered humming, guitar and a drone-like sound. The tapes of these embellishments were played backwards and added to Take 8. A mono mix was made and transferred to an acetate for John. This unique mix of the song is known among collectors as the "Hums Wild" version.

On February 8, all the backwards additions from October 4 were removed from Take 8 to allow for new overdubs, including a new lead vocal from John, organ by Lennon and George Martin, maracas and wah-wah guitar by Harrison, piano by McCartney at the end and backing vocals from John and Paul.

Comedian Spike Milligan happened to be at Abbey Road when the sessions took place and visited George Martin and the boys in the control room to Studio No. 2. At that time he was organizing a benefit album for the World Wildlife Fund. When he learned of the group's decision not to issue the song, he boldly asked the Beatles if they would be willing to contribute "Across The Universe" to the project. Much to his delight, the group agreed to do so. When the song was mixed for mono at the end of the session, bird sound effects were added to the beginning and end of the track. This may have been done at the suggestion of Milligan or Martin.

The March 1968 issue (No. 56) of The Beatles Book reported that everyone who heard "Across The Universe" thought it was "really fantastic and deserved to be the new single;" however, John was not satisfied with the recording and blocked the track from being the issued as either the A-side or B-side to the single.

John's dissatisfaction with the February 1968 recording of "Across The Universe" prompted him to resurrect the song during the January 1969 *Get Back* sessions. Although the song had been donated to the charity LP, John was concerned the album wouldn't be issued and wanted to include the song in the current project. While at Twickenham, he and the group experimented with different tempos and sounds, including a heavier approach with Paul singing along with John, but none of these performances were satisfactory.

On January 23, after the Beatles moved the sessions to Apple, George asked John if they were going to record "Across The Universe." Lennon replied that they were not since the song was coming out on an EP. The extended play disc John was referring to was to include "Across The Universe" as a bonus track along with the four new songs recorded for the *Yellow Submarine* film. The group had received some negative feedback for the just-released *Yellow Submarine* LP because it only had four new Beatles tracks. The EP would give fans a lesser-priced option to obtain the film songs. A tape for the EP was later compiled and banded on March 13, 1969; however, the idea was dropped and the disc was never issued. The mono mixes of the five songs that were going to be on the EP were later released in 2009 on the *Mono Masters* CD.

By the fall of 1969, the World Wildlife Fund album was finally taking shape. The inclusion of an unreleased Beatles recording was a real coup. A line from "Across The Universe" was modified to form the album's title, *No One's Gonna Change Our World*.

On October 2, George Martin, with engineers Jeff Jarratt and Alan Parsons, mixed the song for the stereo LP. Martin sped up the tape of Take 8, shifting the song up a half step from D major to E flat, reducing the running time of the song and raising the pitch of John's voice. He also added the same sound effects of chirping birds and flying birds landing on water that had been used for the mono mix. The next day he banded the LP, which was released on the budget Regal Starline label as SRS 5013 on December 12, 1969. Although the album was not issued in the U.S., copies were imported. The Wildlife version of "Across The Universe" made its official American debut in 1980 on *Rarities*. It is on *Past Masters Volume Two*.

Because the Beatles were shown rehearsing "Across The Universe" in the *Let It Be* film, Glyn Johns was told to add the song to the *Get Back* album. On January 5, 1970, Johns went back to Take 8 (without the added sound effects) and made a fresh stereo mix with the tape running at its proper speed. He mixed out the Beatles backing vocals but kept the voices of Lizzie Bravo and Gayleen Pease because their vocals were part of the reduction mix of Take 7 and could not be mixed out of Take 8. To give the song its *Get Back* flavor, Johns left in a brief bit of studio chat that precedes the start of the song on the master tape (Lennon's "Are you alright, Ritchie?"). Johns then added the song to his revised *Get Back* LP, which was not issued. For the *Let It Be* album, Phil Spector slowed the tape, dropping the song from D to D flat, and added orchestration and choir. The *Let It Be...Naked* album uses Take 7 prior to its embellishments.

You Know My Name (Look Up The Number)

Recorded: May 17 & June 7 & 8, 1967; April 30, 1969 (Studio 2)
Edited: June 9, 1967; November 26, 1969
Mixed: June 9, 1967; April 30, 1969; November 26, 1969

Producers: Geoff Emerick (May 17); George Martin (June 7 & 8);
Chris Thomas (April 30, 1969)
Engineers: Geoff Emerick & Richard Lush (1967); Jeff Jarratt & Nick
Webb (1969)

John: Lead vocals; piano
Paul: Lead vocals; guitar(Casino); bass; tambourine; cymbal; piano
George: Guitar (Epiphone Casino); vibraphone
Ringo: Drums

Brian Jones: Tenor saxophone
Mal Evans: Gravel sound effects

Embellishments: Bongos; tambourine; handclaps; percussion;
crowd noise; applause

During the time the Beatles were knocking out songs for the "Yellow Submarine" cartoon film, they spent a few evenings recording the backing track for a free-spirited piece of nostalgic nightclub nonsense, "You Know My Name (Look Up The Number)." The song was recorded in several parts that would later be edited together. John lifted the title from a phrase appearing on the front cover to the 1967 London telephone directory: "You have their NAME? Look up their NUMBER." Although John envisioned the song as nothing more than the title repeated over and over again in the style of the Four Tops' "Reach Out I'll Be There," the end result was more reminiscent of Goon Show lunacy or the Bonzo Dog Doo-Dah Band than Motown soul. In his Playboy interview, John described the song as "a piece of unfinished music that I turned into a comedy record with Paul."

The Beatles began work on Part One on May 17, 1967. The group recorded 14 takes consisting of John on piano, Paul on guitar, George on guitar and Ringo on drums, supplemented by bongos, tambourine, handclaps and vocals. The group returned to the madness on June 7, adding overdubs to Take 9 and recording a separate rambling rhythm track that would not be used. The next evening the group recorded Parts Two through Five of the song. In addition to the usual instruments, such as Paul's piano and overdubbed bass, the song contains George on vibraphone and Brian Jones of the Rolling Stones on tenor saxophone. The next evening (June 9) the song was edited together and numbered Take 30. The 6:08 rhythm

track consisted of Take 9 of Part One, Take 12 of Part Two, Take 4 of Part Three, Take 6 of Part Four and Take 1 of Part Five. The song was mixed for mono and left alone while the group moved on to a more important project—the recording of "All You Need Is Love."

After ignoring "You Know My Name" for nearly two years, John and Paul entered Abbey Road studio on April 30, 1969, to overdub vocals, percussion and sound effects, including crowd noise, applause and Mal Evans shoveling a bucket of gravel. To add to the nightclub atmosphere, John asks the crowd for a big hand for Denis O'Bell, a name obviously derived from Denis O'Dell, who produced the *Magical Mystery Tour* TV film. Paul then takes on the persona of fictional crooner Denis O'Bell for the lounge act segment of the song. "You Know My Name," still running 6:08, was mixed for mono at the end of the session.

Earlier that evening, George overdubbed a new improved guitar solo onto Take 27 of "Let It Be." At that time, the group had no idea that the two songs would be issued together as the Beatles last British single nearly one year later in March 1970.

In November 1969, John decided that if the Beatles wouldn't release "What's The New Mary Jane" (a *White Album* reject) and "You Know My Name," he would issue the songs as a Plastic Ono Band single. He booked a session at Abbey Road on November 26 (serving as co-producer with Geoff Emerick) to remix and edit the songs. Mono Remix 3 from April 30, 1969, of "You Know My Name" was copied and renamed Remix 4. It was then edited down to 4:19. "What's The New Mary Jane" was mixed for stereo and edited.

Apple made test pressings of a single containing the songs, assigned a British catalog number (APPLES 1002) and announced a rush release date in England of December 5, 1969. An Apple press release stated that the disc featured John and Yoko backed by "many of the greatest show business names of today." This, however, was not to be. The single was put on hold on December 1 and was never released because the recordings were really Beatles songs and the release of the single was objected to by the other Beatles.

While "You Know My Name" would have been difficult to program onto a Beatles album, it was interesting enough to merit release. John finally succeeded in getting the song issued when it was placed on the B-side to "Let It Be."

Anthology 2 contains a new version of the song that restores much of what John edited out in November 1969. For the first time the song is in stereo and runs 5:42. The additional running time exposes more of the song's infectious comedic aspects.

YELLOW SUBMARINE ORCHESTRATIONS

Recorded: October 22 and 23, 1968
Mixed and edited: October 24 and 25 (stereo only)

Producer and conductor: George Martin
Engineers: Jack Clegg (CTS session)

Performed by: The George Martin Orchestra

For his side of the disc, George Martin decided to re-record selections from his score, which had originally been recorded for the film at CTS Studios (Cine-Tele Sound Studios) with Jack Clegg serving as engineer. According to Martin, "It was more convenient to do so – and no more costly since the original orchestra would have had to be paid twice anyway if we had used the soundtrack for the record." Six tracks were recorded at Abbey Road studios on October 22 and 23, with stereo mixing and editing taking place over the next two days. Out of the six songs, five were written by Martin, and one was his arrangement of Lennon and McCartney's "Yellow Submarine."

The first George Martin selection on the album is "Pepperland," a majestic-sounding classical piece featuring strings and horns. Martin successfully matches the dreamworld setting of Pepperland with a theme that is light and lilting, with a happy feeling at the end.

The medley of "Sea Of Time & Sea Of Holes" (identified as separate tracks on the LP jacket and on the first labels prepared for the U.K. albums) is an eerie-sounding track that mixes Indian and classical music, much as George Harrison had done on his *Wonderwall Music* LP. The opening segment is reminiscent of Harrison's "Within You Without You." Martin acknowledged Harrison's influence on the score, adding, "I used a tanpura drone as the background, and I wrote my strings with bendy notes that sound like the Indian dilrubas."

"Sea Of Monsters" is a quirky-sounding piece that starts off with classical touches, throws in a spaghetti-Western theme and ends with backwards tapes to match the images of the Vacuum Cleaner monster sucking up everything in sight. Martin recalls writing an entire section of backwards music for the orchestra to get the desired effect.

"The March Of The Meanies" is a sinister-sounding song that switches between a staccato sound and swirling strings. Martin acknowledged that he was influenced by Bernard Herman's scores for Alfred Hitchcock films. "I was using all the brass instruments in the orchestra, tubas and trombones, and gave a very staccato feel to the strings, a very choppy beat to it...."

The theme of "Pepperland Laid Waste" is one of hopelessness and devastation. Martin used his score to "convey there was the kind of wasteland that was left after the war."

The album closes with a spirited George Martin arrangement of the title song named "Yellow Submarine in Pepperland." The track is very upbeat, starting off in march tempo before slowing down for a poignant passage of verses. When the song returns to the chorus, the tempo increases and the full orchestra joins in to pound out the ending in the style of a marching band playing in unison. According to Martin, "It was a triumph in the end and everyone was happy and the 'Yellow Submarine' was a good tune to blare out."

1967 Tape Prepared for Cartoon Film

On November 1, 1967, George Martin, assisted by engineers Geoff Emerick and Richard Lush, prepared a tape of mono songs for use in the film, including "It's All Too Much," "All Together Now," "Only A Northern Song," "Yellow Submarine," a new mix of "All You Need Is Love" and a strange version of "Lucy In The Sky With Diamonds." For this special remix, John's vocal for the song's opening lines was replaced with Dick Emery "singing" new lyrics in his voice for the film character Jeremy Hilary Boob: "Picture yourself just of nuclear fission with library cards and a metaphor skies/ Somebody quotes you, you read from a source book, a concept with microscope eyes." Fortunately this was not used in the film.

Album Mixes and Banding

The four new Beatles songs recorded for the *Yellow Submarine* album were initially given only mono mixes. On October 16, 1968, "It's All Too Much" was given a new mono mix and its first stereo mix. The song was edited down from over eight minutes to 6:27. The remaining tracks, "Only A Northern Song," "All Together Now" and "Hey Bulldog," were given stereo mixes on October 29, although due to technical limitations, "Only A Northern Song" was a fake stereo mix. "All You Need Is Love" received its first stereo mix that day.

The *Yellow Submarine* album was issued only in stereo in the U.S. The album was released in a limited mono edition in the U.K., but it contained fold-down mixes of the stereo album. While this made sense for the George Martin tracks that were only mixed in stereo, one wonders why existing mono mixes were not used for the Beatles songs on Side One.

MAGICAL MYSTERY TOUR INCIDENTAL MUSIC

The instrumental track "Flying" began life known as "Aerial Tour Instrumental" and was most likely intended for use as incidental music in the TV film's soundtrack. Instead, it was not only featured in the film, but also ended up being issued as a song on the *Magical Mystery Tour* EP and LP. Only one other track of incidental music was recorded at Abbey Road.

Shirley's Wild Accordion

Recorded: October 12, 1967 (Abbey Road Studio 3)
Mixed: October 12, 1967 (mono only)

Producer: John Lennon
Engineers: Ken Scott; Richard Lush

Shirley Evans: Accordion
Reg Wale: Percussion
Paul: Maracas
Ringo: Drums

On October 12, 1967, "Shirley's Wild Accordion" was recorded for use as incidental music in the film. The composition, written by John and Paul and initially known as "Accordion (Wild)," was arranged and notated by Mike Leander, who scored the strings for the Beatles recording of "She's Leaving Home." The song was performed by Shirley Evans on accordion, accompanied by her musical partner and husband, Reg Wale, on percussion. Towards the end of the session, Ringo overdubbed drums and Paul added maracas and shouts.

The song was recorded for use as backing to a dream sequence in the film where Scotch comedian Nat Jackley chases a group of girls in swim suits around a pool as accordionist Shirley Evans plays on. The scene, directed by John on September 13, did not make the final cut of the film, although it was included in the bonus material of the 2012 reissue of *Magical Mystery Tour*, complete with "Shirley's Wild Accordion" without Ringo and Paul's contributions.

Although Shirley's poolside performance was edited out of the film, she still has a scene in the show. After Ringo sings a bit of "I've Got A Lovely Bunch Of Coconuts," she leads the bus passengers through an accordion sing-along that includes "Toot, Toot, Tootsie (Goo' Bye!)," "Frankenlied" (also known as "Valderi, Valdera"), "When Irish Eyes Are Smiling," "Never On Sunday" and "The Galloping Infernal" (also known as "The Cancan Song"). (In another scene, John briefly sings "There's No Business Like Show Business.")

Jessie's Dream

Another piece of incidental music, "Jessie's Dream," was used in the film during a scene where Ringo's Aunt Jessie dreams she is being fed mounds of spaghetti on a shovel by a waiter played by John. The track, credited to McCartney/Starkey/Harrison/Lennon, may have been recorded at John's house and features piano, Mellotron, sound effects and voices. It sounds like something out of the soundtrack to a science fiction space film, but more disjointed. "The Song Of The Volga Boatmen" is heard towards its end.

Mellotron Music and Sound Effects

Other bits of Mellotron music and sound effects weave in and out of the film, most notably during an early scene on the bus and the segments involving the five magicians played by the Beatles and Mal Evans. These scenes in the Magician's laboratory above the clouds have bubbling and electronic sound effects mixed with Mellotron. These bits may have recorded at John's house.

Instrumental Beatles Songs

The film uses an instrumental version of "She Loves You" from the Decca EP *Irvin's 89 Key Marenghi Fair Organ Plays Lennon & McCartney* (during the tug-of-war and wrestling midgets scene) and an orchestral version of "All My Loving" from the EMI HMV album *Beatle-Cracker Ballet* by Arthur Wilkinson and His Orchestra (during the tender love scene featuring Aunt Jessie and Buster Bloodvessel).

Instrumental Recordings

The film includes recordings licensed from de Wolfe Music, including "Circus Fanfare" (Keith Papworth) from *The Big Top* (DW/LP 3035) and "Winning Hit" (Herbert Chappell) from *Marching Highlights* (DW/LP 2972). The soundtrack also includes "Zampa Overture" recorded by The G.U.S. (Footwear) Band with Stanley Boddington.

Strip Club Music

The film contains a scene where the Bonzo Dog Doo-Dah Band performs "Death Cab For Cutie" while Jan Carson does a striptease.

Formats and Later Releases

Although *Magical Mystery Tour* was not the first Beatles album to be issued in the 8-track format, it was the first 8-track to receive billing in Capitol's advertising for a particular album. (Capitol began issuing albums in the format in late 1965 and continued doing so through the summer of 1982.) The company's trade magazine advert for the LP (shown on page 57) contains the notice: "Also available on 8-track Stereo Tape Cartridge." By the time the album was released in late 1967, the 8-track was gaining greater acceptance and was moving beyond being a format aimed primarily for use in motor vehicles. It was now becoming part of the lucrative home hi-fi market.

The 8-track format contained four segments of songs, known as programs, that needed to be approximately the same length of time. In order to satisfy this requirement, the running order of the songs was often changed, leading to the 8-track release of an album having a different running than that of the vinyl LP. In some cases, a track would be added to the 8-track version to better balance the four separate programs, particularly if the vinyl LP had 11 selections. And while the different running order was problematic in and of itself, the most annoying aspect of the format was that sometimes it was necessary to have a song split into two parts, with its first part appearing at the end of a program and the second part being placed at the start of the next program, separated by a very noticeable clinking sound.

For *Magical Mystery Tour*, the 8-track's running order totally destroyed the separation of the film songs from the singles. About the only similarity was that both formats opened with "Magical Mystery Tour" and closed with "All You Need Is Love." For Americans who experienced the album in the 8-track format, this is what they heard:

PROGRAM 1	PROGRAM 2
Magical Mystery Tour	Strawberry Fields Forever
Blue Jay Way	Baby You're A Rich Man
Your Mother Should Know	I Am The Walrus (Part 1)

PROGRAM 3	PROGRAM 4
I Am The Walrus (Conclusion)	Flying
The Fool On The Hill	Penny Lane
Hello Goodbye	All You Need Is Love

Magical Mystery Tour was the last Beatles LP to be issued by Capitol in mono. By December 1967, the vast majority of pressings of newly released albums were in stereo. Record store orders for the mono version of the album were so low that Capitol ended up with a surplus of mono *Magical Mystery Tour* albums, which were later shipped to Brazil where the conversion to stereo was lagging.

Capitol used true stereo mixes for the six film songs, "Hello Goodbye" and "Strawberry Fields Forever," but created fake stereo "duophonic" mixes for the other three tracks because no stereo mixes had been made for them at the time the album was compiled.

In England, *Magical Mystery Tour* became the first Beatles EP to be issued in mono and stereo. All previous extended play discs had been released exclusively in mono. By this time, stereo was gaining greater acceptance in the U.K. by both the record-buying public and by recording artists, producers and engineers. Stereo mixes were no longer afterthoughts made for the few Hi-Fi freaks who bought stereo albums.

While the Beatles and U.K. critics considered the mono *Sgt. Pepper* to be the definitive version of the album, reviewers praised the stereo EP. In the November 25, 1967, Melody Maker, Bob Dawbarn wrote that: "The stereo recording increases the effect of the Beatles harmonies and the action-packed arrangements." Norman Jopling wrote in the December 1 Record Mirror that the single "I Am The Walrus" sounded even better in stereo.

When EMI's West German branch, Electrola, initially compiled its *Magical Mystery Tour* album in Fall 1971, it used the Capitol prepared master with its three duophonic mixes. A few months later, the company requested and was sent stereo mixes for "Penny Lane," "Baby You're A Rich Man" and "All You Need Is Love." The remastered album with all stereo mixes was issued in February 1972.

⑧ EIGHT-TRACK CARTRIDGE
8XT 2835   3¾ IPS

THE BEATLES
MAGICAL MYSTERY TOUR

PROGRAM 1
Magical Mystery Tour
Blue Jay Way
Your Mother Should Know

PROGRAM 2
Strawberry Fields Forever
Baby You're A Rich Man
I Am The Walrus (Part 1)

PROGRAM 3
I Am The Walrus
(Conclusion)
The Fool On The Hill
Hello Goodbye

PROGRAM 4
Flying
Penny Lane
All You Need Is Love

Produced in England by George Martin

MANUFACTURED BY CAPITOL RECORDS, INC., HOLLYWOOD AND VINE STREETS, HOLLYWOOD, CALIF.
FACTORIES: SCRANTON, PA., LOS ANGELES, CALIF., JACKSONVILLE, ILL.

CARTRIDGE MUST NOT BE LEFT EXPOSED TO DIRECT
SUNLIGHT. REMOVE FROM PLAYER WHEN NOT IN USE.

EMI allowed British record dealers to sell imported copies of Capitol's *Magical Mystery Tour* LP. By early 1968, over 50,000 copies (mono and stereo) had been ordered. The album charted for two weeks, peaking at number 31. EMI officially released the album in the U.K. in November 1976 on the Parlophone label. Although true stereo mixes for "Penny Lane," "Baby You're A Rich Man" and "All You Need Is Love" were available by that time, EMI used Capitol's master tape for the album. The Capitol-created *Magical Mystery Tour* album is now considered part of the Beatles core catalog.

Meanwhile, back in the U.S.A. in 1969, the *Yellow Submarine* 8-track had a bonus cut, "Lucy In The Sky With Diamonds," which was added to the start of Program 3 to create similar running times for each program. The Beatles songs are on Programs 1 and 2 in their correct running order. The George Martin Orchestrations are on Programs 3 and 4, with a slightly different running order.

By the time the *Yellow Submarine* album was issued, a new format was available, the cassette tape. Side One of the *Yellow Submarine* cassette matches that of the vinyl album. Side Two has the same running order of the George Martin orchestrations, but has "Lucy In The Sky With Diamonds" at the start of the program to get the running time of Side Two (21:44) close to that of Side One (21:55).

The *Magical Mystery Tour* film was first issued for the home video market in 1978 in both VHS and Betamax tape formats. Both the video and audio of the film were poor quality. An improved video of the movie was issued in 1988 in both the VHS and Laserdisc formats. The soundtrack was digitally remixed and remastered in stereo by George Martin. In 1997, the film was issued in the DVD format for the first time.

Magical Mystery Tour was finally given the deluxe treatment in 2012 with a spectacular Blu-ray release with bonus material. The soundtrack and songs were mixed in stereo and 5.1 surround at Abbey Road Studios by Sam Okell under the supervision of producer Giles Martin and project coordinator Allan Rouse. "I Am The Walrus" was given stereo and 5.1 mixes for the entire song. The picture was restored under the supervision of Paul Rutan, Jr. at Eque.

The Blu-ray edition contains considerable bonus material, including: Director's Commentary by Paul McCartney; The Making Of Magical Mystery Tour; Ringo The Actor; and Meet The Supporting Cast. There are also new edits of "Your Mother Should Know," "Blue Jay Way" and "The Fool On The Hill," which contain footage shot during the filming of the TV show that was not included in the film.

Of particular interest are scenes that did not appear in the film. Nat's Dream was directed by John and features Nat Jackley and accordionist Shirley Evans, who are joined by a bevy of bathing beauties in swim suits. The soundtrack to this scene is "Shirley's Wild Accordion." It's unfortunate this didn't make the final cut, but at least it can now be appreciated. There is also a scene of Ivor Cutler playing organ and singing "I'm Going In A Field," which was filmed in an empty field. The song's lumbering pace explains why it was not included. The Traffic video of "Here We Go Round The Mulberry Bush" would have worked just fine if Paul could have figured a way to work it into the film's "story line."

The BBC refused to broadcast the Beatles promotional clip for "Hello Goodbye" because it violated the Musicians Union ban on miming. Instead the BBC showed images from *A Hard Day's Night* during its airing of the song on the November 23, 1967 Top Of The Pops. When the show featured "Hello Goodbye" again on December 7, 1967, the program ran a black and white video that mixed scenes of the Beatles editing *Magical Mystery Tour* (shot on November 21) with unrelated BBC footage of four young people around a car in the snow who keep appearing and disappearing. This strange video is included on the 2012 *Magical Mystery Tour* Blu-ray.

The deluxe Blu-ray *The Beatles 1+* video contains three promotional clips of "Hello Goodbye" filmed at the Saville Theatre, complete with miming. The package also includes videos of: "All You Need Is Love" (colorized footage from Our World); "Lady Madonna" (utilizing film of the group recording "Hey Bulldog"); and "Hey Bulldog" (filmed on February 11, 1968). The songs were mixed for the release by Giles Martin in stereo and 5.1 surround.

The *Yellow Submarine* film was first released for the home market in the VHS tape and Laserdisc formats on August 28, 1987, to coincide with the release of the *Yellow Submarine* album on CD. Unfortunately the film was prepared with the U.S. theatrical version, which did not contain the "Hey Bulldog" sequence that was edited out for the American market. The home videos were only available for a limited time due to disputes over the rights to the film.

In 1995, Bruce Markoe, vice-president with MGM-UA, sought a video copy of the *Yellow Submarine* cartoon to show his five-year-old daughter. He rented a Laserdisc copy and was disappointed in how the film looked and sounded. Markoe wanted to "renovate" the film by "improving it while remaining true to the integrity of the original piece." When he inquired into whether MGM-UA still had the video rights to the film, Markoe learned that his company was involved in a legal dispute with Apple over the rights. He convinced UA president John Calley that the film should be re-released. The companies then settled their differences and Markoe successfully pitched his renovation project to MGM-UA and Apple.

EMI engineer Peter Cobbin, who was experienced in pop and orchestral music as well as 5.1 surround mixing, was given the task of remixing the songs for the film in 5.1. Assisted by Paul Hicks and Mirek Stiles and project coordinator Allan Rouse, Cobbin spent a month mixing the songs at Abbey Road in 1997. The results of his efforts are stunning, giving the songs a new freshness. Cobbin then prepared stereo mixes of the songs for a new album.

Yellow Submarine Songtrack was released simultaneously with the video reissue of the *Yellow Submarine* cartoon on September 13, 1999, in the U.K. and a day later in America. The album contains the six Beatles songs from 1969's soundtrack LP plus nine more songs featured in the film. In the U.K., the album was issued in the CD, cassette and vinyl formats, while Capitol released the album only on CD and cassette, choosing neither to manufacture nor to import vinyl records. Beatle fans and collectors in America were on their own to find imported copies of the British vinyl album.

The British album sold 19,000 copies in its first week, leading to a chart debut and peak of number eight. In America, the album entered the Billboard chart on October 2, 1999, at number 15, its peak position, during its 15 weeks on the charts. SoundScan reported first-week sales of 67,939 copies. On November 2, 1999, the RIAA certified the album gold, indicating sales of 500,000.

Paul McCartney was very pleased with the album, stating "it's great you can buy all the songs that were in the movie on this one new songtrack album." Perhaps still sensitive to criticism about the original *Yellow Submarine* LP, Paul said that the Beatles "always try to give people good value for money...and pack the albums with good stuff so you don't feel cheated." *Yellow Submarine Songtrack* certainly gave listeners good value for their money and showed how much better the Beatles catalog would sound when it was later remixed and remastered using the latest technology. The *Yellow Submarine* film was restored and issued on Blu-ray on June 4, 2012.

VISIT
www.beatle.net
for more books by Bruce Spizer

SUBSCRIBE TO BRUCE'S EMAIL LIST

FOR MORE EXCLUSIVE BEATLES ARTICLES AND CONTENT

THE BEATLES ALBUM SERIES ALSO AVAILABLE IN DIGITAL, HARD COVER AND SPECIAL COLLECTOR'S EDITIONS

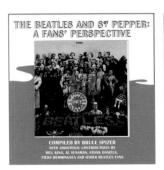

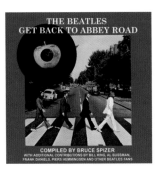

OTHER TITLES: DIGITAL EDITIONS, FIRST EDITION HARDCOVER AND SPECIAL COLLECTOR'S EDITIONS

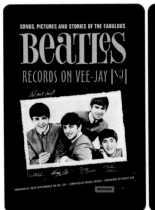

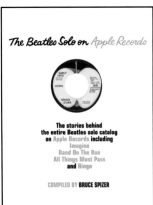

Yellow Submarine